INVESTIGATING THE UNEXPLAINED

INVESTIGATING
THE
UNEXPLAINED

MELVIN HARRIS

PROMETHEUS BOOKS
Buffalo, New York

For Mo—the incomparable!

90 89 88 87 86   4 3 2 1

Library of Congress Cataloging-in-Publication Data

Harris, Melvin.
    Investigating the unexplained.

    1. Psychical research—Case studies. I. Title.
BF1029.H37 1986   133   86-20542
ISBN 0-87975-367-6

CONTENTS

Chapters 2 and 3 are best read in that order. Likewise
with Chapters 12 and 13, and with Chapters 16, 17,
and 18.

PREFACE

This book was not conceived as part of a crusade against the paranormal. Rather, it grew out of the natural exercise of my dual occupation as professional broadcaster and professional researcher. These two occupations inevitably interpenetrate. As a result, many of my investigations have arisen out of a search for program material.

Sometimes I initiated this search myself. Often television companies asked me to review various stories and check them out.

In all cases, I began investigating with a cautious but open mind. I really didn't know if the accounts in front of me were true or not. So I went back to primary sources. I checked and checked—and in the end I was able to say over and over again and with authority: "Sorry—you've been duped!"

My thanks to the helpful people who dragged out books and files for me to delve into. In particular, thanks to Alan Wesencrast, Guardian of The Hally Price Library [University of London]; Nick Clarke and Eleanor O'Keeffe of The Society for Psychical Research; Tony Ortzen, editor of *Psychic News;* and Mike Hutchinson, Secretary of The British Committee for the Scientific Investigation of Claims of the Paranormal.

Special thanks to Simon Welfare who was repeatedly bludgeoned with the full weight of my enthusiasms!

1

THE AMITYVILLE HORROR-MONGERS

The Exorcist started the trend. Unbelievable, horror-filled books and films, featuring possession, began to appear on the market. Unbelievable, that is, to the alert, informed, and rational mind. Unfortunately, far too many people have never had a fair chance to develop the questioning and reasoning part of their minds. They stand crippled by fears, phantasms, cruel superstitions, and distorted values picked up during their vulnerable childhoods. Cash-hungry authors thrive on their credulity. Possession is real. Demons stalk the suburbs. Supernormal horror *can* visit uninvited and unexpected. That's horror fiction's dollar-earning, irresponsible claptrap in essence.

But does *The Amityville Horror* fall into this category? After all, it is unambiguously presented as a real-life documentary, "More hideously frightening than *The Exorcist* because it actually happened!" Real life? Let's see.

Was there ever real horror at Amityville? Yes, and it erupted on the early morning of November 13, 1974, when a twenty-four-year-old New Yorker named Ronald DeFeo ran screaming into a bar near his home. Someone, he sobbed, had broken into the house and slaughtered his family. The police discovered that his mother, father, two sisters, and two brothers had been shot dead as they lay in their beds. But the authorities refused to take the idea of an intruder seriously, and Ronald DeFeo was brought to trial charged with the crimes.

The prosecution saw the motive as a wild attempt to lay hands on $200,000 worth of life insurance plus the sizable funds in the family cashbox. The defense attorney, William Weber, countered by bringing on a parade of psychiatrists to back up his client's plea of insanity. The jury rejected that plea, and Ronald DeFeo was sentenced to six consecutive life-terms.

With the trial over, the tarnished DeFeo house was put up for sale. It was an imposing three-story Dutch Colonial building located on Ocean Avenue, Amityville, Long Island. A valuable piece of property by market standards, its history led real estate agents to offer it at the bargain price of $80,000. Even so, it stood empty for almost a year, until, on December 18, 1975, the Lutz family moved in.

At 28, George Lutz was the owner of a land-surveying company. His wife Kathy had a full-time job looking after her two young sons and five-year-old daughter. The rambling house seemed an ideal place for a lively family to flourish. Yet the Lutzes "fled from the place" after only 28 days—victims, so they said later, of a relentless, nameless terror.

The full story of their ordeal appeared in *The Amityville Horror,* written by Jay Anson and based on many interviews with the Lutzes themselves. The book became a best-seller and was hailed as "One of the most terrifying true cases ever of haunting and possession by demons . . . breathless . . . heart-stopping . . . chilling."

According to this account, it all began when the house became filled with overpoweringly foul stenches. Simultaneously, the bathroom porcelain became stained with a black slime that resisted household cleansers. Then came the flies—hundreds of them swarming into a second-floor bedroom.

Following this, the massive front door was discovered wrenched

How the public were sold the Amityville hoax. Scenes from the motion picture.

wide open and hanging from one hinge. George found that his whole body seemed chilled to the bone, despite the huge blazing fire that roared in the living-room. And to complicate things further, a four-foot-high ceramic lion began moving around the house without any human help!

Within days, cloven-hoof tracks were spotted in the snow around the house. When followed, they led directly to the garage and stopped dead in front of the door. The door itself hung almost torn off its metal frame—a feat that would "require a strength far beyond that of any human being." At last, it began to dawn on the Lutzes that their dream-house was a place of nightmares—haunted by malignant presences.

Kathy Lutz was the first to be truly terrorized by the entities. Invisible arms embraced her and tried to gain possession of her body, "Escape was impossible and she felt she was going to die."

Meanwhile, others were being hit by the "Horror." A priest who'd befriended the Lutzes was stricken with an enervating, unknown infection, while the rectory that he lived in was smothered by a horrible odor that drove all the priests out of their rooms into the open air!

Back on Ocean Avenue, George now began to experience his own private horror—the sound of a marching band parading around the house, boots thumping, horns blaring. "There must be at least fifty musicians," he thought. Yet not a single one was ever seen, though the chairs, couch, and tables were found pushed back against the walls, as if to make room for the many marching feet.

The loathsome green slime that started to appear proved harmless enough, but the red weals that shortly erupted on Kathy's body were hideously painful. She looked as if she'd been slashed with a red-hot poker. But it was simply the "entity" indulging in its sadistic play. And then, of course, there were the personality changes, the levitations and the demons.

By rights it should all have ended after the Lutzes made their dramatic exit from the house on January 14, 1976. But according to the sequel, *The Amityville Horror—Part II,* the evil followed them on to their succeeding homes. It stayed "coiled malevolently around them. Holding them with its unstoppable power. . . ."

An incredibly grim story, if true, but so like fiction that it prompts the question: Was there ever an authentic horror in the first place? Competent investigators unite in their answer—emphatically they say no!

Doctor Stephan Kaplan, director of the Parapsychology Institute of America, has written: "After several months of extensive research and interviews with those who were involved in 'The Amityville Horror' . . . we found no evidence to support any claim of a 'haunted house.' What we did find is a couple who had purchased a house that they economically could not afford. It is our professional opinion that the story of its haunting is mostly fiction" (*Theta*, no. 4, 1977).

Jerry Solfvin of the Psychical Research Foundation visited the house and wrote: "The case wasn't interesting to us because the reports were confined to subjective responses from the Lutzes, and these were not at all impressive or even characteristic of these cases" (*Skeptical Inquirer*, Summer 1978).

But the most damning report of all originates with investigators Rick Moran and Peter Jordan. They went to Amityville and interviewed people mentioned in the book. The results were startling. To begin with, the police rejected the book's claim that they had investigated the house. In particular, Sergeant Cammorato denied that he'd ever entered the place while the Lutzes were in residence. Yet the book has Cammorato touring through the house and even inspecting a "secret room" in the basement—tales that turned out to be so much eyewash.

Then Father Mancuso (real name Pecorara), who's featured throughout the book, also flatly denied that he'd ever entered the Lutz home. So, that tale about his blessing the building and about the phantom voice that ordered him out is quite bogus. As well as that, the pastor of the Sacred Heart Rectory dismissed as "pure and utter nonsense" the Lutzes' yarn about "an unrelenting, disgusting odor that permeated the Rectory"—the alleged "Scent of the Devil" that was supposed to have driven the priests out of their building.

In fact, little in the book stood up to close scrutiny. Local repairmen and locksmiths knew nothing of the paranormal damages they were supposed to have rectified. Not even the story that the Lutzes were driven out of the house by hauntings stood up. The real reasons for their exit were much more prosaic—a cash crisis and a near breakdown.

Naturally, the Lutzes have responded to these revelations by staging a pantomime of bluff and bluster; but, significantly, they have repeatedly avoided meeting informed critics on radio or TV. They have good reason for these evasions, for the first accounts put out by them

James Brolin and Margot Kidder portray the unfortunate Lutz couple who, after purchasing what they considered to be their "dream house," fled in fear for their lives after just 28 days of living with horrible, unexplanable manifestations in American International's taut film adaptation of Jay Anson's non-fiction best-seller, *The Amityville Horror.* Also starring Rod Steiger (pictured here), *The Amityville Horror* was directed by Stuart Rosenberg from a screenplay by Sandor Stern. Released in the UK by ITC Film Distributors.

spoke only of things felt and sensed—never anything about objective phenomena.

Indeed, little notice would have been taken of the couple if they hadn't been pushed into the limelight by attorney William Weber. Weber's motives were unconnected with psychical research. He was simply aiming to win a new trial for his client Ronald DeFeo. Ronald had spoken of a voice that urged him to kill, and Weber hoped to establish that the Ocean Avenue house contained some force able to influence the behavior of anyone who lived there. So he began to pin his hopes on the Lutzes and won them time on New York's Channel 5 "Ten O'Clock News" program.

At first, Weber's involvement seemed to be on a purely professional basis. It was only much later that he admitted helping to sensationalize the Lutzes' story. In an Associated Press release of July 27, 1979, he said: "We created this horror story over many bottles of wine that George was drinking. We were really playing with each other."

Yet the case against the Lutzes doesn't rest wholly on these statements by outsiders. The Lutzes themselves have provided ample proof of their unreliability. The proof is contained in the interviews they gave before the book came into being.

For a start, there's the account published in the *Long Island Press,* on January 17, 1976. In this article George Lutz sets out his experiences at 112 Ocean Avenue. But his story centers around things that were "sensed" and not seen. In fact, he contradicts earlier stories about "flying objects," moving couches," and "wailing noises." The only physical phenomenon mentioned concerns a window that opened of its own accord. (Later investigations were to show that the window's counterweights were simply too heavy for this to have happened.) So, at that date, the Amityville happenings were tame, purely subjective, and hardly worth noting.

Just over a year later, though, George Lutz came out with a new version of the events. He related it to journalist Paul Hoffman and it appeared in the April 1977 issue of *Good Housekeeping.* This is a vital text worth studying in detail, for it shows just how the whole tale was progressively embroidered. What's more, it contradicts George's earlier account and is in conflict with the Anson book as well!

In *Good Housekeeping,* the story begins with a Roman Catholic priest blessing the house. On leaving, he warns the Lutzes about one of their bedrooms, saying, "Don't let anyone sleep in there. Keep the door closed. Spend as little time as possible in there." But in the book the priest does nothing of the sort. His alleged advice about not using the room is given one week after the blessing—and then, only following a whole series of nasty events.

After the priest, the next person to be affected by the house is said to be Kathy Lutz's aunt—described in *Good Housekeeping* as "a normally placid ex-nun." When she came to visit, the article says, she behaved quite out of character. She became hostile toward George, who says she "sat there and cut me down for three hours." In the book though, this event is reshaped to make it more dramatic, for the aunt can only stay in the house for a very short while. There's no three-hour harangue—she simply inspects the house, refuses to enter certain rooms, and leaves. In fact, she "hadn't been in the house for more than a half-hour when she decided it was time to go"—and go she did!

This same revamping technique is used with the "old crone" incident. In *Good Housekeeping,* George states that on Saturday, January 10, 1976, he woke up at night "with a compulsion to flee the house." He yelled at his wife and shook her, but just couldn't wake her up. Then, as he watched, his sleeping wife "turned into a 90-year-old woman." Her hair became "old and dirty," she dribbled, and creases and crow's feet formed on her face. "It took several hours before she returned to her normal self."

When this story appears in the book, however, it contains major differences. To begin with, it's placed four days earlier, on Wednesday, January 7. And George doesn't wake up wanting to flee the house. On the contrary, he's unable to get to sleep and, in this wide-awake state, has the urge to go out to the local tavern for a beer. He doesn't shake or yell at his wife, for when he turns to speak to her he finds her levitating "almost a foot above him." He pulls her down to the bed, where she wakes. And it's then, while awake, that she turns into a 90-year-old woman. But this state only lasts for a minute or so—not several hours.

Now in the book, this levitation of January 7 is the second that's alleged to have happened. The first had "taken place" on January 4 and then Kathy floated "two feet above the bed." A further levitation happens on January 15, only this time both Kathy and George float around at the same time. Yet nothing was ever said about these remarkable levitations in the *Good Housekeeping* account. The only claim there is that on Sunday, January 11, George "awoke to find Kathy sliding across the bed, as if by levitation," which is very different from the "floating in the air" claims and also involves a different date.

The ultimate horrors in the book are the visitations by the "gigantic hooded figure in white," who's also described as a "demon with horns" with half its face shot away. In *Good Housekeeping* there's not even a hint of his visits. There is mention, though, of Kathy turning white and stating, "I just saw some eyes at the window." But these are described as "red, beady eyes"—and that's the end of the incident. Yet, when this story reaches the book, it becomes a point of high drama.

This drama is set in a second-story bedroom at night. The Lutzes' young daughter points to a window and both George and Kathy see "two fiery, red eyes! No face, just the mean, little eyes of a pig" looking in. Then Kathy rushes at the window "screaming in an unearthly voice." She smashes the glass with a chair and then they hear an "animal cry of pain, a loud squealing—and the eyes were gone!" This squealing goes on for a while, out on the grounds of the house. But George doesn't go looking for the flying pig. Instead, he comforts his wife, who sobs out, "It's been here all the time! I wanted to kill it! I

James Brolin as George Lutz in *The Amityville Horror,* produced by Ronnie Saland and Elliot Geisinger for American International Pictures.

wanted to kill it!"

Plainly, the story has undergone a most remarkable transformation. And it's the same with event after event in the book. These findings then, coupled with the investigators' reports, make it certain that the whole bizarre tale is beyond belief.

So what sparked the whole thing off? Well, without a confession from the Lutzes we'll never have a complete answer. But we do know that George Lutz was a man with problems. When his first marriage broke up he tried group therapy, then turned to Transcendental Meditation. His second marriage seemed to help for a while, but even that brought along its own problems. And *before* he moved to Amityville he was already facing a crisis. The two boys tried to run away. His business was in difficulty. And the Internal Revenue people were acting tough. Then, to crown it all, he became completely irresponsible. Instead of cutting back on expenditures, he decided to buy a house that was much above his means.

Once in the new house, matters came to a head fast. Lutz grew so apathetic that for a while he didn't wash or shave and he stopped going to the office. He even lists his problems in the book.

They were: "a second marriage with three children, a new house with a big mortgage . . . taxes in Amityville three times higher than in

Deer Park. Did he really need that new speedboat? How the hell was he going to pay for all this? The construction business was lousy on Long Island . . . so who the hell needs a land-surveyor?" And before long "he was beginning to choke with the pressure of mounting bills for the house . . . and for the office where he would shortly have a very serious payroll deficit."

All this turmoil soon took its toll. He began to blame his inertia, his bad temper, and his worries on the house. When he was short with his employees, or when he hit the children, it became the fault of the house and not his lack of control. And in that frame of mind George Lutz began to identify with the murderer, Ronald DeFeo. He even became convinced that he was the physical double of Ronald. When he first saw Ronald's picture he recorded: "The bearded twenty-four-year-old face staring back . . . could have been his own!" And if a physical double, why not a mental double? There's little doubt that George felt murderous black thoughts in that house. But they came from his own plight and deep frustrations, not from any paranormal agencies. That house and its ghastly reputation served initially as nothing more than a catalyst for morbid ideas. Later, they were to serve as a catalyst for cash-register ideas!

After his exit from Amityville, his imaginings started to grow out of control. The meeting with Anson finalized this process, and the many fantasies were crystallized and put into a sensational and salable form.

And sell they did! *The Amityville Horror* spent eight months on the best-seller lists. By the end of 1979, some 3½ million copies had been sold and a film version was well under way. Such was its impact that, during the production of the film, American International Pictures received more than 13,000 inquiries from members of the public eager for progress reports.

The Lutzes had discovered that gullibility equals gold—but only because their fiction masqueraded as truth. As fiction pure and simple it would have ended up in the ever-yawning wastepaper basket. And rightly so!

2

THE CELESTIAL BUS-CONDUCTORS

Honestly, I promise I've not invented that headline. It comes from *Psychic News,* June 10, 1978, where it leads into a story about the famous medium Doris Stokes. She has recently completed the third volume of her life story, another best-seller for the lady. So, obviously, hordes of people believe or want to believe in mediumship. Yet, strong beliefs are not enough. Is there any firm proof that mediums are a link with another world on another plane? A world peopled by the spirits of those who are nominally dead?

If you search for the answers to these questions on the lengthy shelves of spiritualist writings, prepare to feel dispirited. The pomposity and sheer dreariness of much of what you'll find there can try one's patience to the limit. Consider this gem from Wordsworth penned in spiritland:

> You walked upon the earth in darkness
> You walked out of the earth in light
> And now you know that angels
> Are round you ever bright
> When you yourself do right
> Their gentle wings unfurl
> Not feathers, but pearl after pearl
> A blessing falling down upon the earth
> Peace, beauty and gentle mirth.

Does this insult to the inside of a Christmas cracker lift your heart? Do you really believe that the poet is in love with doggerel and has lost all touch with his genius? Still, if you grit your teeth hard enough, it becomes possible to wade through the incredible literature.

You'll find that, since 1848, the world has been offered a changing variety of mediumistic experiences. Slate-writing was once a high point of spiritualistic fashion. Henry Slade and William Eglinton, the top Victorian mediums, were noted for practicing this phenomenon. Apparently, the spirits would inscribe blank slates with messages and drawings, completely unaided by the medium. He was there simply to help them concentrate their powers.

Eventually the slate craze passed out of fashion when magicians like Maskelyne and Davey and researchers like David Abbott and Hereward Carrington showed how the baffling stunts were engineered. Carrington forcefully concluded:

> If we were to read carefully through the historical evidence for the phenomena of slate-writing, we should find it to consist in one long and practically unbroken series of exposés of fraud and trickery, with no real evidence worth mentioning for the genuine manifestations of any supernormal power, nor any indication of any force or agency whatever at work beyond the muscles of the medium.
>
> In short, there is no good evidence, in the whole history of spiritualism, for the occurrence of writing on slates by other means than such as might have been produced fraudulently by the medium; and I have gone carefully through a vast bulk of spiritualistic literature before making this statement. *(The Physical Phenomena of Spiritualism)*

Longer lasting than the slate-writing phase was the era of materializations. Spirits would apparently take on a temporary solid form and cavort around the dimly lit séance rooms. The most famous of these cases was that of Katie King, who was conjured up by Florence Cook, and actually posed for the photographer. Others of her kind posed as well but with gloomy results—the fakery was shown up by the camera.

As early as 1892, spiritualist W. T. Stead regretfully owned up: "I have made great efforts to obtain the services of a trustworthy materializing medium who has not at any time been detected in fraud. . . . The net result of my inquiries came to this: that, in the whole of the United Kingdom, so far as was known to the spiritualist community, there was only one person of the undoubted materializing faculty and undoubted character who could almost always secure the presence of phenomena, and who had never been detected in a trick of any kind . . . I refer to Mrs. Mellon, late of Newcastle-on-Tyne, whose success as a materializing medium is undoubted."

Unfortunately, even his Mrs. Mellon was caught out at last in a circle staged in Sydney, Australia, on October 12, 1894. A Mr. T. S. Henry grabbed the figure of the alleged spirit and found that he "held the form of Mrs. Mellon, and that she was on her knees, and had a white material like muslin round her head and shoulders."

In the following years, similar exposures became commonplace. The mediums who weren't caught out were the ones who took special care that the curious and the informed investigators were kept at a distance. Among those ranking as "unexposed" are Estelle Roberts and Isa Northage.

Estelle Roberts used to materialize her guide, the American Indian known as Red Cloud. People saw him and were even allowed to feel his hair and his short, soft, silky beard. Apart from his being the only bearded redskin I know of, I was enthralled to see a photograph of spirit Red Cloud. For some strange reason every time I look at it I see a very Western face wearing a feathered war-bonnet. What is equally strange is that I find the face looks just like that of Estelle Roberts at her most grim and earnest. Of the beard, there is no trace. Very strange.

Altogether as strange is the case of Isa Northage. In 1939, she materialized a lady who kissed her grieving husband, then allowed the sitters to handle her spirit drapery. Following that, an Egyptian gentleman is said to have materialized and spoken in his own tongue. Good measure, you'd think—but there was more. Along came a monk who left a crucifix behind, and a Chinese lady who brought a valuable incense-burner and a bangle from her own tomb.

In later years, Isa qualified—if you believe the reports—as the most astounding materialization medium ever. Under the glare of a 150-watt light blub, she materialized a dead Irish surgeon, called Dr. Reynolds. This surgeon then carried out spirit operations on assorted patients in full light. Cancers, ulcers, and "malignant growths" were said to have been removed. More than one hundred people were said to have witnessed the operations.

All that was startling, but consider this: at one point the doctor decided that he'd have to fetch something from the spirit world, so he disappeared through the floor and in a few moments reappeared with a special liquid, which he used to control a hemorrhage.

You may well ask where the world's press was when all this was going on. And why was it that the medical profession didn't turn up in busloads? Your guess is as good as mine. But I have noticed this, that when I look at a painting of Dr. Reynolds—yes, he posed for one—I'm reminded of the experience with Estelle Roberts. For, strangely enough, Dr. Reynolds looks remarkably like Isa Northage with her hair scraped back and an unbelievable stage beard glued in position.

Am I being unfair? Hardly! The claims these people make violate all logic and are at loggerheads with everyday experiences. If they are true, then it's up to them to demonstrate the truth. Yet these claimants never submit themselves to informed and impartial examination. They reserve their antics for the believers. And tragically, believers have a terrible tendency to go on believing—come what may.

This compulsive need to believe was shown in the months following the Paul McElhoney affair of March 1983. McElhoney first made news in 1978 as a spiritual healer. By 1981, he had graduated to a more exalted level.

The delighted editor of *Psychic News* wrote: "The age of physical psychic phenomena is not over. Last week a young materialization medium gave his first ever sitting for a newspaper. All told, several feet of brilliant white ectoplasm gushed from his mouth. Two roses were apported into the room."

From then on, Paul's ectoplasm and flower factories seemed to be working on an overtime basis. And there were sizable metal apports as well, ranging from a model of Cologne Cathedral to a copper and bronze statue, to an ornate 9-inch brass bowl decorated with dolphins. It was all so breathtaking.

Unfortunately, Paul's guide Ceros began mouthing a series of "philosophical teachings." The Ceros teachings were a worn-out, embarrassing collection of mock-simple homilies and platitudes. Each paragraph had the buoyancy of a lead balloon.

Take this as a sample: "I say to all people in friendship it must always be remembered that the flowers and fruits of your earth are always growing even if at times you may not be able to see them."

Unbelievably, these trite sayings were solemnly printed issue by issue in the spiritualist *Two Worlds*. They were then collected into book form and recorded on cassette!

Despite the handicap of Ceros, Paul became "Medium of the Year" in 1981. But his triumph was short-lived. The intense rivalry and envy among the psychics led to his downfall. Spiritualist minister Ronald Baker and president of the Spiritualist National Union, Gordon

Higginson, joined forces in a bid to see if Paul could pass a crucial test.

It was a weird set-up, for Higginson himself had earlier been accused of fraud by fellow-spiritualist Mrs. Phyllis Simpson of Bristol. However, in March 1983, it was Paul who was under judgment, and the Sunday newspaper *News of the World* agreed to cooperate in setting up a test séance—without, of course, the knowledge of the medium.

The fatal séance took place at a house in Osset, Yorkshire. This house was owned by a 69-year-old widow, Mrs. Joan Stubley. She believed implicitly in Paul. She had donated generously to his brainchild, the United World organization. And she was now on the point of signing over the deeds of her house to the medium. By that gesture, her property would "benefit world harmony."

Mrs. Stubley was warned in advance and gave her consent. If Paul was genuine, he had nothing to fear from the test.

The medium walked into the séance room, put his tape-recorder down, and prepared to mentally limber up. At that point, he was informed that Mrs. Stubley wished to speak to him up in her third-floor flat. He nervously left the room and immediately the examiners entered and began searching. Spiritualist David Edgar took charge of the tape-recorder and noticed a heavy black tape bound around the battery compartment. He slowly unpeeled it and opened up the back of the machine. Inside he found a row of carnations taped to a plastic strip, a key-ring flashlight small enough to place in the mouth, and other objects.

The finds were quickly witnessed and photographed. The recorder was reassembled. And by the time Paul returned everything seemed as normal.

Before the séance began, Paul was stripped and searched. Then the lights were switched off and Ceros took possession of the medium. The Ceros messages began to pour out and then a hymn was asked for. David Edgar was on full alert and heard the back of the tape-recorder being opened. Ceros next ordered the lights to be put out and sitters watched as a carnation dropped out of Paul's lips. Off went the lights, and then back on again so that another carnation could jump into view. Now was the time for decisive action.

Edgar was close to the recorder. He looked behind it and saw that the back was off and only one carnation was still left taped inside. That was enough. He walked over to the light switch and told Paul to leave the lights on.

"The game's up, Paul," he said.

The medium froze on the spot, recovered, and asked what was going on. Edgar explained and asked McElhoney to submit to another search. Then everyone could see what lay behind the suspicious bulge in one of his pockets. Paul tremblingly denied that he had cheated but refused a search. He'd only allow the police to search him. So someone phoned the police. At that point McElhoney ran out of the house into the street, leaving his recorder behind.

The affair made a front-page story for the *News of the World,* complete with photographs of the rigged tape-recorder. Paul, of course, had lost everything, including the house! He tried tears and protests and a promise that once he'd got his strength back he'd stage an unquestionable test séance. But his big August "United World Festival"—his crowning glory—had to be canceled. It was farewell to Paul and silence for his garrulous Ceros. Even so, the spiritualists broke up into feuding camps and Paul, incredibly, still found quite a following among those prepared to believe at any cost.

"Materialization" mediumship, then, seems akin to tightrope walking. But other forms have been just as precarious—like spirit photography. This branch of mediumship excited the spiritualist camp well up until the 1930s. It all started, so it's claimed, as early as 1861 when a Boston photographer, William H. Mumler, is said to have captured a spirit face on a photographic plate. How did he know it was a spirit? Easily—he recognized it as a cousin who'd died twelve years earlier.

Mumler gave up his exacting job as an engraver and opened up a psychic photography studio. He was never short of clients, who flocked in hoping to see their loved ones once more. Many of them left fully convinced that some sort of photographic evidence had been given to them. Even President Lincoln's widow dropped in and was photographed. Days later she received a print that seemed to show a shadowy Abraham Lincoln standing behind her touching her shoulders.

The practice spread rapidly to Europe. In London, Frederick Hudson was the pioneer, followed by the roguish Richard Boursnell of Shepherd's Bush. In France, the supreme practitioner became Edouard Buguet, who accumulated quite a bevy of aristocratic and influential sitters.

And what did they get for their money? Well, most of the time, simple double exposures. At other times, quite elaborate fake set-pieces. But don't take my word for it. Photographs are meant to be looked at, not described in words and I've provided some gems from the master fakers, leaving you to make your own judgments.

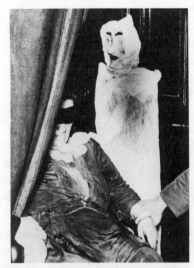

Medium Helen Duncan with friend from spirit land.

If nothing else, many of these photographs are amusing, but they weren't intended to amuse. Their aim was to dupe the gullible and milk those in need of comfort. But the fakers didn't have it all their own way. One after the other most of these photographers were caught either cheating or preparing to cheat. Then, when plate cameras went out of fashion, the practice became much more difficult, and in the 1930s it dwindled almost to the point of extinction.

But, while they reigned, these people were skilled and cunning. So much so, that Dr. d'Aute Hooper, a medium who was never caught out, has only recently been *proven* to be a cheat. One of his famous pictures, of a small spirit girl, was taken back in 1905. The case involved a patient who was staying with him in order to receive spiritual healing. Dr. Hooper reveals the story behind the picture in these words: "One day he (the patient) had been out for a walk, and when he came back, he said: 'Doctor, I feel so queer, I feel as if there is someone with me; will you get your camera and take a snapshot of me?' I got the camera and before I exposed the plate I told him I saw a beautiful child with him. I put a dark tablecloth over the door in the drawing room to form a background and then exposed the plate. The gentleman himself took the plate to the dark room and developed it; and there appeared the beautiful spirit form of a little girl with a bouquet of flowers in one hand and a roll of paper in the other. The exclamation of the gentleman was 'Good heavens! It's my daughter, who died thirty years ago.'"

This picture, together with its touching story, first appeared in print in 1919 and has been celebrated every since.

In 1978, this well-loved story and photograph were included in

Fred Getting's book *Ghosts In Photographs* and a new generation was introduced to the tale. But nemesis was at hand. A year later, Camden Graphics of London decided to reprint some Victorian poster designs in the form of greeting cards. Among their charming selection was a painting by Charles Trevor Garland called "For You." It depicts a young girl with a letter in her right hand and a bunch of roses in the other.

As the greeting cards circulated, sharp-eyed investigators, including Dr. C. M. Cherry of the Society for Psychical Research, felt a tinge of recognition. Comparisons were made and all became clear. Dr. Hooper had conned his patient and his admirers by printing in a degraded photo of the original Garland poster!

That story well illustrates the problems researchers have in showing up deception. Evidence is all too easily concealed, or is difficult to locate. In this case, the deception reigned for more than sixty years.

Not all mediumistic deception is intentional though—often self-deception is at work. The medium allows chains of thought or images to run through the head and interprets them as if they were messages from *outside* the brain. It's easily done, especially if you start off expecting messages.

When I draw on my own experience, I have to conclude that most mediumship shows signs of a mixture of deliberate deception and naive self-deception.

Take the case of voice mediums, like British champion Leslie Flint and U.S. contender Keith Milton Rhinehart. Flint has tape-recorded a host of his spirit visitors. He claims that these voices don't emerge from his mouth but from a spot near him. Apparently an ectoplasmic larynx is created by the spirits for this special purpose. I've listened attentively to his tapes of these voices. Regretfully, I have to conclude that his spirits were awfully mixed up. His Valentino speaks with a stage French accent—shades of Charles Boyer, while his George Bernard Shaw sounds like an irascible English colonel with no trace of Shaw's precise and memorable soft Irish brogue.

Apart from that, his "visitors" have unaccountably lost all the wisdom and charm they exhibited on earth. Does this mean that plain and inadequate mimicry is at work? Is Mr. Flint deceiving himself? He says not. He points to tests where his mouth has been filled with liquid, his lips have been sealed with adhesive tape and still the voices have rung out. In the United States Mr. Rhinehart has also undergone such a test.

Are these tests stringent enough? Are there loopholes? The career of medium William Roy may provide some answers. But before considering him, what briefly can we say about mediums who shun gimmicks and rely on the plain transfer of messages?

Perhaps Doris Stokes is a good example. She packs huge theaters like the Palladium and exudes an air of complete control and conviction. Her audiences seem convinced as well. But only a handful at each gathering ever receive messages. And, of those messages, some show signs of being gained by guesswork or fishing. Yet Mrs. Stokes triumphs because, even though only a few are blessed, the rest take comfort from that. They think one day it will happen to them.

That is part of the key to the lure of spiritualism. It can score over other religions because of its offer of direct comfort—"Your daughter is here at your side," "Your father watches over you and sends his love." This style of comfort wins hands down over the abstractions, the remoteness, and the almost antiseptic utterances of the orthodox clergy.

But even "top-of-the-league" Doris Stokes goes too far at times. She started developing a hotline to dead show business figures in 1983. Her most impressive visitor at that time was John Lennon, who came through to say that he bore his killer no bitterness. By 1985, Doris had seemingly cornered a sector of spiritland Hollywood. Mae West had been through, so had Peter Sellers, Elvis Presley, James Dean, Jimmy Hendrix, Diana Dors, and even mega-star Marilyn Monroe.

The giant publication *Daily Mirror* wanted a piece of the action. It contracted her and ran a double-spread interview on October 2, 1985. She proved true to form. She got through to Marilyn Monroe and found that Robert Kennedy was there as well! She listened intently to Robert's protests. "You were just good friends with Marilyn? Nothing more? I see."

Then it was through to Marilyn herself, to observe: "You didn't mean to kill yourself? You tried to phone Robert that night, but he was out at a dinner party? Yes, I see. . . . You tried to get help, but were too proud to phone the police or hospital? And there was nothing between you and Robert? He just liked to be seen with beautiful women, but he always loved his wife? I understand lovey."

It was incredible gush like this that led the editor of *Psychic News* to make a front-page protest headed "End 'Kiss and Tell' Seances." He wrote (October 25, 1985):

It does Spiritualism no good to give the impression that at the drop of an astral hat mediums can tune in to anyone at will and receive meaningful messages . . . to be candid, whenever famous personalities return they rarely impart information of much import.

They drone on about the mistakes they made on earth, and like someone picking at an angry spot would seem endlessly to examine their earthly lives, their failures, their disasters and, according to some mediums, their love lives . . . I am concerned by her messages said to come from the famed and acclaimed.

I am not saying Doris Stokes is a liar. She is not. I am not saying she is making it up. I am sure she is not. I am not hinting it is all wishful thinking, that Doris is deluding herself.

But—and this applies to all mediums—once again the acid test, the only test, that one can apply is this: what is the evidence, the supporting testimony, that James Dean, for example, truly is communicating.

But editor Tony Ortzen's protest raises a further question. Just what *is* happening in the medium's mind? If she is not able to separate the suspect messages from the others, then what reliance can be placed on anything she says? Tony Ortzen might argue that in the valid cases people recognize the information passed on to them. But, again, what does this mean? Think of Dr. Hooper's patient who recognized a poster image of his long-dead daughter. People with strong yearnings will *force* information into the shape of their hearts' desire. The evidence for this, from psychic photography alone, is overwhelming.

Then again, even if some seemingly exact information is offered, how can we be certain that it is paranormal in origin? Mediums are like sponges when it comes to soaking up details and storing them. And, can we be sure that their information hasn't been deliberately gathered?

We have a right to be on guard, to be doubtful, even suspicious. The history of spiritualism is not a pretty or uplifting one. But does it offer useful lessons for today? Does it show us what to anticipate? Here the William Roy case should be of some help. Some of the answers are there for certain. Remember, he was top-rank. He produced materializations, apports, spirit-voices, and shoals of evidential messages. He even went one better than show business; he ushered from spiritland to the séance parlor none other than Queen Victoria herself!

3

THE DARK FIDDLER

When William Roy died in August 1977, *Psychic News* said of him: "In Spiritualism's long history there has never been a greater villain. He is now in a world where he cannot cheat."

There were many who would not accept that verdict, for over the years Roy had so raised false hopes among his dupes that a good percentage of them could never face the fact that he was phony. And the people he took in were not always simple, ill-educated types—far from it. They included prominent "society" figures—among them the late Mackenzie King.

Mackenzie King's involvement began during World War II, when he was prime minister of Canada. It was a post that he'd held before, but wartime brought with it extra responsibilities, including top-secret visits to London to confer with the War Cabinet. It was on one of these hush-hush visits that he went to consult William Roy—then famed as Britain's greatest medium.

Since King's visit to Britain was *so* secret, he didn't give his true name in advance. So, on the surface, it looked as if Roy could have had no clue as to the real identity of his client. And yet Roy was able to give the Canadian P.M. some pretty convincing messages, and all from top people—from those who, when they lived, would have naturally and easily talked to a head of government. The grandest of all these was Queen Victoria. Dear, deluded Mackenzie was thrilled as he chatted away to "Her Majesty."

More thrills came when Mr. Gladstone came through and gave a message of hope—just the sort of thing to cheer one up in the dark days of war. It was all very satisfying and comforting. So much so, that the prime minister went back for further sessions and was overwhelmed when his dead brother and sister spoke to him.

Mackenzie King returned to Canada overjoyed and without any suspicions whatsoever—completely unaware that he'd been most thoroughly deceived by a scheming rogue. For Roy's "gifts" were nonexistent. His sessions involved nothing more than play-acting, phony voices, and stage-effects, while his revelations were all due to elaborate cunning and trickery. How did he do it?

His tricks were usually based on techniques that had been used way back in the last century. He added a few of his own, of course, but in the main he stuck with stunts that had been well-tried by other tricksters before him.

He'd found most of his tricks carefully explained in a book called *Behind the Scenes with the Mediums*. This enlightening book was written by David Abbott in 1907 and published only in the United States. A few copies, though, were sold in England by the Magical and Unique Novelty Company in London. Roy had the good fortune to find one of these copies, and it set his mind reeling. Here were all the details he needed to set up a lucrative business. From then on, that book was for him like a portable treasure chest.

By the time Roy set himself up as a medium, he'd mastered most of the tricks in the book. He even worked out a few refinements, so his clients innocently walked into a trap every time they visited his home. You see, they were expected to leave all coats and bags in a special cloakroom, and this gave Roy's accomplice a chance to search through their belongings for bits of useful information. What's more, they were kept waiting before each séance began. As they chatted to pass the time away, hidden microphones picked up their words.

By these means, Roy always knew more about them than they dreamed possible. Sometimes he'd even overhear them list the dead relatives they hoped to contact. In this way, every sitting was neatly rigged beforehand. And, when Roy ran out of authentic tidbits, he was adroit enough to bluff his way through the rest of the session.

Part of his bluff was worked by calling on colorful "spirit guides." There was one called Joey, another called Dr. Wilson, and—best of the lot—an American Indian called Tinka. Tinka was not only fashionable, he was invaluable, for if the questions became awkward he would just sulk and grunt, "No can answer . . . Me just simple Indian." And that would quickly smooth over any rough parts of the evening.

The microphones and searches weren't the only preparations made. Once Roy knew the names of the clients he'd check on their families at the Registry in London's Somerset House. He'd look up death notices and entries in *Who's Who*. He'd even contact other fake mediums for extra information.

His most masterly research, though, involved his initial session with Mackenzie King. For, in that case, he had no opportunity to go through the premier's pockets and no chance to listen to his conversation. All he had to prepare with was an advance booking for a "distinguished person." And all he knew about the booking was that it was made by a member of the Duke of Connaught's staff. That clearly wasn't much to go on, but he had to start somewhere—so he read up on everything he could find on the Duke of Connaught and discovered that the duke had been governor general of Canada from 1911-1916. As soon as he read that, Roy made a brilliant deduction—this mysterious visitor could easily be a distinguished *Canadian* friend of the Duke's. And the most distinguished Canadian known to embrace spiritualism was their prime minister, Mackenzie King.

Roy was so convinced that his deduction was right that he began practicing passages in the voices of Gladstone and Queen Victoria. The queen's high-pitched voice was a bit of a strain, but by the time Mackenzie King turned up it was good enough to fool him and make him want to know more.

But Roy wasn't just famed for the messages he gave—it was the way he gave them that brought him renown. He could make a luminous trumpet float through the air in the darkened séance room and induce "spirit voices" to speak through the mouth of the trumpet. Sometimes there would even be two voices at once. And, remarkably enough, he could even produce extra voices in full light.

When he appeared at public meetings, he worked even more baffling stunts. In 1947, at Kingway Hall, London, his hands were tied to the arms of a chair; his mouth was filled with colored water and his lips were sealed with adhesive tape—yet he still produced spirit voices. And, after the tape was removed, his mouth was found still full of the colored water—so fakery seemed ruled out.

That, of course, is what his audience believed. For they knew nothing about his careful research, and they never realized that Roy was adept at picking up small hints from his clients. He'd delicately pump them for information, then feed it back to them in a new way— and they never realized just what was happening.

As for those voices—well, at the public meetins Roy was responsible for all of them, even when his mouth was filled and sealed up. For him that was just a minor problem. In the darkness he found it easy to bend his head down, loosen the plaster with one tied hand, and eject the water through a rubber tube into a small container in his breast pocket. At the end of the event the water was sucked back up again, the plaster was smoothed back into place, and everyone was overawed.

The private séances were somewhat different. Although most of the voices were Roy's, some were provided by his assistant, while others were tape recordings. In that way he was able to produce more than one voice at a time. And the methods he used apart from the tape recordings were all drawn from that invaluable handbook by Abbott.

First of all, the trumpet flew through the air on the end of a telescopic rod—just as Abbott described. Also, an assistant next door passed information through to Roy by telephone—again exactly as in the book. Of course, that telephone conversation was made without cords, for that would have given the game away. Instead, Roy wore copper plates on the soles of his shoes and these were soldered to thin wires which ran up his trouser-legs and through his jacket to a small earphone on his wrist. To link up with his assistant, he only had to put his feet onto metal carpet tacks and he was connected, for the tacks were wired up to cables running through the wall.

That cunning system worked beautifully, especially when voices were produced in the light, for the earphones would double as a tiny loudspeaker. But it had its limits, so a second connection to the other room was called for, and this was provided by a dummy power-socket on the wall. It wasn't wired to the main circuits, but to an amplifier so Roy could plug a cable into it and energize a miniature loudspeaker fixed on the tip of his telescopic rod. While his assistant's voice came through the speaker, Roy imitated one of his "guides" and threw occasional comments in his own voice. Small wonder that he was famed for his spellbinding sessions.

We all know about Roy's trickery because in 1952 he fell out with his assistant, who promptly paid a call to the offices of *Psychic News*. There he opened up a large suitcase and took out the apparatus used to fake the séances. It was all there, from the telescopic rod to the shoes fitted with copper-plates, and it looked like the end for Roy. His exposure seemed inevitable.

But later on there was a problem, for the assistant didn't want the matter to go any further. Following his assistant's revelations, Roy promised to give up mediumship and leave the country, saying that he wanted to make a new start in South Africa. In fact, he did leave England and the whole sorry affair was silently laid to rest—or so it seemed.

Yet, his old habits proved hard to kill, and within a few years Roy was organizing séances in South Africa. He then had the supreme cheek to return to Britain and start up again. This proved too much for the rest of the spiritualist fraternity, and one of their publications, *Two Worlds,* named Roy as a fraudulent medium.

Dramatic results followed this newspaper report. Roy's wife attacked the editor with a riding-crop, and Roy himself started a lawsuit against the editor. Roy's wife was fined three pounds for the assault, and Roy paid the fine with a smile, for he knew that his lawsuit meant that he could go on milking his clients since his action prevented any further newspaper comment on the case until *after* the court hearing. Further, court actions can sometimes take years before they get to be heard, and that's just what happened in Roy's case.

He carried on his fakery until February 1958. Then he dropped this lawsuit for he knew he couldn't win, and agreed to pay costs to the editor of *Two Worlds.* Following that, he brazenly sold his story to the *Sunday Pictorial.* It was published in five installments and the *Pictorial* readers marveled at the way he'd cheated his way to fame and fortune. At the end of the series Roy wrote this: "I know that even after this confession I could fill the séance rooms again with people who find it a comfort to believe I am genuine."

At the time that sounded like hot air or bravado, but Roy went on to make his boast come true. He set up shop under the name Bill Silver, and for years he ran his old racket without challenge. And, believe it or not, among his clients he numbered people who knew his real identity and who were fully aware of his sordid confessions!

4

THE CLUELESS CRIME-BUSTERS

Six grim-faced detectives surrounded the woman in the armchair. The guarded cellar was darkened and lit only by a single dim red bulb. The silence was deathlike. The men held their breath. "Then their hair almost stood on end as they watched the handsome face of the old lady transform slowly into a visage of dreadful evil. The kindly mouth was drawn back into a bestial snarl; eyes burned like living coals."

It was 1929. The place, the German city of Dusseldorf. Three sadistic murders had brought a mounting fear to its streets. In desperation, the police were seeking help from a "psychic detective."

Her lips moved, saliva dripped from the corners of the mouth, and weird and awful sounds filled the room. It was not the gentle old lady speaking; it was the spirit voice of some horrible creature who in his earthly days had butchered and tortured like a maniac. No sane creature could have mouthed the awful oaths and blasphemies which came from between the snarling lips . . . the senior officer pulled himself together, and asked in steady tones:

"We want to know who is killing our people here in Dusseldorf. We shall not harm him. Will you tell us?"

The awful voice shrieked, "No! No! Let him kill them—it is good. I like blood—blood—blood!". . . . The medium licked her twisting lips at the mention of the word, squirming in her chair like some fearful vampire. . . .

"I know him. I control him. He does what I command. When I want blood he drinks it for me," the maniacal tones shrilled. "But you shall not find him. You shall not take him from me."

Suddenly the medium sprang to her feet and leapt like a tigress upon the detective . . . hands like steel claws gripping his shoulders . . . it took four strong men, used to rough-and-tumble fighting, to shake off those clawlike hands.

More than fifty years ago, such melodrama introduced the public to psychic sleuthery. The quotation is from "the first book to be written on the relationship of crime to the supernatural." This volume was appropriately "ghost-written" for ex-Detective Sergeant Edwin T. Woodhall—late of Special Branch of the CID and Scotland Yard.

In *Crime And The Supernatural,* the wily Woodhall (we'll meet him again!) gave false authority to a string of dubious yarns. Since then, "psychic detective" tales have proliferated. But are they to be taken seriously?

Unfortunately, while a lie can be coined in minutes, months may be taken up in exposing that lie. And therein lies the difficulty of grappling with accounts of psychic detection.

Let's accept these difficulties. Let's set legitimate doubts to one side and take some recent, well-reported cases as examples. Given adequate documentation, we may be able to judge fairly and firmly.

The case of the Dartmoor Air Cadets provides a good starting point. In April 1981, this odd affair took up many columns of the national and local newspapers in Great Britain.

Each year hundreds of children and teenagers descend on Dartmoor in Devon during the last week of April. They come in organized groups to practice for the Ten Tor Expedition held in May.

The groups have to cover some fifty-five miles of inhospitable moorland following predetermined routes. It's a test of skill and endurance under the best of conditions. Unfortunately, in late April 1981 freak blizzards hit Dartmoor.

Rescue teams set out and brought the most isolated groups back to safety. Other groups made their own way off the moors. But one group of five air cadets from Cornwall remained missing—lost somewhere in the raging snow. The police organized search parties. A systematic sweep of the moors began and, after about fifty hours, the cadets were located at Brat Tor, near the northwest edge of Dartmoor.

Then the story broke: "Medium's message leads to lost boys," wrote the *Daily Telegraph* of April 28. "Medium's 'Psychic Guide' leads the Dartmoor boys to safety," proclaimed the *Daily Express* next day. It went on to ask, "Can we explain these amazing powers?" Most of the other papers chimed in on a similar theme.

Apparently, Mrs. Frances Dymond, a 55-year-old mother of seven and a medium, had directed the baffled search party to the right place and just in the nick of time!

A radio newsflash had reported that the boys were missing. Minutes later Mrs. Dymond was on full mental alert: "My guide kept telling me that I had to save the boys," she said. "It made me so upset.

I did not really know what I could do. I just had to give up cooking the Sunday lunch. My mind was in a turmoil."

She telephoned the police. They took no notice. Sunday night proved sleepless: "The messages kept coming from my guide. I could see an old man and he was living in a tumbledown cottage on the Moor and he kept pointing to a monument with spikes on the top."

She went to the police station near her home at Perranporth. There she poured over their Ordnance Survey map and put two fingers on the place where the boys could be found.

Her information, so she claims, was passed at once to the rescue team in this area. The team followed her lead, headed for the spirit-inspired location, and the boys were found. Their equipment and tent had kept them alive and reasonably fit.

Press statements by William Ames, secretary of the Dartmoor Rescue Group, seemed to back up Mrs. Dymond's story: "There was only one place that matched that description, Widgery Tor, and we were clutching at straws because we had searched over a hundred square miles. . . . But this lady's description of the monument was too clear to ignore."

Police statements, on the other hand, presented a very different picture. They revealed that when the boys were found they were walking toward the edge of the moor. In ten or so minutes they would have reached the main Okehampton-Tavistock Road. Even if the boys had not reached that road they would have been discovered by one or other of the search-parties working in that section, for the moors were not being combed haphazardly but systematically square by square. And this all-embracing sweep was nearing completion.

So, our medium had every natural factor in her favor since all such late forecasts draw on the "drought factor." In other words, the longer a drought goes on, the closer we are to rain. And it's just so with a systematic search of the type mounted at Dartmoor.

Now, Mrs. Dymond lives more than fifty miles west of Dartmoor. Despite this, the main landmarks of the moor are extremely well known to people in her area and are frequently featured in newsreels and documentaries shown on the local television channels in southwest England.

The lady does live, though, just seven miles from Truro, where four of the cadets came from. From the beginning of the drama, details of the search were the talk of Truro town. And the radio and television coverage kept the matter to the fore. Any information the medium needed about the boys themselves or about the stages of the search was, therefore, freely available.

Devon & Cornwall Constabulary Public Relations Officer Robert Busby summed up the medium's contribution in this way:

> During the operation, Mrs. Dymond did contact the search headquarters by telephone and described certain landmarks on Dartmoor. Her information fitted about forty locations on the Moor and was of no practical use whatsoever. The problem arose in that when the boys were finally located by a team from the Dartmoor Rescue Group an enthusiastic volunteer informed the press that they had been guided to the spot by Mrs. Dymond's vision, thus establishing her credibility. She then sold various stories to national newspapers including a £400 feature for the *Sunday Mirror*.

But could this just be pique on the part of the police? Not a bit of it. There's nothing to show that Mrs. Dymond was anything but a rank opportunist. At the time, checks were made on her at the offices of *Psychic News*. This paper carries files on all mediums great and small, but Mrs. Dymond was not listed. In fact, when *Psychic News* telephoned one of their Cornish contacts with an extensive knowledge of the spiritualist movement in that area, they found that Mrs. Dymond's name meant nothing.

Yet this lady, who was *so* little known and who had presumably done nothing newsworthy in her life before, was within days announcing that the *first volume* of her autobiography was going to be published that summer! Further statements showed that five papers were competing for "exclusive" interviews.

But, in typical opportunistic fashion, the lady overreached herself. She gained further press and radio publicity when she announced that she knew strange things about other murders. She claimed to have psychic insights into the killings of black youths in Atlanta, Georgia. She further claimed that she knew about the true fate of the missing Devon schoolgirl Genette Tate.

Genette had disappeared in August 1978. Mrs. Dymond now announced that Genette had been strangled and her body had been walled up in a house in the Exeter area. The house belonged to the killer. It had bay windows and the upstairs window had been repaired.

The police called her bluff. There was little they could do about the Atlanta killings, but the Genette Tate case was within their province. An officer called at Mrs. Dymond's house in Perrenporth to take a statement. After all her boasts, she backed down and refused to expand on her public claims. Her excuse? She said that "her spirit guide had told her not to cooperate." From now on she had to "stick to faith-healing." All the hopes she'd raised were dashed earthward.

So ended the meteoric career of Mrs. Dymond. Yet few people know of this outcome. The newspapers that yelled long and loudly on her entrance took care to only whisper about her exit!

Lone Ranger Dymond wasn't the first "psychic detective" to dabble in the Genette Tate case. There were many others right from the start in August 1978.

On the early afternoon of Saturday, August 19, Genette cycled off on her newspaper route—a route that took her along the quiet country lanes circling the village of Aylesbeary in Devon. Hours later her abandoned bicycle was found at the side of Within Lane. Of Genette there wasn't the slightest trace or sign. The alarm was raised. The hunt began.

A police helicopter slowly scanned the fields, farmlands and woods for miles around the area. Seven thousand rubber-booted searchers trudged across the ground, probing in every ditch, hedge, and copse. But even "Genette's Welly Army" (as the press dubbed them) failed to find a single worthwhile clue.

The crass materialists, with their sole reliance on physical methods, were clearly at a loss. But the psychics were more than confident that their extra-special knowledge could crack the case. There were telephone calls and letters to the police and to the Tate family. Then came the visits. As Genette's father John Tate affirms: "A dowser turned up . . . and took away with him personal items belonging to Genette. He then locked himself away at the police incident centre to study the items and area maps. . . . He came up with a number of suggestions which were duly followed up, they all proved false hopes. . . . Many people came to us offering threads of hope. We clutched at them desperately in the early days. . . . But the promises of the psychics were all lies. They raised false hopes in us. At times we really believed we were onto something. The suggestions and ideas preyed on our minds. . . . But always, when it came to the crunch, the so-called leads and ideas led absolutely nowhere but into a pit of despair."

One of the callers at Tate's house stated that he was the reincarnation of a 5,000-year-old Eastern god. He prophesied that Genette would be beamed down from Venus into a nearby field at 2:30 the following Thursday.

Another caller was a woman who arrived clutching a bamboo table. As credentials, she affirmed that she was the slave of a masterful Indian spirit. "She bounced this table up and down for three hours calling up her master and going through the alphabet each time to spell out the words."

In all, almost five hundred psychic theories and suggestions were put forward, and the police have stated that they had a schedule of more than two thousand items of information from such sources in their case index. The possibility for inspired guesswork and permutations was certainly great. And yet all the "insights" led nowhere. Some of the police comments are worth noting. Roger Busby has this to say:

One of the first psychics on the scene, a medium from Cornwall, shook like a leaf when he visited the scene, much to the amazement of the DCI who was accompanying him, and then predicted that Genette's body would be found within two days and the offender arrested the following day. . . . When his predictions failed to come to pass he was not seen again (although at a much later stage he did claim in a newspaper interview to have been called in by the police).

Another psychic awakened by a vivid dream at his home in Leicester, jumped into his car in the early hours of the morning and drove over two hundred miles to the incident room where he told an officer: "I've solved it. Genette's in the boot of a car. . . ."

"Can you tell me what make of car?"

"I'm sorry I can't."

"Registration number?"

"Afraid not. . ."

He was given a cup of tea and then drove home.

There were many such instances in which psychic information was offered and I must add that much of it was certainly in good faith, which was just too vague to follow up. "She's in a country cottage with honeysuckle near the door," was a typical example. Plenty to choose from in Devon. "She's been devoured by a wild animal which escaped from a zoo. You won't know the animal's escaped because it ate its keeper first"—that was one of my favourites.

At one stage, dowsers (they're the ones who dangle objects over maps) were queueing up to have a crack at the case.

We decided in view of the psychic interest in the case that we would approach . . . Dr. Croiset of Utrecht, through an intermediary, i.e., the "Daily Express.". . . He duly came across but after an inconclusive day during which he provided some quite startling observations on the case, even down to describing the offender and the sequence of events surrounding Genette's disappearance, he finally confessed that he had no way of knowing whether the information he received through his extra sensory powers related to the past, present or future. Again, a problem for accepted police procedure.

Needless to say the Genette Tate case is still unresolved and if the Ufologists (flying saucer experts) are to be believed, it will stay that way. They maintain she was kidnapped by a Venusian space craft evidenced by a crescent shaped scorch mark from its exhaust in a field adjacent to the lane. A somewhat more mundane explanation came from a local farmer who said he had inadvertently spilled a little too much lime in that corner of the field.

Don Crabb, now police superintendent at Newton Abbott, writes: "We never invited psychics in, but when we said we'd listen to anyone who might help we opened the floodgates. We had early 1,200 letters from people claiming to be mediums or possessing ESP and many more of them turned up. . . . Some suggested she was bricked up in chimneys; some said she was in roadworks; some said she was in water. One thought she was under a bridge. We listened to them all, but they didn't do anything to help our enquiry."

There was even a highly respectable "psychic search party" set up in December 1978. It was headed by television script writer Andrew Wilson and had the cooperation of ex-Detective Chief Inspector Dick Lee. They tried to take some of the crankiness out of the atmosphere, but for all their "scientific" pretensions, they simply wasted much time and money on wild-goose chasing. Nothing of value was contributed by this group.

As far as Genette is concerned, perhaps her father should have the last word. He says: "We soon found that the psychics who came up our garden path were 'foot-in-the-door' types who, once they had wormed their way in, were very reluctant to leave again. They were strong characters who were not afraid to assert themselves. They rode rough-shod over our feelings—which were in a desperate state already. In one week, our emotions and normal grip on life had gone through a wrenching upheaval, and the influence of psychics started to have an unpleasant effect. Even when we didn't want them they were there, on our doorstep, always expecting to be met with an open door."

And he bitterly adds later: "We discovered that the work of the psychics was not just ludicrous and laughable. It was sinister and evil. Once we got into that web of deceit—and that was what it was—we found it very hard to struggle free. None of it ever led anywhere except to despair and disappointment, misery and confusion. We had become enslaved to the suggestions of the psychics."

Talk of the sinister and evil naturally brings us back to our starting point—to the melodrama enacted in Dusseldorf in 1929. How did it end? Well, despite all those mediumistic writhings and mouthings the killer went on killing. At least six more victims were slaughtered. In the end the Dusseldorf Ripper was delivered to the police by none other than—his wife!

He was an outwardly calm, stuffily respectable, middle-class citizen who was also a secret admirer of London's Jack the Ripper. His name was Peter Keurten. Remember it. It will resonate. It ties in strangely with the psychic flimflam surrounding the Yorkshire Ripper murders.

Now *there* was a real challenge to the psychic detectives of the world. They had a full five years to focus their powers. So, just *how* did they face up to that challenge? And what was their final score?

5

THE YORKSHIRE RIPPER
AND THE PSYCHIC CIRCUS

The trail of terror began on the morning of October 30, 1975. On that bleak, wet day, Wilma McCann was found murdered on a deserted playing-field in the Chapeltown area of Leeds. Her skull had been smashed by two vicious blows. Her body was marred by fifteen stab-wounds. The Yorkshire Ripper had chalked up his first killing.

He was to kill twelve more women before he was caught, more than five years later. For the greater part of those five years the air was thick with rumors and theories about his identity. The police were constantly baffled and at loggerheads with one another. The pressmen were eternally speculating. And the gaudy psychic circus brought out its clowns great and small!

The police have never released the number of psychics who approached them with examples of their "special insights," but in the less spectacular Genette Tate case more than 450 "mediums of one sort or another" were known to have been in touch with the detectives. In the Ripper case, it would be fair to guess that the number was equally as great, and possibly even greater.

The most prominent among this group have fortunately gone on record, sometimes more than once. That allows us to make a fair judgment of their forecasts when compared with the real events as they unfolded.

One of the most dramatic forecasts of this type was printed in the *Sunday People* of July 1, 1979. It was the lead on the front page and its startling headline set in large type read: "Face of the Ripper." Alongside the headline was a large sketch of "the Ripper" drawn by artist Bob Williams. The account went on to say that "famous clair-voyant Doris Stokes has 'seen' the face of the Ripper." The remarkable sketch was based on her description as given to the newspaper's artist.

According to this description, the Ripper had a "scar below his left eye which twitches when he gets agitated." He was five feet, eight inches tall. He was called Ronnie or Johnnie with a surname beginning with the letter M. He lived in a street named Berwick or Bewick.

In detail, the sketch shows the Ripper as clean-shaven with long, straight hair—"mousey hair which covers his ears." The hair is parted on the right, where "there is a small bald patch which he tries to cover up."

In filling in the Ripper's background, Doris Stokes claimed that she had got through to his mother, Molly or Polly, who told her that the killer was married, but his wife had left him. Doris was also able to add that she believed the Ripper had received treatment at a hospital, "possibly Cherry Knowle Hospital at Ryhope, near Sunderland, which specializes in mental cases."

It should be noted that Mrs. Stokes terms herself a clairaudient, rather than a clairvoyant. In other words her information comes in the form of voices instead of visions or pictures. Nevertheless, this didn't stop her from being certain that the artist's impression really matched the face of the Ripper. Her certainty led her to repeat this information on Tyne Tees Television.

Mrs. Stokes's description led to considerable anger on the part of a Mr. Ronnie Metcalf. The poor man unfortunately lived at Berwick Avenue, Downhill, Sunderland. He had a Wearside accent and was a long-distance lorry driver, working for an engineering firm. These matched some of the features the police were looking for in their hunt. And, to top it all, his travels took him regularly to Yorkshire and Lancashire where all the victims had died. In a statement to the press, Metcalf said: "It's not me, so just lay off. I seem to fit the bill almost exactly. At first I didn't mind having my leg pulled but this is no laughing matter. There are bound to be people who take this clair-voyant stuff seriously and who will be pointing their finger at me. I haven't been seen by the police, but I have no doubt that I could quickly convince them that the Ripper and I are two completely dif-ferent people."

Doris Stokes's conviction that the Ripper lived on Tyneside or Wearside came after she'd heard a broacast of a tape-recording said to have been made by the killer. We now know that the tape was nothing but a cruel hoax. At the time, though, even the police gave the tape full credence. As a result, the police took Mrs. Stokes seriously or, so it seems; for Brian Johnston, Northumbria's chief constable, was quoted as saying that the police would be checking on all the places with the names Berwick and Bewick in their region.

Five months later, the Dutch "psychic detective" Gerard Croiset made *his* solemn pronouncement. Remarkably, he seemed to agree broadly with Mrs. Stokes. In *The Sun* of November 28, 1979, he said that the Ripper had "long hair cut straight across the neck." He limped, due to a damaged right knee, and he lived in the heart of Sunderland in a large block of service flats over a garage. Croiset added that, when about six years old, the Ripper had been in "a kind of institution for psychologically disturbed children."

Quite different conclusions were reached by clairvoyant Flora Mackenzie. She forecast that the killer would live in the Barnsley-Sheffield area. This brought her into direct conflict with a Mr. Patrick Barnard who seemed to have seen more than anyone else and in much more detail.

Mr. Barnard's story took over the front page of the Southend *Evening Echo* of November 24, 1980. "I Have Seen the Ripper" yelled the headline. Then Mr. Barnard went on to describe how he'd looked down on the Ripper "as if from my bedroom window." The killer was a man of average build with dark hair, either wavy or curly.

"I could only see his back," he said. "But on the shoulders of his black duffle coat were the white letters R.N. It seemed that he was walking out of a submarine dockyard. I felt that it was in Scotland and I got the impression he was working on a nuclear submarine.

"Wouldn't that explain everything? A crewman on a sub, at sea for months at a time, while the police are chasing their own tails looking for him ashore?"

In his visions, Mr. Barnard saw an old and abandoned green railway coach in an overgrown and disused building. This was the place where the Ripper came after each murder to change his clothes. He even saw the Ripper's home, a place also close to a railway—a top flat in fact, in a dilapidated gray house situated over a railway tunnel. And one more place was visible to him. An old wartime air-raid shelter. In this shelter was a cardboard box, and he sensed that inside it were parts of the Ripper's victims!

Mr. Barnard had no doubts whatever about the accuracy of his visions. "I have seen these things as plainly as slides projected on a screen," he insisted. "I am not a nutter."

Despite his certainty, the Leeds police were not impressed. They first reacted by saying: "We get thousands of people like this, all ringing us up and telling us something different." And they added,

"Railway coaches in these parts don't have green livery."

Yet two days later an *Evening Echo* reader reported that he had seen green railway coaches on a disused line close to "a remote coastal road near Hull." Since Hull is close enough to Leeds to make the information exciting, the *Echo* rang Hull police. Inspector Terry Lamb, at Hull, took the tip-off seriously enough to send out officers to trace these coaches—but later reports show that the searches led nowhere.

In the days following Patrick Barnard's disclosures there came a crop of forecasts. The *Daily Star* ran a front-page lead story and devoted a double-page spread to what it termed an "amazing dossier." This dossier was supplied by an anonymous medium who claimed that the Ripper was between forty and forty-five years old. He was of stocky build with blue eyes, moles on his face, and fair hair that could have recently been dyed. He was born in London, but moved north when six years old. By trade he was possibly a plumber, but he'd once worked as a miner. He was unmarried, partly owing to the influence of his mother—a domineering and religious woman "probably in her eighties."

A list of twelve "psychically supplied" names of acquaintances was included, together with other fine details—one being the remarkable fact that the Ripper perhaps owned a parrot!

This "amazing dossier that comes from beyond the grave," was illustrated by seven drawings supplied by a "famous psychic artist." An eighth drawing, of the Ripper himself, was held back in case it hindered police investigations.

The next development came when the medium David Walton went into print in *Psychic News* on December 6, 1980. His information included the tidbit that the Ripper "sometimes disguises himself as a woman." Walton also believed that he had contacted the Ripper's dead father and had homed in on a terraced house where the killer occupied a small back-room.

Following that, Joan Gricks called at the *Psychic News* offices and revealed information that she'd passed on to the police. In her view, the killer "disguises himself and has, on occasion, dressed as a woman."

In reporting these things, *Psychic News* wisely made no attempt to list all the other confident claims made up to that date. Had the paper done so, it would have also recorded statements by Alfred Cartwright, Simon Alexander, Reginald du Marius, and others. So, in the interests of fairness, let's consider these people as well.

Starting with Alfred Cartwright, we find he told the police: "As soon as I saw a picture of this girl (Jayne MacDonald) I began to see pictures of the man who killed her. He is an ordinary working man, aged about 28 or 30, who lives in Bradford. In four weeks time he will strike again in the Chapeltown area but he will then be caught."

In reality, the Ripper struck ten days after Mr. Cartwright's statement, and went on to kill eight more women.

Seventeen days after Mr. Cartwright's intervention, clairvoyant Simon Alexander was taken to five of the murder sites—one in Bradford and four in Leeds. He then said: "I think the first death was probably an accident, after the man was taunted, and it has built up from there. Obviously there is something very wrong with the man, but I don't think he'll murder another woman."

But there was obviously something very wrong with Mr. Alexander since the murders continued for three more years.!

Reginald du Maris, by contrast, was refreshingly precise. He was a Manchester astrologer who sent his deductions to the police on July 26, 1979. He announced that the Ripper strikes "when the moon is positioned in an orbital course of 22 degrees." This allowed him to know that the Ripper would "strike tomorrow, Friday night"—that is, on the twenty-seventh. He was also able to add, "I've also deduced that the Ripper was born at 9:30 P.M. on September 15th, 1946—making him 32 years of age." For the record, there was no attack on Friday, July 27, 1979—and the Ripper was born sometime after eight o'clock on June 2, 1946.

Not all the psychic detectives, however, were British. In August 1979, Dutch engineer Wim Virbeek said that the Ripper was a 27-year-old washing-machine mechanic living in Aberdeen. At the same time, another Dutchman, the clairvoyant Dono Meijling, actually came to England and spent his Christmas and New Year prowling around Chapeltown in search of clues. He was finally able to supply fairly specific leads—none of which were of any use. The most controversial of these was the suggestion that the Yorkshire Ripper was in some way related to Detective Chief Superintendent Jim Hobson!

They all seemed to be at it—with pendulums and maps, crystal balls, trances and séances and group meditations, to list just some of the strange methods employed. Even the self-styled "King of the Witches," Alex Sanders, felt impelled to chip in with a pearl of wisdom. One of his trances had brought him into contact with the spirit of the killer; so, with authority, he announced, "He lives alone in a flat in

South Shields, overlooking railway arches." Regrettably, he forgot to list the street name and house number.

So many words, so many theories, and so much conviction—yet it was all nothing but pretentious blather. The arrest and conviction in 1981 of Ripper Peter Sutcliffe showed every published psychic forecast had been hopelessly wrong. The "clean-shaven" man, who was alleged to have posed as a woman, had sported a dense black beard and moustache all along. His "dead father" was very much alive—his "living", dominant mother was two years dead. Far from being a bachelor skulking away in a small back-room, he turned out to be a married man owning a large detached house. He was thirty-five, with a thick mop of black curly hair and no scars or moles on his face. Born a Northerner, he was living at Bradford in his native Yorkshire!

Now the sincerity of these forecasters is not in doubt. But the inescapable conclusion is that five years of psychic probings failed to bring to light one single useful clue as to the Ripper's identity or whereabouts. On the contrary, the "psychic information" was wholly misleading. If taken seriously, it would have led to the waste of thousands of hours of police time. As such, it ranks as arrogant and mischievous nonsense.

6

THE MURDERER AND THE MEDIUM

Eighteen months before the police arrested Peter Sutcliffe, the York-shire Ripper, Kent medium, Nella Jones, drew a picture of him, described where he lived and worked and accurately predicted two more murders before he was caught . . . Eventually Nella went to Yorkshire and accompanied police to help them locate clues and places. Her mental pictures were always accurate.

Nella could exactly describe details of a location before they ever arrived on the spot. Police were amazed the psychic could direct them to places she had never seen. (*Psychic News,* June 5, 1982).

Note the words of that report. The exaggerations are already creeping in. A new myth is already being minted. The real truth is only to be found in Mrs. Jones's writing—the logical starting point.

On the surface, her Ripper forecasts seem to score an inexplicable number of significant hits. Unlike the other psychics we've looked at, her major predictions were never published in advance, still, she insists that they were *witnessed.* So, in her case, every detail warrants the closest possible scrutiny.

We begin, though, with a handicap. I've written to Nella Jones and asked her to deposit copies of all her original forecasts involving these murders with the Society for Psychical Research. In that way, they could be analyzed at leisure by believers and skeptics alike—a very fair proposition.

To date no documents have been deposited—and Mrs. Jones has chosen not to reply to my polite letter. You may draw your own conclusions from this. So, in proceeding, we're forced to rely on twenty-one pages in her book, *Ghost Of A Chance,* and the various newspaper reports of Nella's sayings. Fortunately, even this incomplete record shows up the fatal flaws. There's enough left to demonstrate that her apparent "hits" are ultimately derived from analogies with similar crimes, and from published information. Now, I don't make those statements lightly—consider the proofs.

Dark-haired Jacqueline Hill was murdered in Leeds on the rainy night of Monday, November 17, 1980. Nella's book claims that this death had been foreseen fourteen months earlier—early in September 1979. Then she'd said: "The next victim will be found on a small patch of waste ground."

Nearer to the date she'd added: ". . . I suddenly saw with tremendous clarity, the scene of the Ripper's next attack. It was a small piece of wasteland. . . . The girl I knew without seeing, had dark hair. . . ."

Amazing foresight? Let's see. Prior to Jacqueline's death, only one woman had died in a bedroom. Of the others, one was found on a rubbish-pile, one in the grounds of a wood-yard, two on sites described as "grassland" and six on *wasteland*. Of the Ripper's twelve victims, *ten* had dark hair. Clairvoyance was hardly needed to infer that the same pattern would recur!

Of the Ripper himself, she said: "I believe he lives in Bradford and that he is a long-distance lorry-driver. . . . I had the strongest feeling that the police had already spoken to him." In the end, all these things turned out to be true. But where is the psychic element?

As early as October 1975, the police had announced that they were looking for a *lorry-driver* in connection with the murder of Wilma McCann.

On October 26, 1977, after the murder of Jean Royle, a team of Manchester detectives swept into the Bradford area. They announced that together with detectives from West Yorkshire, "We will be visiting factories in the Bingley, Shipley and Bradford areas and are interviewing all male employees."

On the following day the police gave their reasons. A near-mint five-pound note had been found in Jean Royle's handbag. The note had been traced to its bank of issue—the Shipley and Bingley branch of the Midland Bank on the edge of Bradford.

Following this announcement, the police launched a massive appeal to all workers in Bradford, Shipley and Bingley to check their wage packets for five-pound notes within a short range of serial numbers. They searched for a full three months. Over five thousand people were interviewed. In the end, Detective Superintendent Jack Ridgeway was able to say (January 17, 1978), "It is more than likely that we have interviewed the person who received the fiver."

So, everything she'd spoken about had been given national publicity ages before. Anyone interested in the Ripper killings could have toyed with those ideas. For example, take author David Yallop. By looking at the published material and without any psychic indulgences, he was able to deduce that, the clues ". . . pointed unquestioningly to the Baildon/Bingley/Shipley areas near Bradford as the killer's place of work and almost certainly residence."

He was so sure of this that on Wednesday, June 25, 1979, he met up with Assistant Chief Constable George Oldfield at the police offices in Wakefield. As Yallop testifies in his *Deliver Us From Evil:* "I put it to George Oldfield that in my view, the five pound note had come from the killer, that he most certainly worked in the Baildon/Bingley/Shipley area and equally certainly lived there, that he was probably a lorry-driver."

Yallop has a tape-recording of the interview. His deductions refute the view that Mrs. Jones' visions gave her extraordinary and valuable information.

She had another try in 1979, when she declared, "He's older than the police think—about thirty-six." At that time, the Ripper had just turned thirty-three. But it's easy to see how she arrives at *her* figure, for a year earlier, Dr. Stephen Shaw had developed a possible profile of the Ripper. This profile appeared in the *Yorkshire Post,* the newspaper Nella was cooperating with. The significant age mentioned by Shaw was thirty-five. At the same time as Nella's guess and without clairvoyance, writer Michael Nicholson guessed the Ripper's age as thirty-two.

Was she any better at revealing his killing and mutilation techniques—or even his height? She seems to think she was. She says, "The murders, it was disclosed during the trial, *did* involve the use of a hammer, among other weapons. . . ." She put his height at, somewhere between five foot seven or five foot eight.

The hammer reference presumably refers to her horror dreams of August 1979. However, these plagued her only after newspaper articles had already made the information public. First, consider the prominent article in the *Daily Express* of June 30, 1979. It said the killer, "uses work bench equipment to mutilate his victims."

Twelve days later the *Bradford Telegraph & Argus* revealed the truth for the first time. It stated: "Kills with an engineers' ball-pein hammer. Wears size seven boots. . . ." So, from July onward, the hammer-weapon and his small size became national knowledge.

Her "foreknowledge" concerning the Ripper's house is presented as being right on the mark. She pictured ". . . a grey house with a wrought iron gate in front . . . the impression of a small garage nearby." The house number was six.

When it was revealed that Ripper Sutcliffe lived at number six, Garden Lane, Heaton, Bradford, an exact correspondence was chalked up. Yet, the Garden Lane house had exterior walls of a *light pinkish* hue. And the "physically revealed" address was *not* one in Garden Lane; it was number 6, Chapel Street, Bradford.

There are four Chapel Streets in Bradford, as well as a Chapel Walk, Chapel Lane, Chapel Place, Chapel Fold, and Chapel Road. None of these places had the slightest connection with the Ripper!

That leaves us with just a few items that seem to be different in quality. At one point the name Ainsworth had leapt into her mind—and it turned out that the last-but-one murder actually occurred in the grounds of a Leeds magistrate named Hainsworth. Then, she'd had the name Peter in mind. And long before the murder of Jacqueline Hill she'd recorded the initials J. H. Finally, weeks before Jacqueline's death she predicted that the Ripper would strike in November, possibly on the seventeenth or the twenty-seventh. Jacqueline was murdered on Monday, November 17.

So, how does anyone pluck such information out of thin air? They don't. This is past knowledge recycled as future knowledge. It becomes extra-convincing by sheer coincidence, as we'll see.

Consider the mind of the psychic. He or she constantly looks for cycles, patterns, or portents linked with their current interests. When these things are discovered, they are projected forward and used as a framework for picturing future events.

Sometimes, this is a conscious search. Sometimes, it is subconscious. At other times, it will be a mixture on both levels.

Next, consider the special interest factor. In short, we all take extra notice of anything that reflects or impinges on our special interests. So, naturally the psychics will register anything that falls within their field—even marginally. Books and articles dealing with the spiritualist or occult worlds are inevitably taken notice of. Whether the interest is deep or superficial matters little, for even a superficial glance at a text can be enough to register ideas and images in the subconscious. Hold this well in mind. It is often the key to psychic revelations.

Since the revealer is essential to the revelation, what sort of person is Mrs. Jones? Her own statements show that she has been levitated by invisible hands; been transported twice to a phantom village; has seen the ghost of a cowled monk; has practiced faith healing and psychometry; and has initiated exorcisms.

In a less enlightened age she would have been accused of witch-craft. Indeed, as a schoolgirl she was ostracized by her school-mates. When she asked why they wouldn't talk to her any more, one yelled: "Because you're a witch. You said that old lady would die . . . and she did. Witch! Witch, witch, witch . . ."

So much for her psychic background, but has she a good memory for detail? Certainly. Her book records "I was just beginning to discover what a good memory I had. Our school-teacher had read 'Hiawatha' to us twice in class and just from those two readings I had memorized the whole poem."

And that poem involved 22 sections spread over 70 pages, broken down into 140 columns and involving roughly 5,320 lines. These lines in turn embody 130 unfamiliar Indian names!

So, she brought a phenomenal memory to bear on the Yorkshire Ripper case. And there was no lack of material around to fire her imagination. At the time, psychics and non-psychics alike were looking back at earlier Ripper-style murders in a search for some sort of guidance—for significant patterns.

They first looked far back to the original Jack the Ripper murders; then, forward to Jack's notorious imitator, the Dusseldorf Ripper of the 20s—Peter Keurten. Peter Keurten's name and record were mulled over repeatedly.

In 1979, in the very first book on the Yorkshire murders, Michael Nicholson devoted four pages to Peter Keurten's crimes, emphasizing: ". . . it is possible to draw several lessons from his pattern of behaviour which may be helpful in an interpretation of the Yorkshire killer's psychology and motives."

We see then that, in truth, the *only* Christian name constantly associated with the Ripper murders was the name *Peter*. That it popped up in Nella's mind is hardly electrifying.

The name of Ainsworth, though, looks quite baffling. Does it present an insoluble problem? To begin with, we find that only one person with the name Ainsworth has achieved national and popular fame in Britain in the last two centuries. That was novelist W. H. Ainsworth. At one time his books were best-sellers. Now they are out of favor, which is why they often turn up for next-to-nothing in street-markets, junk-shops and thrift-shops.

We already know that Mrs. Jones is deeply involved in all things occult. Consciously or subconsciously, she will take note of anything she meets up with in this field. It's her special mental circle of interest.

Now, one of Ainsworth's frequently seen titles is *The Lancashire Witches*. To Mrs. Jones its significance may not be great. But it's strong enough for the title to register. The subconscious is a marvelous magpie.

Once this connection between Ainsworth and the occult has been made, the name Ainsworth gains extra importance to Mrs. Jones. Any future titles by him will be noted and mentally filed. Later on, a completely unconnected set of events sets up a resonance. The mental files are shuffled and the mind brings up the author's name—seemingly out of nowhere.

In this particular case, the vital resonating factor is provided by the only Christian name shown on the covers of Ainsworth's novels. That name is Harrison, a name in common with the Ripper's second victim—Joan Harrison, killed in 1975.

But why should *this* victim's name be especially significant for Mrs. Jones? Well, incredible as it may seem, the published picture of Joan Harrison shows a woman whose face resembles that of Nella Jones. This is not fleeting resemblance. It's one so close that the picture could be passed off as a snap of a younger sister. The ultra-significant killing of Harrison took place in Lancashire in the town of Preston.

We now have in front of us all the evidence we need to show the essential interconnections.

The Lancashire connection brings to mind the novel *The Lancashire Witches*. And Preston, as a place of violence, resonates with another of Ainsworth's titles, *Preston Fight*.

Then the three factors, the name of the county, the name of the town, and the name of the victim, couple inexorably with the name of the author. In Nella's mind the name Ainsworth is erected as a mysterious mental signboard.

It doesn't stop there. The Harrison murder is behind other mental leaps. Nella conceived the idea of a November killing involving the intitials J. H. Those, of course, were Joan Harrison's initials. And she, in fact, *was* killed in November.

This is a splendid example of the past being refurbished as a glimpse of the future. It was only the coincidences surrounding Jacqueline Hill's death that gave this forecast a spurious splendor. But note this: earlier on, the Christian name produced in connection with the initials was not Jacqueline, but Jean—which is simply another form of Joan!

All that's left are the dates, the seventeenth and the twenthy-seventh. How were they arrived at? Firstly, a murder prediction involving the twenty-seventh of the month had been advanced by Mr. du Marius in July 1979. His forecast appeared in the press and on page 114 of Michael Nicholson's book. On the *same page,* Nicholson reports Nella Jones's forecasts. There's one possible sparking point.

Next, in the whole range of attack-dates considered by her, the bulk of them fell in the last fortnight of the month. There were missing days, but the only ones of significance to her were the twenty-seventh, for which she'd already been primed by du Marius, and its logical associate, its ten interval partner, the seventeenth.

This is not far-fetched reasoning. On the contrary, such elementary numerical pattern associations are common. In more elaborate forms they are freely employed by stage magicians.

Having noted all this, we now need a realistic perpsective. What *in total* did she claim? By that I mean to include all the things that had been left out.

In July 1979 she claimed she'd, "been inside the mind of the Ripper." More than once she'd had a view of his face. Time and again she'd seen the Ripper walking, trailing a woman through rain-drenched streets, "drinking tea out of a thick white china cup" in a cafe, "eating a chocolate eclair". She witnessed him having trouble with the axle of his lorry, even saw "his lips moving as he spoke to another man" at a depot. Finally, she "saw" him murder Jacqueline Hill and mentally followed him for some hundreds of yards as he walked away.

The result of *all* these clairvoyant viewings led her to make a drawing of the Ripper's face. The drawing shows that all along she'd seen a long-nosed, straight-haired, completely clean-shaven man. A man able to dress as a woman and get away with it. And she alleged he *did* dress as a woman.

It needs to be emphasized that there's no resemblance whatsoever between this psychically observed man and the real murderer, Peter Sutcliffe. He was bearded and had been throughout all the killings.

In July 1979, she dramatically forecast that his next victim would be a young boy of fifteen or sixteen. It turned out to be a young woman aged twenty. Her unwarranted confidence led her on to say: "I don't think he has ever married, but I believe his mother is dead and that his father was a cripple . . . I have the feeling that he was taken away from his mother when he was ten or eleven years old."

Yes, Sutcliffe's mother was dead but the rest was rubbish. Equally false is the statement that she had, "accurately forecast two more murders before he was caught." There were three more murders before he was arrested—those of Barbara Leach, Marguerite Walls and Jacqueline Hill.

As for the killing of Jacqueline Hill, Jones's complete psychic picture was as follows. She said that, on the night of the murder, the Ripper had left his car in the city center of Leeds, then travelled out to Headingley. There he killed Jacqueline, walked along Chapel Street and down an unmade road leading to the railway station at Headingley. He then boarded a pay-train to Leeds city center where he collected his car and made his getaway.

Nella insisted that this is what had happened. She even convinced a newspaper that there was something in it. They took her north to retrace the Ripper's path from the attack point along the dirt road to Headingley Station.

It was an absurd scenario from start to finish. Sutcliffe would never have risked having to travel on public transport. He could never be sure just how dishevelled or blood-stained he'd be. When the full story emerged, it turned out that at 9:30 on November 17 he was sitting in his car *in Headingley* outside the Arndale Centre. There was a bus stop opposite and he spotted Jacqueline as she left the bus. He watched her cross the street and turn into Alma Road. He followed her in his car, overtook her and sat waiting until she walked by. When she was a short distance in front, he got out of his car, trailed her, chose the right moment, leapt forward and struck her across the head. He dragged his unconscious victim onto a piece of waste ground where he stabbed her repeatedly with a sharpened screwdriver.

Those are the facts—everything set down by Nella Jones was sheer fiction.

The fiction doesn't end there. In her book she records her "final" forecast: "He is killing indiscriminately now. But he is coming to the end of the road. He will try to do another, but it will go wrong and he won't finish the job. He will be caught before he gets the chance."

That was made in early October 1980, and after the murder of November 17, Sutcliffe did come to the end of the road. But the account in the book clashes with the real statements she made to the press after the murder of Jacqui. Nella said: ". . . he will strike again almost immediately. I see him coming back to claim another victim within the week."

This statement was made to the *Daily Mirror* (November 21, 1980). The *Mirror* then went on to summarize, "She said the next victim would be a youngish woman, but refused to give further details. 'I do not want to frighten the life out of some poor girl with a similar description.' "

There was no murder within the week. And the November murder was, in fact, the last of Sutcliffe's killings. So Nella Jones was wide of the mark to the very last. Unfortunately, few people take the trouble to examine all her statements in detail. Therefore, I forecast that her legend and myth will grow despite all the absurdities that can be brought to light.

It can be said with certainty that at no time did she supply a single name, location, address, or description connected with any of the murders that was of any use to the police. The impression that she in some way cooperated usefully with them and supplied valuable information is false. If they'd gone chasing around, trying to tie real people and places to her nebulous descriptions, they would still be on the search. And if they'd taken her psychically inspired drawing as evidence, they'd still be hunting for that imaginary long-nosed, straight-haired, clean-shaven culprit.

Fortunately for us all, the police are wiser than that! Their blue lamp needs no astral light.

7

I CAPTURED JACK THE RIPPER!

Both Jack the Ripper and the Yorkshire Ripper excited the avid interest of mediums and clairvoyants. It's even claimed that the Victorian case was eventually solved by the timely intervention of a gifted medium—the late Robert James Lees.

This claim rests on a document "dictated by the medium" and released after his death in 1931. Its validity is strengthened by the further claim that his story has never been contradicted by the police.

According to the spiritualist movement, Robert Lees developed his amazing powers during boyhood and they were so outstanding that Queen Victoria consulted him when he was a mere thirteen years old. Other royal consultations are said to have followed. By the time of the Ripper murders Lees's sensitivity was at its peak and this unexpectedly led to a "loathsome clairvoyant experience."

His posthumous statement records that, shortly after the third Whitechapel murder, while writing in his study, Lees became convinced that the Ripper was about to strike again. He had a vision of an East End location—a narrow court with a gin-palace nearby. He could see the name of the court clearly, he could even see that the bar-clock stood at 12:40 A.M.—pub closing time.

A man and a woman entered a dark corner of the court. The man was cold sober—the woman the worse for drink. In her drunken state she leaned against the wall for support and the man quickly closed her mouth with his hand, drew a knife and slit her throat. Then he let her drop to the ground, stabbed her repeatedly, coolly wiped his blade on her dress and walked off into the night.

All this was seen in full harrowing detail. Shaken, Robert Lees hurried to Scotland Yard to warn them, but he was treated as a harmless lunatic, although to humor him the duty-officer wrote down the time and place of "the forthcoming murder."

The following night, the Ripper slew a prostitute in the very manner, at the very time, and in the very court named by Lees.

The news of this murder disturbed Lees so much that he found himself unable to sleep at night. His health suffered badly and his doctor advised a holiday abroad—so Lees moved for a while to the Continent. During this vacation, the Ripper murdered four more women, but Lees was untroubled by visions and he returned to London renewed in health.

About a year later, he came face to face with the man seen in his vision. At the time, he was riding with his wife on an omnibus bound east from Shepherd's Bush. At Notting Hill a medium-sized man boarded and sat near them. Lees took no notice at first and then he experienced the strange sensations that heralded his vision. He looked hard at the man, turned to his wife and said, "That is Jack the Ripper."

At first she took his words lightly—as a foolish fancy—but his sincerity finally convinced her. They kept watch surreptitiously until the man alighted at Marble Arch; then Lees leapt off the bus and followed his suspect down Park Lane. About halfway down the lane, Lees spotted a policeman and told him that the Ripper was just yards away from them and should be arrested. The policeman simply laughed and threatened to run Lees in as a nuisance. By then it was too late to take any other action, for the Ripper became frightened in front of Apsley House and jumped into a passing cab, which sped off rapidly along Piccadilly.

A minute or so later Lees met up with a police sergeant and poured out his suspicions to him. The sergeant reacted with dismay and anger. "Show me the constable who refused to arrest him," he cried. "Why only this morning we received news at Bow Street Station that the Ripper was coming in this direction."

That night Lees had another premonition. This time the vision was far less clear than his first, but he was able to see the murdered woman's face. He also noted the peculiarity of the mutilations—one ear completely severed, the other left clinging to the face by a mere strand of flesh.

On recovering from the trauma of his trance, Lees visited Scotland Yard again. There he insisted on seeing the head inspector of police, and in great anguish told his story. This time his tale was received with awe. From his desk, the inspector drew out a shabby postcard and handed it to Lees.

The card was written in red ink and adorned with two bloody fingerprints. It read: "Tomorrow night I shall again take my revenge, claiming, from a class of women who have made themselves most obnoxious to me, my ninth victim. JACK THE RIPPER. P.S. To prove that I am really Jack the Ripper I will cut off the ears of this ninth victim."

The Inspector now looked on Lees's story as a warning sent from heaven, since no one but he himself knew of the postcard message. Extra police were drafted into Whitechapel and by the next day the alleys and courts of the area were swarming with plainclothes men. But despite these precautions the Ripper struck. As in the vision he left his victim with one ear severed and the other hanging from her face.

Robert Lees suffered a further breakdown in health and left for a rest on the Continent once more. While he was abroad, the Ripper killed his sixteenth prostitute and informed the Yard that he was to go on until he reached a score of twenty—then cease.

Shortly afterward Lees returned to London and dined at the Criterion with two Americans. Halfway through the meal Lees cried out "Great God! Jack the Ripper has committed another murder." They checked the time as 7:49 P.M.; then all went post-haste to the Yard.

The police there knew of no such murder, but before Lees could finish dictating his statement, a telegram arrived stating that a body had been found in Crown Court. The time of discovery was given as ten minutes to eight!

An inspector at once drove to Crown Court with the medium. On reaching the court, Lees pointed across to a dark corner and said: "Look in the angle of the wall. There is something written there." The inspector ran forward, struck a match and, for the first time, saw that chalked on the wall were the words—"Seventeen, Jack the Ripper."

The inspector needed no more convincing. He now seemed to see Lees as "an instrument of Providence" and he became determined to make use of the medium's "marvellous though incomprehensible powers."

To fully appreciate the policeman's attitude "it must be borne in mind that the madman had for years baffled all the resources of the greatest police force in the world."

After an earnest appeal from the inspector, Lees "consented to try to track the Ripper much in the same way as a bloodhound pursues a criminal. There seemed to be some magnetic wave connecting him . . . with the fugitive."

All that night Lees allowed that strange magnetic influence to guide him. He moved swiftly through the London streets, guiding the inspector and his detectives. At last, at four in the morning, Lees stopped. He pointed to the gates of a West End mansion and gasped: "There is your murderer—the man you are looking for."

But the inspector simply stood there, dumbfounded, for he recognized the house as the residence of one of the most celebrated society physicians. It was unthinkable to link such a distinguished man with the East End slaughter. Still, the medium vehemently insisted the Ripper was inside.

Lees's insistence made the inspector waver, and he set the medium a new task. "Describe to me the interior of the doctor's hall and I will arrest him, but I shall do so at the risk of losing my position." Without hesitation Lees said: "The hall has a high porter's chair of black oak on the right hand as you enter it, a stained glass window at the extreme end, and a large mastiff is at this moment asleep at the foot of the stairs."

The police waited until the servants rose at seven o'clock, then they rang the doorbell. The door opened to disclose a hall exactly as described by Lees, except for one thing—there was no dog in sight. But, as the servants explained, there *was* a mastiff in the house and it did sleep at the foot of the stairs, but every morning it was let out into the garden as soon as they rose.

"This is the hand of God," whispered the inspector, and he asked for the doctor's wife to be called.

Under examination the wife sobbed out an incredible story. Her husband was a dual personality. To the outside world he was always a kindly and sympathetic man. Only she knew that at times he became a brutal and uncontrollable sadist.

His favorite sadistic pastime involved the systematic torture of helpless animals. He would often cut the eyelids from captive rabbits and then expose them to the blinding sun, reveling all the time in their agonized contortions. One night she'd even found him slowly burning a cat to death.

There had even been times when she had locked herself and the children into a bedroom to escape his vicious side. Then came the most horrible part of all. The Ripper murders began and she "noticed with heart-breaking dread that whenever a Whitechapel murder had occurred her husband was absent from home.

After hearing the wife's account, the inspector called in two experts on insanity and the doctor was sent for. When confronted, he admitted that his mind had been unbalanced for some years and there were times when he had complete lapses of memory. Once he'd found his shirt-front soaked with blood, but he attributed this to a nosebleed during one of his stupors.

A search of his house brought proof that the Ripper had been found at last, and the doctor was overcome by horror and remorse. He begged to be killed at once, since he "could not live under the same roof as a monster." But this was never seriously considered. Instead, twelve doctors were summoned to constitute a Commission in Lunacy —the Ripper was declared insane and all parties to the proceedings were sworn to secrecy.

The mad doctor was promptly removed to a private asylum for the insane in Islington, where he was lodged under an assumed name. In order to account for the doctor's disappearance, a sham death and burial was arranged and the public was convincingly duped. Even the asylum deepers and inspectors never dreamed that they had custody of the infamous Jack the Ripper. To them, he was simply inmate 124, even until the day he died!

This detailed and elaborate account gained a massive circulation when it was published in the *Daily Express* in March 1931. From then on it was repeated in newspapers, magazines, and books throughout the world. Its very wealth of detail made it look authentic. It was treated seriously by investigators of standing, such as Hereward Carrington and Dr. Nandor Fodor. The leading spiritualist editor, Maurice Barbanell, often retold it and never had any doubts about its accuracy. Yet, for all that, this story is completely untenable. There is no possible way of matching it up with the real facts of the murders and their investigation.

To begin with, there were not seventeen murders, but five. It's true that some earlier and later murders were at times muddled in with the Ripper's, but that was solely due to a circulation-hungry press and a sensation-hungry public. Sir Melville Macnaghten of Scotland Yard was adamant that "the Whitechapel Murderer had *five* victims and five victims only."

Also, the murders were not spread out over a period of years, as alleged, but took place over the short period of a mere ten weeks— beginning on August 31, 1888, and ending on November 9.

Police records show that none of the murders took place at the times quoted and no murder took place at Crown Court. And no postcard was ever received bearing the quoted message. There was a postcard written in red ink with red smudges, but this was posted in London on October 1, after the double murders of September 29, and after details of these murders had become public knowledge. The writer of this card and of a previous letter was, in fact, the first to use the name "Jack the Ripper." It was believed to have been the work of some seamy journalist out for some extra copy.

Finally, the police have denied that Lees was involved with the Ripper hunt. In fact, Robert Lees's own diary entries contradict this part of the tale. They show that he didn't approach the police until October 2, 1888—three days after the murders on the twenty-ninth.

His diary records:

> Tuesday 2 Oct. Offered services to Police to follow up East End Murders—called a fool and a lunatic. Got trace of man from the spot in Berner Street.
>   Wednesday 3 Oct. Went to City Police again—called a madman and fool.
>   Thursday 4 Oct. Went to Scotland Yard—same result but promised to write me.

Now these are not the words of someone already involved with the police. Neither are they the words of someone who has already forecast two murders. His reception confirms this. With two correct prediciitons to his credit he would have been received with respect—and welcomed. But he was simply treated like any of the other psychics and clairvoyants who were clamoring to have their "special knowledge" taken seriously.

In that case, what prompted Lees to dictate this grossly absurd statement? The answer is amazing—there never was such a statement! That claim can now be shown up as a deplorable journalistic device used to sell the story.

The truth is that the *Daily Express* story of 1931 turns out to be nothing more than a slightly modified reprint of a hoax article dating back to the end of the last century. This original article first ran in *The Sunday Times-Herald* of Chicago, as long ago as April 28, 1895.

Superficially, this Chicago piece posed as sound information. Its small opening section was said to be based on the revelations of "Dr. Howard, a well-known London physician . . . who sat on the commission in lunacy", while the greater part was supposed to have been supplied by "a London clubman living in Chicago" who knew the inside story and was willing to unseal his lips. Despite these credentials, the whole piece was reckless, pseudodramatic fiction. Yet, there was a reason for this. Openly stamped throughout the text were all the hallmarks of a deliberately concocted hoax. In truth, not a single event in the whole story corresponds with any of the real-life events of the Whitechapel murders!

What remains true, however, is that Lees did independently state that he'd cornered the murderer. But others made similar claims. Robert Clifford Spicer, for one, claimed that he'd arrested the Ripper; while Dr. Forbes Winslow asserted that it was his actions alone that had brought the murders to a halt.

Those killings certainly bred a good many illusions and delusions. And in the case of Robert Lees there is not a scrap of proof to show that his firm belief was anything more than just one of his many cherished and carefully nurtured delusions.

8

THE UNQUIET GRAVE OF PRINCE LOUIS

It was a cruel, callous murder! Political assassination cunningly engineered by Freemasonry! Perhaps even Queen Victoria had a hand in the affair!

Outlandish rumors along these lines percolated through French society in the summer of 1879. Louis Napoleon, the Prince Imperial, had been slain in British Africa. The last fond hope of a French monarchist revival had perished in the service of the British Army.

But what was a French prince doing on British soil? Well, his family were domiciled in England. As they viewed it they were there, marking time, until the day came when the French people would once more clamor for a monarchy.

The Napoleons had fallen into disgrace after the Franco-Prussian War. Napoleon III had striven to imitate his famous uncle. He was desperate to cover himself in military glories, but he had none of his uncle's brilliance. In 1871, his campaign against the Prussians was feeble and pathetically ill-planned. As a result, he suffered a humiliating defeat and lost his throne. France reverted to a republic and the ex-emperor and family scuttled acrosss the Channel into exile.

Once in Britain, they dreamed of their glorious return, and this dream came to be of paramount importance to Napoleon's son, Prince Louis. Indeed, after his father's death, the Prince's dream was encouraged by the French royalists. In their eyes, Prince Louis was now Napoleon IV.

In order to win more support in France, Louis began to polish up his misty image. He knew that the French adored military prowess, so he looked around for ways to gain experience in battle. This was far from easy, and for six years he had to content himself with military studies. His only fights were the occasional mock-battles staged during the army maneuvers. It was during this period that the hostile French Press dubbed him Napoleon III½!

Then, in 1879, came the chance to prove himself, and the prince was grimly determined to end the Republican sneers. In South Africa the British were locked in a war against the Zulus, and Louis won permission to join up with the British troops. It was made clear, though, that he was to keep out of danger. He was there to observe and make a map or two, but not allowed to ride into the fighting line.

Before he left for Africa, he made a moving appeal to his mother:

> Owing to the accident of my birth I am not my own master. God has willed it so . . . Whether I like it or not I happen to be the nominal and eventually the effective head of a great party which believes itself to be. . . . truly representative of France . . . but I can say that in France, although my name may be an emblem, my personality and my moral value, such as they are, are unknown . . . At the age of twenty-three I am still a child to them. . .
>
> I am continually having it thrown at my head that the Orleans Princes have seen fighting, and that I have not seen any. My enemies have even gone so far as to call me a coward, simply because I have never had the opportunity of proving the contrary . . . In Africa I shall be able to show that I am no coward, and that when I have proved that I am willing to risk my life for a country which is not my own, but to which I owe a debt of gratitude, I shall *a fortiori* have proven that I am equally ready to risk it in the service of my own country when she has need of me.

Once in South Africa, the guidelines issued for Louis' safety were ignored. In practice he was allowed to join a number of forward patrols in Zululand, and each one of these placed him in potential danger. Indeed, the patrol he joined on Sunday, June 1, led to his tragic death.

On that day, he and his companions had dismounted and dallied for half an hour in a deserted kraal. They brewed coffee, smoked, and corrected their maps. But they stupidly neglected to post a lookout, so they were easy prey for a small band of Zulus. The British troops tried to make a hasty getaway but in doing so they left the prince behind. He desperately tried to mount his charger, which had panicked and was galloping off. He kept pace with the horse and grabbed at the holster-strap on the saddle. He swung upwards to the saddle, but the strain was too much for the strap. It broke and the prince rolled under the hooves of his horse.

When he reached his feet, he knew he was doomed. His sword had been lost, his revolver held only a few cartridges, and he was alone, facing seven fearsome Zulus. Seventeen spear thrusts left the prince dead and mutilated.

The thorough investigation and army hearings that followed his death were reported in every detail in England. But even so, this didn't stop the rumor-mongers. The wildest stories persistently circulated—including the claim that the prince was still alive. Most persistent were the allegations that he was the victim of a plot. In France, the atmosphere was so hostile that, for a while, Englishmen found it wise to stay out of sight.

With time, though, the fantastic tales died down. Yet, as they submerged, an even more fantastic tale surfaced. It features the Empress Eugenie in the incredible role of a psychic detective!

It seems that Eugenie yearned to bring her son's body back from Africa to rest beside his father in the family vault. The problem was to *find* his body. The exact spot where he'd fallen and been hurriedly buried was not known.

The ex-empress turned to Field-Marshal Sir Evelyn Wood for help. A year after Prince Louis's death, Eugenie and Sir Evelyn landed in South Africa and the search began.

At first they tried offering a rerward for information that would lead them to the grave. A number of natives came forward, eager to help and enrich themselves. But, in each case, the information they offered was either worthless or badly invented. One claimant even took them on a weeklong trek to the "burial site." He knew the place well—but the trip ended when he completely lost himself in the tangled bush.

Eugenie was exhausted by the journey and deeply frustrated by the lack of dependable help. So Evelyn grew concerned enough to beg her to give up the quest. She stayed determined. She would carry on until she found the grave. "In the end we shall find it," she insisted. "I know it."

Then it seemed to her that her faith was to be rewarded. A giant Zulu approached Sir Evelyn and offered his help. He claimed to have been one of the party involved in the attack on the British in which Prince Louis had died. This made him certain that he could guide them to the site of the skirmish.

It meant a three-day journey into the bush, but the safari set out in high spirits. When they finally reached the place there the Zulu said the action had been fought, they grew dispirited. The whole area was covered in dense undergrowth.

Under these conditions, finding an unmarked grave seemed an impossible task. The Zulu guide himself had lost all sense of certainty. He was sure that they were in the right area, but unsure as to the direction of the final search.

The stalemate was ended by Eugenie. "My son lies somewhere in that direction," she said, and she moved off stumbling through the bush. The search party followed her wonderingly.

Once she halted and asked if they could detect an unusual scent. But her followers could only detect the normal scents of the bush. Eugenie, however, insisted that she was picking up the strong scent of violets—her son's favorite perfume. "He always said he loved it because he remembered me wearing it when he came to kiss me good night as a little boy."

At that point people in the search-party began to have doubts about her sanity. Indeed, the public at large had been entertaining such doubts for some time, for the persistent quest of the ex-empress for her son's grave "had been making news headlines." It was feared that the triple tragedy she had suffered—the loss of throne, husband and son—had unbalanced her mind.

Despite their doubts, the searchers faithfully trudged behind her. For two hours she led them on, guided she claimed by the mysterious perfume. The scent that only she could detect. Finally, completely exhausted, she stopped and pointed at a patch of scrub. There was nothing to distinguish it from the rest of the bush that they'd passed through. But the empress was unshakable.

"Under there," she said, "we shall find the body of my son."

The men drew their cutlasses and slashed through the undergrowth and soon the markings of a grave became visible. The picks and spades went to work, and a body was discovered. There was no possible doubt about its identity. It was Prince Louis.

So there we are. The quest was one "that made news headlines." The search was "proclaimed by public appeals." And in later years the empress "confirmed" that a paranormal perfume had led her to her son's corpse.

In other words, it is a story that can be researched and verified in every fine detail. Let's turn to the press then. Let's see what it has to say.

The date and manner of Louis's death are confirmed. The press gave the tragedy the fullest possible coverage. It also reported the events of June 2, the day after the tragedy.

But rather than quote one newspaper, let us look at the official report sent by Captain Molyneux to Lord Chelmsford. He wrote:

> In accordance with your instructions, I this morning accompanied
> the cavalry commanded by Major-General Marshall to find the body
> of His Highness the Prince Imperial. Surgeon-Major Scott, Lieu-
> tenant Bartle Frere, and the servants of His Imperial Highness were
> with me. . . . We went first to the kraal where the attack took place
> . . . and speedily came upon the bodies of the two soldiers of the
> Natal Horse. At nine o'clock, Captain Cochrane drew my attention
> to another body at the bottom of a donga, which on examination
> was recognised as that of His Imperial Highness.
> He was about two hundreds yards north-east of the kraal. . . .
> The body stripped bare except for a gold chain with medallions,
> which was about his neck. His sabre, his revolver, his helmet and
> other clothes had disappeared, but we found in the grass his spurs
> with their straps, and a sock marked N. . . .
> The body had seventeen wounds, all in front, and the marks on
> the ground as on the spurs indicated a desperate resistance. At ten
> o'clock a bier was made of lances and blankets, and the body was
> brought out of the donga. . . .

Louis's corpse was carried in front of the mounted procession for
an hour. Then an ambulance wagon from the camp at Itelezei met up
with them, and the Prince Imperial was transferred to its interior.

On June 2, at twilight, the prince's body was laid on top of a
fieldgun at the camp. The whole camp took part in a memorial procession to honor the dead prince. At the end of the ceremony the body
was taken to the field hospital and handed over to the camp surgeons.
The surgeons undertook the task of embalming the corpse, using
whatever materials they had on hand—it was crude but, they hoped,
effective. Meanwhile the sappers using saws, cold-chisels and hammers,
crafted a metal coffin out of empty zinc tea-chests.

Early in the morning an ambulance wagon loaded with the zinc
coffin set out for the coast—escorted by a body of the 17th Lancers.
The ambulance reached Pietermaritzburg on Sunday night, June 8,
and there the body was transferred to a lead-lined, wooden coffin. The
next day the sad procession moved under escort to Durban.

By the fifteenth the coffin was on board HMS *Orontes* bound for
England. She reached Plymouth on July 10. There the royal coffin was
unloaded onto the deck of the Admiralty yacht *Enchantress,* which
steamed out of the backwater bound for Woolwich.

At Woolrich, the remains of the Prince Imperial were placed on board a gun-carriage and taken to the great Hall of Woolrich Arsenal, where a group of doctors examined the body.

The funeral of the prince took place the next day. Queen Victoria was present. Four royal dukes, including the Prince of Wales, were among the pall-bearers. Three batteries of the Royal Artillery fired minute-guns. Other regiments lined the route. And some 40,000 mourners and onlookers crowded into the tiny village of Chislehurst, in Kent, where the Napoleons lived.

After a short Mass in the local Roman Catholic church, the prince was taken to the private memorial chapel erected by Eugenie in 1873. There he was laid to rest beside his father—just three weeks after his death.

So there never was a missing grave in Zululand! No missing grave means no quest. No public appeals. No rewards. No time-wasting applicants. No giant Zulu guide. No exhausting trek. And *no* paranormal perfume!

"Here are the *stories,* here is the *evidence*—collected, examined, verified." So claims *The Reader's Digest Book of Strange Stories, Amazing Facts.* And then it goes on to offer the paranormal perfume baloney! Brad Steiger presents it as "a dramatic case study of a ghostly scent." And Fred Archer, one-time editor of *Psychic News,* vouches for the story, saying of it: "Sight, hearing, touch, even smell can operate as a psychic sense." I won't bore you by listing all the other appearances of this asinine yarn.

But I can imagine someone asking, "Isn't there just a teeny, weeny bit of truth in this lovely legend?" Well, there is. It's true that Eugenie made the trip to South Africa a year after her son's death. And that's all the truth there is.

The empress yielded to an irresistible urge, she wrote: "I feel myself drawn towards this pilgrimage as strongly as the disciples of Christ must have felt drawn towards the Holy Places. The thought of seeing, of retracing the stages of my beloved son's last journey, of seeing with my own eyes the scene upon which his dying gaze has rested, of passing the anniversary of the night of the 1st of June watching and praying alone with his memory, is for me a spiritual necessity and an aim in life. Since the end of the war has allowed me to regard this possibility more hopefully, it has become my dominant thought. . . . This thought sustains me and gives me fresh courage; without it I should never have sufficient strength to endure my life, and I should allow myself to become submerged in my sorrow."

Eugenie arrived in Cape Town on April 18, 1880. By the evening of May 25th, she had seen the kraal where her son fell. There wasn't the slightest uncertainty about the location. The kraal was less than two hundred yards from the east bank of the River Ityotyosi. In fact, nothing was uncertain about the prince's end. The fatal spot where he'd fallen had been marked by a cairn of stone the day after his death. And, shortly before Eugenie's arrival, Queen Victoria had arranged for a stone cross to be erected at the spot.

So, when Eugenie left her tent that evening and walked toward the place of Louis's death, she was saddened and disappointed. She felt that her own sorrowful intuition would guide her irresistibly to the exact spot, but she was thwarted. The Queen's Cross stood there; all traces of the grass watered by her son's blood had disappeared beneath a layer of white cement. And surrounding the area was an iron railing. The place had all the peaceful and orderly appearance of an English cemetery.

This *authentic* mission of hers was extensively covered by the world's press. In fact, few lives are as fully documented as that of this empress. It's dramatic, tragic, even doom-laden. It can well do without the tawdry inventions of psychic penmen.

9

REGIMENT OF THE DAMNED?

"In the course of the fight . . . there happened a very mysterious thing." Those were the opening words of a curious dispatch sent to Lord Kitchener in 1915. The dispatch came from the Dardanelles and was written by General Ian Hamilton. He had the soul of a novelist, and the tone of his dramatic dispatch set off a long train of unwarranted speculation. For he was concerned with the complete "disappearance" of a body of British troops. And, for some, here was a golden chance for a spot of "out of this world" tomfoolery.

In 1965, the tomfoolery reached its peak and the Dardanelles became the setting for an awe-inspiring paranormal mass-kidnapping!

The Dardanelles venture itself began with a hare-brained scheme to knock Turkey, then Germany's ally, out of World War I. The plan involved seizing Turkey's long sea channel that stretches from the Mediterranean to the Black Sea. If the Allies had been successful the direct links between Germany and Turkey would have been severed. The Russian grain ships could have steamed freely to and from the Black Sea. And the Turks would have been so weakened and demoralized, they might even have sued for peace.

It was all a grand dream that turned into a ghastly nightmare. The planning was hasty, improvised, and totally unrealistic. General Hamilton had this to say about his marching orders: "Within twenty-four hours I must hand over a command three times larger than the British Expeditionary Force; receive my instructions; select a staff; get the hang of the Dardanelles and of the nature and whereabouts of my new force and bundle off. Equally serious was the fact that there was no time to get my staff together. I had to start without any of my administrative officers, whether for supply, medicine or discipline. They were not destined to join me for more than three weeks, until they came and I and my small group of General Staff officers had to undertake their work, including matters so remote from our experience as unloading and reloading ships and making arrangements for the wounded."

Throughout March and April heavy naval guns hammered the

Turkish forts and defense lines. And on April 25, the first landings were made. The conditions were appalling. The beaches were yawning death-traps. By the time the troops were able to secure a foothold they were too exhausted to move forward. Then, while they rested and regrouped to build up their strength, enemy reinforcements were free to move up to counter them. Almost everything favored the enemy. They knew the area and they had ample water supplies. So they simply dug in and held the Allies at bay.

For more than three months the Allied forces remained pinned down, suffering in the furnacelike heat. Then, in an attempt to break the deadlock, fresh landings were made in August. One of these took place at Suvla Bay. And among the troops landed there were officers and men of the Norfolk Regiment. This is the regiment that's alleged to have suffered the paranormal kidnapping.

John Keel says of it: "The one Fourth Norfolk Regiment marched into a 'peculiar brown cloud that hugged the ground in their path.' The cloud rose up, joined a group of similar clouds and sailed off *against* the wind! And the regiment had vanished—'eight hundred men gone— or taken—from the face of the earth!'" *(Our Haunted Planet)*

Robin Collyns tells a similar story and suggests that the abduction could have been the work of a giant spaceship. Otto O. Binder, "the renowned UFO and space expert," puts forward the view that the regiment was kidnapped by a long cigar-shaped UFO surrounded by mysterious mists.

The story crops up in books by many other writers. There are discrepancies in the numbers of troops involved. The numbers vary from eight hundred down to two hundred and fifty. But all the writers agree on one thing, that the event was witnessed by twenty-two soldiers of the New Zealand forces. Few of them take the trouble to quote the exact statements made by these New Zealanders. One writer who *does* quote the eyewitnesses is Charles Berlitz, one of the "Bermuda Tri-angle" merchants. The first thing to take note of is that twenty-two men did not make statements, or even agree to a single statement. The whole story rests on one statement only, drafted by one man, ex-Sapper F. Reichardt, and countersigned by two of his former comrades who claimed that they were witnesses as well.

As quoted by Berlitz, Reichard's document reads:

The following is an account of a strange incident that happened . . . in the morning, during the severest and final days of the fighting which took place at "Hill 60," Suvla Bay, "ANZAC." . . .

The day broke clear, without a cloud in sight, as any beautiful Mediterranean day could be expected to be. The exception, however, was a number of perhaps six or eight "loaf of bread" shaped clouds— all shaped exactly alike—which were hovering over "Hill 60." It was noticed that, in spite of a four or five mile an hour breeze from the south, these clouds did not alter their position in any shape or form, nor did they drift away under the influence of the breeze. They were hovering at an elevation of about 60 degrees as seen from our observation point 500 ft. up. Also stationary and resting on the ground right underneath this group of clouds was a similar cloud in shape, measuring about 800 ft. in length, 200 ft. in height, and 200 ft. in width. This cloud was absolutely dense, almost solid looking in structure, and positioned about 14 to 18 chains from the fighting in British held territory. All this was observed by twenty-two men of No. 3 Section of No. 1 Field Company, N.Z.E., including myself, from our trenches on Rhododendron Spur, approximately 2500 yards south west of the cloud on the ground. Our vantage point was overlooking "Hill 60" by about 300 feet. As it turned out later, this singular cloud was straddling a dry creek bed or sunken road (Kaiajik Dere) and we had a perfect view of the cloud's sides and ends as it rested on the ground. Its colour was a light grey, as was the colour of the other clouds.

A British Regiment, the First Fourth Norfolk, of several hundred men, was then noticed marching up this sunken road or creek towards "Hill 60." It appeared as though they were going to reinforce the troops at "Hill 60." However, when they arrived at this cloud, they marched straight into it, with no hesitation, but no one ever came out to deploy and fight at "Hill 60." About an hour later, after the last of the file had disappeared into it, this cloud very unobtrusively lifted off the ground and, like any fog or cloud would, rose slowly until it joined the other similar clouds. . . . On viewing them again, they all looked alike "as peas in a pod." All this time, the groups of clouds had been hovering in the same place, but as soon as the singular "ground" cloud had risen to their level, they all moved away northwards, i.e. towards Thrace (Bulgaria). In a matter of about three-quarters of an hour they had all disappeared from view.

The Regiment mentioned is posted as "missing" or "wiped out" and on Turkey surrendering in 1918, the first thing Britain demanded of Turkey was the return of this regiment. Turkey replied that she had neither captured this Regiment, nor made contact with it, and did not know that it existed. A British Regiment in 1914-18 consisted of any number between 800 and 4000 men. Those who observed this incident vouch for the fact that Turkey never captured that Regiment, nor made contact with it.

That, then, is the only "first-hand" testimony to an event that is said to have happened on August 21, 1915. What you should know about it, though, is that this testimony is suspicious from the start. This statement as quoted by Charles Berlitz in his *Without Trace* is incomplete. A *vital* sentence has been left out. That missing sentence shows that this so-called evidence wasn't written down until 1965—fifty years after the paranormal exit!

But could it still be true despite that suspicious fifty-year gap? Writer Brad Steiger certainly thinks so. He labels it "one of the most horrifying incidents ever recorded" and cites "official records" to support his view.

He writes: "The official record on the Dardanelles campaign state: 'They (the First Fourth Norfolk Regiment) were swallowed up by an unseasonable fog. This fog reflected the sun's rays in such a manner that artillery observers were dazzled by its brilliance and were unable to fire in support. The two hundred and fifty men were never seen or heard of again.'"

Having produced his evidence Steiger then sarcastically comments: "An 'unseasonable fog' capable of snatching up two hundred fifty British soldiers certainly makes the most noxious of our industrialized smog clouds seem extremely feeble in comparison. How do the authorities explain such a disappearance with any degree of satisfaction to the survivors of those who vanish into 'fog clouds?'"

Yet all this talk about official confirmation is nothing but bluster. There is not the remotest possibility of the testimony being true. In the first place, the First Fourth Norfolks wasn't a regiment, it was simply one battalion within the Norfolk regiment itself. What's more, it didn't disappear on Turkish soil, or anywhere else, but went on fighting right up until the end of the Great War.

It's true, though, that a minor disaster did hit part of the Fifth Battalion of the Norfolks. The Fifth Norfolks were included in the 163rd Brigade, which set out to occupy the strategically important heights of Kavak Tepe and Tekke Tepe. These were commanding heights to the east of Suvla Bay. And the original plan was to seize them before the Turkish reinforcements could arrive and entrench on their summits.

The action began on August 12, and the Fifth Norfolks were ordered forward at 4:45 P.M. together with the rest of the 163rd. Optimistically, they intended to clear the way through the jungly, tree-covered ground at the foot of the mountains, but they met with tenacious opposition, and the enemy fire grew heavier and more deadly.

When the brigade reached the farm called Anafarta Ova, the Fifth Norfolks found themselves ahead of the rest of the force. Then occurred a galling setback that prompted the famous dispatch from General Hamilton. In full it reads:

> In the course of the fight, creditable in all respects to the 163rd Brigade, there happened to be a very mysterious thing. The 1/5 Norfolks were on the right of the line, and found themselves for a moment less strongly opposed than the rest of the brigade. Against the yielding forces of the enemy Colonel Sir H. Beauchamp, a bold, self-confident officer, eagerly pressed forward, followed by the best part of the battalion. The fighting grew hotter, and the ground became wooded and broken. At this stage many men were wounded or grew exhausted with thirst. They found their way back to camp during the night. But the Colonel, with 16 officers and 250 men, still kept pushing on, driving the enemy before him. Amongst these ardent souls was part of a fine company enlisted from the King's Sandringham estates. Nothing more was ever seen or heard of any of them. They charged into the forest, and were lost to sight or sound. Not one of them ever came back.

General Hamilton's somewhat mystical streak led him to color his words a little too garishly. Others at the time were much more realistic. War-correspondent H. W. Nevinson wrote of the Norfolks: "One cannot doubt that their bones lie among the trees and bushes at the foot of that dark and ominous hill and the last real hope of Suvla Bay faded with their tragic disappearance."

Nevinson gave his opinion in 1918 and, sure enough, a year later corpses of the missing Norfolks were uncovered. They had been tossed into a ravine by a local farmer who had found the bodies scattered on various parts of his land. It's true that only 122 bodies were those of the Norfolks. But 122 is still a large enough number to demolish the idea of a mass disappearance. And there's little mystery about the bodies that were not located. Under the atrocious conditions of that campaign it was more than easy for bodies to vanish without trace. One only has to think of the prowling animals, the crevasses, the countless shell-holes and the dense forests of the battle area to realize how. Apart from that, any Norfolks captured and imprisoned stood little chance of surviving, especially if they were wounded. The Turkish prison camps were hellish. The Turkish regard for prisoners was nonexistent. The treatment of the prisoners taken at Kut proves this. Nearly five thousand prisoners captured at Kut died in Turkish hands, since "the dull brutality of the Turks, who treated their own soldiers like dogs, had no mercy for sick or starving prisoners."

So the undisputed real-life disaster that overtook the Norfolks had no supernormal or extraterrestrial features. In that case, what on earth prompted the strange tale that surfaced in 1965? Well, the date given for this claimed event provides the essential clue. For, on August 21, 1915, another set of odd circumstances surrounded a further large-scale action by the Allied Forces.

On that day the scheme of attack involved a series of advances aimed at securing control of Scimitar Hill and Hill 60. The master plan was wrecked by a perfectly normal but dense out-of-season mist. As Sir Ian Hamilton reported: "By some freak of nature Suvla Bay and the plain were wrapped in a strange mist on the afternoon of August 21st. This was sheer bad luck, as we had reckoned on the enemy's gunners being blinded by the declining sun and upon the Turkish trenches being shown up by the evening light with singular clearness, as would have been the case on ninety-nine days out of a hundred. Actually we could hardly see the enemy's line this afternoon, whereas out to the westward targets stood out in strong relief against the luminous mist. I wished to postpone the attack, but for various reasons this was not possible. . . ."

Tragically, the attack went ahead with the basic strategy unaltered, and the brigades of the 29th Division, supported by the Yeomanry, drove forward against the Turkish defenses. Shell-fire threw up plumes of smoke and dust that thickened the mist. Then, raging bush-fires added thick, acrid black clouds of smoke and smut. The Allied troops found themselves half-blinded and when they attacked Scimitar Hill they were easy targets for the Turks, who were in elevated strongholds to the north and southwest. As a result, the British were cut to pieces by sustained and vicious crossfire from the enemy's rifles and field guns.

When I first researched this story I drew the provisional conclusion that the three New Zealanders had talked over old times and quite innocently confused the two different military actions. The thick, unexpected mist that hit the 86th Brigade on August 21 was remembered as if it was the cause of the Norfolks disaster, nine days earlier. By combining the two separate events, their final tale became shaped along the lines of the flying-saucer mysteries that were becoming popular in the 1960s.

In short, I believed it to be a comparatively recent confusion. Then in 1982, Frederick Reichardt's son wrote a letter to *The Unexplained* which said:

> The statement, I can assure you, *was* made by him throughout his life, from the earliest days I can remember (I was born in 1932).
>
> Because of this the story was not written down until the reunion on the fiftieth anniversary of the landing, when he came in contact with the other witness—for the first time, I believe, since the First World War. . . . I have written this for the sake of an old man who, when he died at the age of 84 years, still firmly believed in what he saw.
>
> Signed, W. A. Reichardt

This nullified the idea (put forward by Paul Begg) that Reichardt had possibly picked up information from the *Final Report of the Dardanelles Commission,* edition of 1965. As a supposition it was, in any case, unnecessary and unlikely, as we'll see.

For all the pleading by Reichardt's son, the odor of fakery and manipulation hangs thickly around his father's story. In the first instance, the quote from official documents advanced by Steiger and others is a forgery. It will not be found in any legitimate government document. When it is analyzed, it can be shown to be a parody of some of the words used by General Hamilton on two distinctly separate occasions. The opening sentence, "They (the First Fourth Norfolk) were swallowed up by an unseasonable fog," is based on Hamilton's report of August 21, with the "regiment" name filled in. The second sentence again refers to August 21. But the final sentence, "The two hundred and fifty men were never seen or heard of again," is based on the dispatch of August 12.

Secondly, Mr. I. C. McGibbon, former historian at the New Zealand Ministry of Defence, has taken a special interest in this matter and made his own investigation of the people involved. In 1982, he wrote:

Information that has recently come to light in New Zealand throws further doubt on the "sighting." Newnes, one of the alleged "witnesses," turns out to have been a trooper in the Auckland Mounted Rifles rather than a sapper in the New Zealand Field Engineers. A person who forgets which unit and arm of service he was in can hardly be regarded as a reliable witness. Neither Newnes nor Newmann. . . was on Gallipoli at the time given in the original statement—'in the morning" of 28th August, 1915. (The date originally published in the New Zealand UFO Magazine "Spaceview.") Both were evacuated because of illness—Newman on 5th August and Newnes on 21st August. These facts, drawn from their service records at the New Zealand Minstry of Defense, immediately throws serious doubts on the authority of the statement.

The intrusion of an extra date of August 28, can be dismissed without much problem, since Reichardt's story refers unmistakably in its substance to August 21. This view holds good even though McGibbon's research shows that Reichardt wasn't present on Rhododendron Spur on the twenty-first. But McGibbon throws extra light on my original idea that the story had been influences by the UFO craze. He writes:

Reichardt had attended a public meeting in Rotorua to discuss UFOs early in 1965. Following the meeting, he approached Gordon Tuckey and "intimated that he had a story of his own to tell." A meeting was subsequently arranged at a private house and Reichardt recounted his story. He refused to allow a tape recording to be made, but some weeks afterwards provided a written statement. "It was in his own handwriting," recalled Tuckey, "and was signed by himself and the two other alleged witnesses." Tuckey never met the latter. Reichardt had obviously seen them at the 50th jubilee of the ANZAC landing, which took place at Rotorua between 24th and 26th April 1965. (Signing the statement would have been one of Newman's last acts, for he died on the 26th!)

McGibbon then gives his own view of the birth of Reichardt's story. It is a view that corresponds so closely with the view I had reached in 1978, that it's worth quoting:

It seems most unlikely that such a visually striking cloud formation could have been present all day—Reichardt implies that it was visible at daybreak—without attracting widespread attention from the thousands of men in the vicinity. The fact that a mere three "witnesses" have so far belatedly come forward suggests that few saw the clouds.

My own conclusion is that Reichardt's memory had become confused. I believe that he may have seen a unit march into a patch of ground mist at some stage of his service at Gallipoli and that the men of the unit may have taken cover, perhaps, viewed from a distance, given the illusion of having disappeared.

Probably he heard accounts subsequently of the battle on the 21st August, in which several battalions in the Sulva Bay area lost their direction and inclined too far north. He may have heard rumors of the "disappearance" of the Norfolks and later read accounts of the "lost battalion." As time passed he may have convinced himself that he had witnessed the "mysterious" event described in the dispatch sent by Sir Ian Hamilton. . . .

This explanation is given added weight by the importance Reichardt attached to the account of the incident, along with two earlier "disappearances," that he claimed to have seen "in one of the official histories of the Gallipoli campaign." No official history recounting such events has ever been located.

More probably, Reichardt saw accounts of them in some popular book dealing with unidentified flying objects or military mysteries and mistakenly decided thath they were authoritative accounts. He was not a well-read man. . . and possibly fell victim to one of the more sensational descriptions of the loss of the First-Fifth Norfolks. . . ."

There were indeed plently of chances for Reichardt to pick up sensational treatments of the Fifth Norfolk's disappearnce. It was one of the events that constantly cropped up in the many popular histories of the Great War that were churned off the presses between 1918 and 1940. For example, the story occurs in *Deeds That Thrill The Empire,* the popular series published by Hutchinson, and *Twenty Years After,* another immensely popular series.

An extract from *Twenty Years After* will give a good idea of the graphic and sensational treatment employed. Of the action of the twenty-first, it says: "No one knew exactly what the position was, where the enemy were, or how far their own comrades had got. Nevertheless, they plunged into the din of the battle and the clouds of mist and smoke and fire that veiled the field. Stumbling blindly forward, they too reached Scimitar Hill, and a gallant handfull pushed on beyond, and were never heard of more."

In the end, it all boils down to a synthetic mystery created by the muddled mind of one old Anzac veteran, a man charismatic enough to have successfully carried two other old-timers along with him in his fantasy. I don't think we should blame these old soldiers too much though—memories can play exceedingly strange tricks. Just try thinking back over the years and you'll be surprised how hazy and muddled the past can seem. And these men, remember, were thinking back more than half a century to a time of enormous stress, anguish, and confusion. So they can be excused. But how can we excuse the many writers who've made capital out of this tale?

A prime example is Brinsley le Poer Trench—otherwise known as the Earl of Clancarty. He's presented this hokum as authentic military history.

Clancarty will pontificate for hours on UFOs—he even initiated a debate on this topic in the House of Lords. The War Office is just across the road from the Lords, while the Imperial War Museum lies just over the River Thames, mere minutes away. A few checks with these institutions would have alerted Clancarty to the absurdities of this Dardanelles horror story.

But, then, if he and his fellow obscurantists were reckless enough to do too much research—or even a little—their books would forever remain as thick, blank wads of paper.

10

THE ANGELS WITH NEWSPAPER WINGS

Did God take sides in the Great War of 1914? Did flights of angels wing their way over the Belgian landscape? Were miracles wrought among the blood-drenched battlefilds of Flanders?

It was in Flanders that the first major battle of the war was fought. And there, at Mons, the British troops held back a numerically superior German force and fought with an amazing ferocity. But, in the end, the pressure of numbers became too great; and, in order to avoid being trapped, the British were instructed to make an orderly withdrawal. And they did this successfully, even though they suffered heavy losses.

Now there were two main reasons for their success. In the first place, there was the devastating markmanship of the riflemen. In fact, their rapid-fire techniques were so spectacular that at times the Germans imagined they were facing machine-gunners. Then, secondly, every soldier carried a special entrenching tool in his haversack. With this tool, protective ramparts of earth could be thrown up in minutes. Thus, even in exposed places, the troops could shield themselves and then fight back. So there was nothing in any way uncanny about the whole episode. The uncanny "explanation" only crept in later.

It began with a short story by Arthur Machen called "The Bowmen." This was printed in the afternoon and evening editions of the London *Evening News* on September 29, 1914; and it proved to be the most influential piece that Machen ever wrote. Here is a brief outline:

It opens with the description of a large-scale retreat of the British Expeditionary Force. Then, in the heat of battle, one of the soldiers remembers a restaurant he used to visit. He recalls the blue and white plates with their pictures of St. George. And he shouts out the motto that ran round the edge of the plates, *"Adsit Anglis Sanctus Georgius"* (St. George Help the English).

Suddenly, the battlefield is shaken as thousands of voices call out the name of St. George. And there, facing the Germans, stands a long, shining line of Agincourt archers. Then the air is dark with arrows that cut down the advancing enemy troops—the day is saved. Ten thousand dead Germans lie scattered on the battlefield, but not one of them bears a single wound!

Now that tale wasn't one of Machen's best. And he, for one, thought it would soon be forgotten. But within a few days, Machen received letters from the editors of *The Occult Review* and the magazine *Light,* who asked whether the tale had *any* foundation in fact. They were, naturally, told that it was just a piece of imaginative writing.

Then, in the following months, various parish magazines wrote in for permission to reprint the story. The editor of the *Evening News* said yes to every one of them for he had no idea the story was already being misused.

But one of these magazines ran out of copies, so the vicar wrote directly to Machen and said that he'd like to re-issue "The Bowmen" as a pamphlet. He also asked Machen to write a short introduction, giving exact authorities for the story. Machen wrote back to say that there were no authorities, since the story was pure invention. But the vicar refused to believe him and insisted that the story *must be true.* It

1914. The British were swamped by angels!

was then that Machen realized that "he'd succeeded unwittingly, in the art of deceit."

Very soon variations of the tale were being told as "established fact." But all the stories were clearly traceable back to Machen's flight of fancy.

Take the version published by the Roman Catholic paper *The Universe* in its issue of April 30, 1915. This was a second-hand account said to be based on a letter from "A Catholic officer from the Front." This letter claimed that: "a party of about thirty men and an officer was cut off in a trench, when the officer said to his men, 'Look here; we must either stay here and be caught like rats in a trap, or make a sortie against the enemy. . . .' The men all agreed with him, and with the yell of 'St. George for England!' they dashed out into the open. The officer tells how, as they ran on, he became aware of a large company of men with bows and arrows going along with them, and even leading them against the enemy's trenches. . . . Afterwards when he was talking to a German prisoner, the man asked him who was the officer on the great white horse who led them? For although he was such a conspicuous figure, they had none of them been able to hit him. I must also add that the German dead appeared to have no wounds on them. . . ."

The Protestant version was just as colorful. As told by the Reverend Fielding Ould of St. Albans, it ran: "A sergeant in our army had frequented a house of Young Men's Christian Association, and had seen there a picture of St. George slaying the dragon. He had been deeply impressed by it, and when at the Front, he found himself in an advanced and rather isolated trench, he told the story of St. George to his men. . . . When shortly afterwards, a sudden charge of the grey-coated Germans in greatly superior numbers threatened the sergeant's trench, he cried, 'Remember St. George for England!' to his men as they advanced to meet the foe. A few moments afterwards the enemy hesitated, stopped and finally fled, leaving some prisoners in our hands. One of the latter seemed dazed and astonished, demanded to be told who were the horsemen in armour who led the charge. Surely they could not have been Belgians dressed in such a way!"

Even the spiritualists had their own variation! Miss Callow, secretary to the Higher Thought Center in Kensington, wrote to *The Weekly Despatch* to say: "An officer has sent . . . a detailed account of a vision that appeared to himself and others when fighting against fearful odds at Mons.

"He plainly saw an apparition representing St. George the patron saint of England, the exact counterpart of a picture that hangs today in a London restaurant. So terrible was their plight at the time, that the officer could not refrain from appealing to the vision to help them. Then, as if the enemy had also seen the apparition, the Germans abandoned their positions in precipitate terror."

After a while, some people grew unhappy with the bowmen. Perhaps they were too militant and too secular for comfort. So transmutation began, and the shining archers were turned into shining angels. Winged creatures who intervened not aggressively, but in an awe-inspiring fashion! A poem, "After Mons," published in *Light* (May 15, 1915), seems to mark this shift of emphasis. It's second verse read:

> You saw, O friend, the forms, the light, the sheen?
> Our foes, their horses, saw; they turned and fled,
> As troops of silent angels filed between
> Our broken ranks and theirs, and stilled our dread.

And so the bowmen were pushed into the background. The angels proved much more reassuring and acceptable. Even so, people were reluctant to give up all the glamour of Machen's tale, and St. George managed to survive in many yarns that untiringly circulated.

From July 1915, angels were in season with a vengeance. Sheaves of articles appeared in the press—so did a mass of heated correspondence. And many clergymen preached sermons using "the Angels" ɛ ɜ the central theme. Even Machen was swept up in the fervor. He was pressed to issue "The Bowmen" in book form—tying it in with some extra stories of "Legends of the War"—and he obliged.

He delivered three more fantastic pieces—one of which was again taken as true. But the best part of his slim book was the twenty-four pages he used to explain how and why the legend had become confused with fact.

The Bowmen—And Other Legends became a best-seller—three thousand copies a day were snapped up, and it was translated into six languages. But this did little to dampen people's ardor for the angelic myth. For suddenly the public was overwhelmed by "testimony and evidence" in favor of the angels. Late in the day, certainly, but there it was, in glorious believable print!

First in the field was Ralph Shirley, editor of *The Occult Review*.

His pamphlet, *The Angel Warriors at Mons,* claimed to be "An Authentic Record" including "Numerous Confirmatory Testimonies." Then, the Reverend Herbert Wood of Liverpool issued his *Wonderful Works of God,* which recounted visions of angels. Other reverend gentlemen followed suit.

After that, Harold Begbie intervened. He was an extremely popular writer of the time. He was also an ardent patriot, and he felt the story was inspiring and had to be defended. So he waded in with a book entitled *On The Side Of The Angels*—the weightiest defense of all.

Begbie was furious with Machen's attempt to set the record straight. He even suggested that Machen may have picked up information about the angels direct from the battlefields—by telepathy! But telepathy apart, both *The Occult Review* and Harold Begbie relied heavily on the statements of a young girl—nurse Phyllis Campbell.

This Miss Campbell was an extraordinary figure, with an extraordinary batch of tales to tell. But they can wait for a while. First, let's consider the fate of the other impressive testifiers.

One of the widely quoted testimonies was that of Miss Marrable, daughter of the well-known Canon Marrable. The copy distributed by the Reverend M. P. Gillson read:

> Last Sunday I met Miss Marrable and she told me she knew two officers both of whom had seen the Angels who saved their left wing from the Germans when they came right upon them during our retreat from Mons. They expected annihilation . . . when to their amazement the Germans stood like dazed men, never so much as touched their guns nor stirred until we had turned around and escaped. . . .
>
> The other man she met in London and asked him if he had heard the wonderful story of the Angels. He answered that he had seen them himself while he and his company were retreating. They heard the German cavalry tearing after them. They had made for a place . . . of safety, but before they could reach it the German cavalry were upon them, so they turned around to face the enemy expecting instant death when, to their wonder, they saw between them and the enemy a whole troop of Angels, and the horses of the Germans turned round terrified out of their senses and regularly stampeded, and tore away in all directions from our men . . . this gave them time to save themselves.

This testimony convinced thousands. For here were the considered words of a "lady of quality" from a committed Christian family. Small wonder then that her statements were used by the Reverend R. F. Horton in a famous sermon often reprinted. And understandable that her claims were embodied in parish magazines, religious pamphlets, and Harold Begbie's book.

Just as convincing was the testimony of Private 10515 Cleaver of the First Cheshire Regiment. He asserted that supernatural intervention had indeed saved the British troops from annihilation. And there was no questioning this, for he'd *been* at Mons himself and *seen* the vision of angels. What's more, he swore out an affidavit to this effect before George S. Hazelhurst, a justice of the peace of the County of Flint.

This sworn and confident statement was seized on by the press—"striking confirmation," *Light* called it. Begbie agreed and triumphantly flourished it in his book. But his triumph was to prove short-lived.

Unfortunately, for all concerned, Magistrate George Hazelhurst picked up some rumors concerning Private Cleaver. As a result, this led to inquiries at the headquarters of the Cheshires. And there the major in charge of records turned up details showing that Cleaver had in fact been *in England* during the battle of Mons and the subsequent retreat! Hazelhurst broke the news in a crestfallen letter to the *Daily Mail*. And he ended with the sad plea: "Will none of the officers who were at Mons and saw the Angels of whom Miss Marrable speaks, come forward and confess it?"

His plea was never to be answered—and Miss Marrable, herself, explained why. In a letter to the *Evening News* she revealed that she knew nothing at all about any supernatural episodes during the retreat from Mons. Those stories, using her good name, were nothing but fabrications.

Despite these exposures, "Miss Marrable's Testimony" continued to circulate—often with her name left out. And Private Cleaver's lying affidavit was still being reprinted eight months after it was discredited. But in September 1915, such exposures made Begbie's "powerful defense" look somewhat dubious.

It's true that he still had other testimonies—but most were third, fourth and even sixth-hand statements. A number of them were patently absurd, and most led back to witnesses who were untraceable. In truth, he was left with only one body of evidence worth considering—those impressive statements of Nurse Phyllis Campbell as featured in *The Occult Review*.

Miss Campbell was no ordinary nurse. She was highly articulate.

Her mother was a novelist, while her aunt was Lady Archibald Campbell, also a writer. So she came from an imaginative family.

When the slaughter began Miss Campbell was living in France. She immediately volunteered as a nurse—took a crash-course—then worked at a dressing-station at one of the railway halts in the forest of Marley. And there she met the men who'd "met the Angels."

There was the Lancashire Fusilier who'd seen St. George on horseback, leading the British. There was the Royal Field Artilleryman who declared: "It's true Sister. . . . We all saw it . . . a tall man in golden armour on a white horse, holding his sword up. . . . then before you could say 'knife' the Germans had turned, and we were after them. . . . We had a few scores to settle and we fairly settled them."

Then there were the two officers and three men of the Irish Guards who told her roughly the same story.

So Phyllis Campbell presented testimony that differed markedly from that offered by everyone else. In truth, she seemed to know more about the angels than anyone else—anywhere! She even added to her claims by asserting that the French soldiers had seen Joan of Arc. Said one: "I know her well, for I am of Domremy. I saw her brandishing her sword and crying, 'Turn! Turn! Advance!' . . . No wonder the Boche fled down the hill."

And, remarkably, other Frenchmen had "seen *St. Michael* on horseback flourishing his sword and shouting 'Victory!'"

Her remarkable knowledge didn't end there. To crown it all she further stated that St. Michael had also reappeared, frequently, during the battles on the Russian front. Her Russian knowledge *naturally* came from the very best of sources—from a letter "received by her friends in France before September 14, 1914" and written by, of *all* people—a Russian princess!

Clearly, this Miss Campbell is the key figure in this whole affair and deserves a very close scrutiny. Such a scrutiny shows that she was no stranger to occult fancies. Her influential aunt, Lady Archibald Campbell, turns out to have been a noted clairvoyant and medium—who believed in fairies. Young Phyllis herself had written two articles on French ghost stories (under the name Phil Campbell) for *The Occult Review,* just before the war. So she had a lively imagination fired by psychic teachings.

She also had a very strange view of evidence. When challenged by Arthur Machen to produce first-hand confirmations, she countered by saying that the troops were forbidden to talk about the events—which was an outright lie. Then she fielded the following quote as proof. It was part of a young officer's letter: "I had the most amazing halluci-nations marching at night, so I was fast asleep, I think. Everyone was reeling about the road and seeing things too, they said . . . marched on for the rest of the night. . . . Most tiring; I again saw all sorts of things, enormous men walking towards me, and lights and chairs and things in the road."

And that passage from Mabel Collins' *The Crucible* was, in Miss Campbell's view, one in the eye for Machen! Yet if anything, it showed the real weakness of her case. When put to the test she offered nothing but a letter which describes the hallucinations suffered by battle-fa-tigued soldiers. Such visions were common on forced marches on many fronts. Simply contrast that letter with the following. It's a report from the South-West Africa Campaign of 1915: "The fatigue became awful. I began to get lightheaded. The sky seemed to become a straight wall in front of us, and the effect of the moonlight through the dust made me imagine I saw great palaces and churches, with the stars as little win-dows. Then I would pull myself together, and look at the men riding in front, and they would turn into funny old giantesses dancing in the moonlight. I learnt afterwards that everyone suffered from these hallu-cinations" (Keith Morris, *A Great Soldier of the Empire* [1915], 52).

In clashing with Machen, Miss Campbell escaped the drubbing she'd invited. For Machen was hampered by his chivalrous outlook and he held back. So she continued to shine as the leading light among the "Divine Interventionists." Indeed, she promised that ". . . evidence exists . . . and when the war is over and when the embargo of silence is removed, Mr. Machen will be overwhelmed with corroborative evi-dence." Having said that, Miss Campbell apparently changed her mind. For there was talk of a book written by her—one which would provide *all the answers.*

That particular book never appeared—not even after the war. But another book of hers came out called *Back of the Front*, and it proves to be a revelation. It gives dramatic insight into her mind. It shows that she was driven by a fanatical type of patriotism. And this led her to ac-cept and repeat every atrocity story that came her way. At no time did she bother to check the truth or otherwise of these tales. What's more, for every atrocity tale that circulated, Miss Campbell had one better. She actually claimed to have *seen* these atrocities for herself!

The atrocity-mongers had shrieked that Belgian women were having their breasts cut off by the Huns. Miss Campbell confirmed this by writing: "In one wagon, sitting on the floor, was a naked girl of about 23. One of her suffering sisters, more fortunate than the rest in possessing an undergarment, had torn it in half and covered the front of her poor body. It was saturated with blood from her cut-off breasts. On her knees lay a little baby, dead."

Then it was said that the Huns cut off the hands and feet of children, tortured women, burned people alive, and impaled and crucified civilians—including priests. Phyllis Campbell "knew all this to be true."

In one railway wagon she saw "women covered with sabre cuts, women who had been whipped, women burned alive escaping from their blazing homes, little boys maimed in the hands and feet."

And she further catalogued the horrors of ". . . priests impaled, of little children done to death in such ways that they cannot be spoken of . . . of crucified sons and fathers."

Her warped patriotism even led her to write of "utter depravity of the German soul. . . .It seemed to me that all the wickedness, all the fear and filthiness imaginable that exists can be summed up in one word: GERMAN."

She was so certain of this that she was drawn to an inevitable conclusion: "When I saw the German prisoners . . . when they stood blinking in the sun with their square heads and putty-coloured faces, their colourless eyes and lashes, it suggested to me a creation of some monstrous spirit of evil. Is it strange that saints and angels should fight against this dreadful foe? I have seen no vision, but in my heart I believe that the Captains of God are leading the Allies to Victory."

And there you have a glimpse of Miss Campbell's secret. The Hun was so loathsome that anything could be used as a weapon against him—*even lies*. Used in a good cause—perhaps the greatest of all good causes—lies, rumors, half-truths, and myths, could stiffen people's resolve. Could make them that much more determined to stamp out the "monstrous spirit of evil."

At the time, of course, no one dared openly call her a liar. The lady was too well-placed. In addition, she was a disarming, beguiling creature. She was described as "extremely pretty, child-like and sensitive." But it was also noted that "she seems to possess extraordinary powers of self control and endurance."

Another factor that stilled people's tongues was her record of devotion in the military hospitals. Yet logically considered, her conduct as a nurse is wholly irrelevant. It may have helped confuse the issues at the time, but it has no bearing on the accuracy of her statements.

On the other hand, we have firm evidence from the First World War that some sweet young ladies and nurses were guilty of inventing the most incredible tales. Just consider two examples.

On September 16, 1914, *The Star* reported the murder of Nurse Grace Hume from Dumfries, Scotland. Her hospital at Vilvorde in Belgium had been overrun by the Germans. She'd been mutilated by two soldiers who'd sadistically cut off her breasts. Before dying she'd scrawled a last note to her sister Kate and slipped it to a friend—Nurse Mullard. Luckily the Allies then liberated the remaining nurses and faithful Nurse Mullard made a pilgrimage to Dumfries to break the news.

Seven leading newspapers took up this grim story and the public was rightly enraged—but not for long. Within a few days it was found that Nurse Hume was living happily and in one piece in Huddersfield! She'd certainly volunteered for service at the Front but had never been called on. She'd never even set foot in Belgium!

Following this, her sister Kate stood trial, and it was proved that she'd fabricated the whole story. The published letters from her sister and from "Nurse Mullard" were nothing but forgeries from her own fair hand.

Later on, ex-Nurse Catto came up with another batch of terrors. She claimed to have actually nursed mutilated Belgians—children with their hands cut off—women with their breasts cut off. She even named the hospital as Ramsgate General. But an investigation at that hospital showed there wasn't a word of truth in her story.

Now those cases merely serve to restore a correct perspective. For the proof of Miss Campbell's duplicity can't be established by analogy. To prove this we need to contrast competent accounts by people who lived through the retreat from Mons. Fortunately, there's no shortage of these.

Just two accounts though, will be sufficient—accounts by men who were ministers of religion working as army chaplains, men who would have *welcomed* news of angelic aid—had it been forthcoming.

The first writings to consider are those of Abbé Felix Klein, a French Army Chaplian attached to the Ambulance Division of the American Hospital at Neuilly, north-east of Paris. He writes that he:

Abbé Felix Klein, 1914. His diary refutes the angels myth.

"... was privileged to go forth to gather in the wounded from the very Front ... we went forth to it in the morning and came back from it in the evening ... the wounded, brought back from them (the battlefields) after twenty-four or forty-eight hours, retain an only too lively impression of them."

From August 3 to December 28, 1914, Abbé Klein kept a lengthy diary. In it he recorded the views and "lively impressions" of the troops and details of the campaigns as they came in—including significant rumors. He even notes the famous rumor about Russian troops coming to the aid of the British Expeditionary Force. But *nowhere* does he mention any talk or rumors of divine intervention in the battles.

This is telling since Nurse Campbell endorsed *The Occult Review's* claim that: "No French paper would have made itself ridiculous by disputing the authenticity of what was vouched for by many thousands of independent eye-witnesses ... whole battalions of French soldiers had seen apparitions of Joan of Arc ... and St. Michael."

Yet Abbé Klein, who was in daily touch with the troops during and after the retreat, had clearly never heard of any such talk—from any quarter. And his diary *La Guerre Vue D'Une Ambulance* (published, January 1915) recorded events as they happened. *The Occult Review,* by contrast, spoke of events over a year *after* they were alleged to have happened. And it failed to produce a single verifiable statement from any of the "many thousands."

The second significant record was kept by the British Chaplain Owen Spencer Watkins. He was attached to the 14th Field Ambulance with the British Expeditionary Force. He was at Mons, took part in the retreat and his account was published in March 1915 *(With Field-Marshall French in France and Flanders).* It's a book rich in detail but without any mention whatsoever of the angels, either as realities or even rumors.

So, was it all imagination run riot? A great mythical tapestry woven from threads of hope, anguish and blind patriotism? No—there was much more to it than that! More than even Machen's crucial story. For beyond the Angels myth lay an even greater myth. One created by the British Government itself—in the interests of recruiting.

This goverment myth went into print on Sunday, August 30, 1914, in a special Sunday Edition of *The Times*. Basically, it was a heart-rending dispatch from Arthur Moore in France. It was headlined "Fiercest Fight in History." It opened with the poignant words—"This is a pitiful story I have to write. Would to God it did not fall to me to write it." And the body of the story spoke of "very great losses"—of "a retreating broken army"—of German troops, so numerous ". . . that they could no more be stopped than the waves to the sea." These were words that shocked the Nation.

Now, normally, such a despairing piece would have been slashed to pieces by the official censor. But *this* dispatch was passed with the full approval of officialdom. You see, the director of the Press Bureau recognized that Arthur Moore had been swept away by fierce emotions. His piece was a misinterpretation, based on muddled, incomplete information, exaggerations, and misunderstandings. The Government itself knew far better. Things were nowhere near as bad as the dispatch made out. And losses were by no means as great as imagined. Yet, there was an awareness that fresh recruits were urgently needed. And the public deserved to be sharply shaken out of its complacency. So, this sincere, but misleading, dispatch was waved through—with blessings!

More than that, it was furnished with a new ending, written by F. E. Smith, director of the Government Press Bureau. This read: "England should realize, and should realize at once, that she must send reinforcements, and still send them. Is an army of exhaustless valor to be borne down by sheer weight of numbers, while young Englishmen at home play golf and cricket? We want men and we want them now."

The ploy worked. Britain stiffened its backbone and the recruits poured in. But from then on, the myth of the Battle of Mons as "the clash that saved civilization," grew in stature, while the contributions of the French and Belgians were overshadowed and under-valued.

This dramatic dispatch inspired two trains of thought that led directly to the Angels legend. Machen's "Bowmen" was written after he was moved by the anguished words of Arthur Moore. Also, people at large began to reason that if the British had escaped from such an enormous force, then it was nothing short of a miraculous event. From then on, nothing could stop the gradual growth of speculation and fantasy.

In short, there was a desperate need to believe in the rightness of the Allied cause. And divine intervention was surely the ultimate proof of such rightness. As the *Christian Commonwealth* observed, proof of angelic aid "would strengthen religious faith, which has been greatly weakened by the war, and would reinforce belief in the justice of the cause for which so many men fell during that magnificent retreat and almost miraculous recovery on the banks of the Marne."

In the years after the war, as the real events at Mons became forgotten, people grew even more reckless. It became easy to find "witnesses" who'd claimed to have seen those angels. And many inventive yarns were spun about their doings. But it was very different in 1915—at a time when these events were supposed to have been "vouched for by many thousands."

As Machen pointed out in August of that year: "It's been claimed that 'everybody' who fought from Mons to Ypres saw the apparitions. If that be so, it is odd that nobody has come forward to testify at first hand to the most amazing event of his life. Many men have been back from the Front, we have many wounded in hospital, many soldiers have written home. And they have all combined, this great host, to keep silence about the most wonderful occurrences, the aspiring assurance, the surest omen of victory."

Twenty-five years later, Machen wasn't so kind. He'd grown weary of the contradictions. Become fed-up completely with the failure to grasp the requirements of worthwhile evidence. And when he looked back on the assorted Angels stories he said, "There was not one word of truth in them, those stories were lies. Everyone of them lies sir!"

For myself, though, I prefer a more charitable verdict. I'd call it "tragic self-deception"—and leave it at that!

11

THE GHOST WITH WET BOOTS!

The two giant battleships were designed like immense can-openers. They were everything that ranked as up-to-date in 1893—armorclad in parts, bristling with formidable guns in revolving turrets and even sporting torpedo tubes. Yet their bows harked back to Roman times, for each one carried an enormous steel ram!

The larger ship of the two was the HMS *Victoria,* flag-ship of Vice-Admiral Sir George Tryon. The slightly smaller ship was HMS *Camperdown,* commanded by Rear-Admiral Markham. They were the pride of the Mediterranean Squadron of the Royal Navy.

On the afternoon of June 22, 1893, Sir George led his squadron northward following the line of the Syrian coast. He intended to turn about on reaching Tripoli and enter the anchorage there.

The fleet steamed along in two parallel columns—five ships in one, six in the other. The five were led by HMS *Camperdown,* while the other column was headed by Tryon's *Victoria.* The distance separating them was a mere six cables—a trifle over 1,200 yards. At that distance many maneuvers were possible, even intricate ones, but not the strange one dreamed up by Sir George. He ordered the two columns to turn inward simultaneously and reverse direction before anchoring. A monstrously inept order by any standards for the turning circles of the ironclads were huge—800 yards easily. This meant that the warships would be set on an inevitable collision course.

This danger was at once apparent to Admiral Markham. He knew that even eight cables would have been scarcely sufficient separation to guarantee complete safety. So he queried the signalled orders—but they were immediately repeated. After that, no one argued—indeed, few people ever dared argue with the arrogant Sir George. Instead, Markham acquiesced, blindly trusting that Tryon had some elaborate master-plan hidden up his gold-braided sleeve, and the *Camperdown* swung inward.

HMS *Victoria* began its turn at the same time. And the two giants steamed toward each other as if they were foes bent on using the vicious steel rams on their bows. No one took evasive action. Admiral Markham still hoped that his chief would prove to be a tactical genius.

But, aboard the *Victoria,* Captain Bourke grew apprehensive. He spoke to the Vice-Admiral and warned of the danger. Yet Tryon remained dumb—almost as if he were locked in a trance. And the ship relentlessly turned on its collision course.

The Captain then urgently asked for permission to go astern at full speed. But Tryon still remained transfixed and silent. The question was repeated again and again until finally, the Admiral answered with one word—"Yes!"

By then it was far too late to save the flagship. For, even though the *Camperdown* had reversed her screws she still drove forward and inexorably smashed into the *Victoria's* bows with her ram. Now, behind that ram was the weight of the ship's 10,600 tons. So the flagship's armor plate was pathetically weak protection. It was caved in and split open by sheer brute force—and the sea poured in.

The end was horrific. The *Victoria* began to turn turtle, and the enginemen were trapped at their posts. Many leapt from the sloping decks. Then came a fresh horror—as an eyewitness put it:

> The powerful engines, deep down in the heart of the ship and enclosed in the water-tight compartments, kept throbbing and working, and the formidable steel flanges of the twin screws whirled round and round at first high up in space, and then gradually came nearer and nearer to the surface of the water until the ship descended in the midst of the mass of human beings struggling for life, when the propeller-blades struck the calm sea and sent an enormous cloud of spray into the air; and then as the ship disappeared the suction increased until it became a perfect maelstrom, at the bottom of which these deadly screws were moving like circular saws, gashing and killing the poor creatures who had battled vainly for life.
>
> Then came the scene that caused the officers on the decks of the remaining vessels of the Fleet to turn sick. Shrieks were heard, and then the waves and the foam were reddened by the blood of the hundreds of victims. Arms, legs wrenched from bodies, headless trunks, were tossed out of the vortex to linger on the surface for a few moments and then disappear.

Three hundred and fifty-eight lives were lost, and among the dead was Tryon. Indeed, Sir George made no attempt whatsoever to save himself. With his death went all chance of knowing what he really had in mind in ordering the fatal maneuver. There are some, though, who claim that he was supernaturally doomed. They say his mind was unhinged by the remorseness working out of a *curse*. Prominent amongst the "curse" advocates is Mr. Richard Winer—one of the "Bermuda Triangle" jokers.

In his *From The Devil's Triangle to the Devil's Jaw,* Winer takes ten dreary pages to tell the story and spices it with the claim that, "There is a 'mummy's curse', and it originated, or began to unfold, on the shores of the Mediterranean." According to Winer, hundreds of Syrian Arabs had waited and watched for the British fleet to be hit by this curse. Apparently, they'd been alerted *a week before* by a local fakir. And he'd ". . . prophesied that Allah was determined to visit the vessels of the infidels."

To add strength to his supernatural view, Winer then relates the amazing tale of Sir George Tryon's last London appearance. It took

"Did this catastrophy beget a ghost?"

place at a late morning tea party organized by Lady Tryon at her Eaton Square home —"The majority of the guests were wives of the Royal Navy's commanders. About noon, Admiral Tryon was seen walking down the stairs and across the drawing room. The Admiral was attired in his full-dress uniform but appeared to be oblivious to the guests in his home."

We then learn that this party was held on that sorrowful June 22 so that the solid-looking Admiral was nothing but a spectre. The real Sir George was, at the time, some thousands of miles away on the bridge of the doomed *Victoria.*

There's no doubt that the author imagines that he's on safe ground in recounting the story. In various forms it has been cited for years by many other authors. People like Peter Underwood, Christina Hole, Ray Lamont Brown, to name a few. They've all presented it without any doubts—indeed, James Wentworth Day even described it as, "one of the best authenticated ghost stories in living London history."

But for all that, I'm afraid Mr. Winer's confidence is misplaced. Like many of the other tales he vends it has no validity. None whatsoever. A careful comparison of the different versions shows that the story has the same mythical quality as the Lord Dufferin saga, which is the subject of the following chapter. And there is the usual conflict over the most basic things.

One account has it that he walked through the reception room at Eaton Square and then disappeared. Another states that he walked through the "crowded ballroom" and was seen by some three hundred guests. Yet another claims that he appeared at a party in the drawing room at the exact time of his death—that is at 3:40 in the afternoon. But the most detailed account of all gives the time of his appearance at 11:30 in the evening. That is, some eight hours *after* his death.

According to this last and lengthy account (by Ian Fellowes-Gordon), Sir George made his entry through the east door of the ballroom, walked across the ballroom floor, and made his exit through the west door. Some fifty or so guests are said to have recognized the Admiral and some even spoke to him. But he didn't reply—just walked in, walked through, and walked out!

So here we have discord over the time, the exact place and the number of witnesses. There is one point of close harmony though, for they all agree that Lady Tryon *saw nothing* of the apparition. The claim that *she did* is Richard Winer's own special variation.

Now these disagreements are significant enough. But even more significant is the total absence of contemporary references or witnesses. When I questioned James Wentworth Day he was amiable enough to admit that he really had no material which would authenticate this story! I looked around for anything and everything that could throw light on this mystery. And for a short while there were two leads that looked very promising.

The first was in an account by Ian Fellowes-Gordon where he quotes from and elaborates on the testimony of an alleged eyewitness. He writes:

Months later Sir Jasper Hoad was to explain what had happened. And his account, verified by every other guest present in the ballroom at eleven twenty-five that evening, would go down in history. "I had to summon up a bit of courage to ask Clementina if she'd seen what I'd seen. But I did. And she let me have it.

"'I don't know what *you* saw, Jasper. I only had the sensation of watching as all my guests ridiculously moved heads, like mechanical toys, from one side to the other. I saw nothing else, not a thing. Yet it seems that they imagined they were seeing something. . . .'

"'But Clementina,' I said to her, 'it was George.' That's what I said to her, and she said, 'Don't be ridiculous, Jasper, George is at the far end of the Mediterranean. If he'd got back, on some sudden leave, well then obviously, I'd have seen him too.'

"'Clementina, my dear. I only hope and pray that this means nothing sad and—supernatural. But I assure you that every man and woman in that ballroom saw your husband walk in the east door and out the west. He turned and smiled at everyone—including you, my dear—but he didn't stop. And when he got to the west door, well, he just vanished.'"

Naturally, something as meaty as that looks mighty impressive. Unfortunately, when I spoke to Ian Fellowes-Gordon, he hadn't the remotest idea where the information came from! He was cheerfully helpful, but, as he explained, his story had been written while he was working for the BBC World Service. Because of pressure of work he was unable to carry out his own research and simply sent a note down to the librarians at the BBC library. They obliged by sending up collections of press cuttings, magazine articles and books and he delved into them to create the story. Somewhere or other he'd come across a mention of Sir Jasper Hoad who'd talked to Lady Tryon about the sighting. From the same source he'd gleaned the statement that there were at least fifty people to back up Sir Jasper's story.

My own search for the elusive Hoad source proved futile, but in the course of events this proved to be unimportant, for on checking the peerage lists for 1893 and afterwards, I discovered that there *never was* a "Sir Jasper Hoad." So, the testimony of a man who never existed amounts to nothing but the rankest fiction.

The second promising lead had a very different feel about it. It was found in the most bizarre account of the Tryon case in print. It's included in Will Eisner's *Spirit Casebook of True Haunted Houses and Ghosts*. This is a book with comic-style illustrations but, nevertheless, a serious intent.

This time dear Sir George appears in the library of his London house in "Bristol Square" where guests found him standing behind his desk. His eyes were riveted on ". . . his globe, his finger pointing to

Sir George Tryon—ghost with wet
boots?

Tripoli . . . on the Mediterranean. They greeted him. He nodded absently . . . trance-like in his movements."

The guests excused themselves and rushed off to tell the glad news to Lady Tryon, and was she astounded! What was Sir George doing back home? He was supposed to be at sea. She ran to the library but it was empty! But on the globe of the world was a still moist fingerprint exactly at the point where the two ships had collided. The ship's clock on Tryon's desk had stopped at 3:44—the exact time of the collision and, most startling of all there was a damp footprint just the Admiral's size on the floor behind the desk!

Bizarre as it is, this version does have the merit of giving a checkable source. It says: "Two months after the incident this account appeared in the August 1893 issue of the *Review of Reviews.*"

Two months after the event makes the account fresh enough to be exciting. Sorry to have to tell you, though, that the reference turned out to be quite bogus. The account in that issue of the *Review of*

Reviews contains nothing but a straightforward report of the collision at sea—there is no mention of the ghostly portent in London. What's more, there's no mention of the event in *any* issue of the *Review of the Reviews* from 1893-1895.

That, in itself, is most revealing. For the *Review's* editor was W. T. Stead—an ardent spiritualist. A man who went out of his way to collect and print any good story which had a supernatural slant. In fact, his Christmas 1892 issues were crammed chock-full of "true ghost stories."

Among these ghost stories is one which, oddly enough, turns out to be the welcome genesis of the Tryon legend! It's entitled "A Ghost In a Ballroom."

The account tells how a Mr. W. walked through, and out of, a ballroom without speaking to any of the people present, including the lady he was due to partner. Then, on the following morning, the witnesses learned that Mr. W. had been found drowned. Remarkably, "his watch had stopped at 10:15," the exact time at which he'd been seen in the ballroom.

So the tale of the drowned ballroom ghost was circulating at least six months *before* the *Victoria's* end. But that end was so spectacular and puzzling that it simply invited rumor, speculation and fantasy. It also gave a new slant to an old story and the shadowy Mr. W. became the beefy and arrogant Sir George—complete with wet boots.

But how about that curse? Does *that* stand up to scrutiny? Not for one moment! As Admiral Colomb has testified, Sir George acted "with a strong and frequently expressed impatience of all mathematical calculations and mechanical certainties." And he also had a mathematical blindspot. For he occasionaly confused the *radius* of a ship's turning circle with its *diameter*. This confusion had almost led to a disaster some three years earlier. Then he'd signalled precisely the same fatal maneuver during the 1890 naval exercises off Plymouth. But at that time, Rear Admiral Tracey had refused to comply and Tryon eventually cancelled the orders.

As for Tryon's "trance state," he'd been ill for some time—plagued by a painful ulcer on the leg which refused to heal. And the medication and pain-killers he was using were more than probably laced with laudanum and opium derivatives. Enough to slow anyone's reflexes and double-glaze the eyeballs!

So I'm afraid that the Tryon tales have to be filed along with all the many other bright stars of the "factual-fictional" firmament.

Inevitably, this won't please Richard Winer, who's been impetuous enough to write: "Could an Arab fakir have caused one of the greatest peacetime tragedies in the annals of the Royal Navy? Could the Admiral of one of the ships involved have been removed spiritually from the bridge of his ship until seconds before the tragic event occurred— by which time it was already too late? . . . the answer is yes."

But the real, and politely restrained, answer is surely "Hogwash!"

12

DEATH BECKONS LORD DUFFERIN!

Fate was exceptionally kind to the first Marquis of Dufferin and Ava. He died peacefully on February 12, 1902—nine years after "a dramatic escape from violent death." An escape only made possible by supernormal intervention—or so some of his chroniclers tell us.

His career was one of sustained brilliance. After a short Parliamentary period, Lord Dufferin became in turn, governor-general of Canada, ambassador to Russia, ambassador to Constantinople, viceroy of India, ambassador to Rome and, finally, the ambassador to France. In all, his was a bustling active life punctuated by spells of leave in his beloved Ireland.

The awesome part of his saga begins in the 1880s, at the country-house of Tullamore in County Wexford, Ireland. He was there enjoying a welcome break from the incessant whirl of diplomatic life. And the great house seemed to provide an ideal refuge for anyone seeking tranquility. But one night, the whole atmosphere of the place changed and Lord Dufferin woke up sick with terror.

His sleep had been cruelly broken into by strange sounds from the grounds outside—terrifying sounds. Yet, terrifying as they were, he was no coward. So he climbed out of bed to investigate. With racing heart and trembling body he reached the french windows and peered out.

From his window he overlooked the trim lawns bathed in moonlight. Almost every section was in plain view except for a spot where tall trees cast long black shadows. From the direction of these shadows came the sounds that had awakened him—heartfelt sobs, more animal than human.

He fumbled with the window-latches, but as he did a man staggered out of the shadows into the moonlight. He was agonizingly bent over under the weight of a load on his back. At first sight, it looked like a long linen-chest. Yet, as he drew closer, it suddenly became clear that his burden was a crudely-made coffin.

At that, Lord Dufferin threw open the windows, ran across the lawn and shouted at the man to halt. Until then, the man's face had been held down and hidden, but on hearing the shout, the man lifted his head and turned it towards Lord Dufferin. And the moonlight fell on a face loathesome and unforgettable and so contorted with hate that Lord Dufferin stopped dead in his tracks. Then, he drew on his reserves of courage, advanced on the man and walked—right through him!

Simultaneously, the man disappeared, coffin and all. With his disappearance the gloom lifted, and the house and grounds became as calm and restful as ever.

Lord Dufferin returned to his bedroom shaking and puzzled. Then, after writing a complete account of the event in his diary, he managed to snatch some sleep.

At the breakfast table he read out his account and appealed to his host and fellow guests for an explanation. But no one could help. The description of the man matched no one in the area past or present. There wasn't even a local ghost to blame—so the event remained an inexplicable mystery.

Over the years, the memory of that night stayed with Lord Dufferin, but it no longer puzzled him. He grew to believe that it really might have been nothing more than an extra-vivid nightmare. And that's how things stood for the next ten years. Then, in 1893, the vision took on a new significance.

Lord Dufferin—a miraculous deliverance?

By that time, Lord Dufferin was the British Ambassador to France, and was obliged to attend a diplomatic reception at the Grand Hotel in Paris. When he entered the hotel foyer he found it jam-packed with impatient guests, for the lift was taking ages to make its trips to the reception area on the top floor. So, together with his secretary he joined the queue for the lift. After a long time, he reached the head of the queue, the lift arrived, its door squealed open, and the lift-attendant waved the guests in.

Lord Dufferin blanched,

stood fast and refused to enter. He mumbled an excuse to the officials with him, then stepped backwards, pulling his secretary after him. Nothing would persuade him to use *that* lift, for the lift-attendant was the exact double of that hideous man he'd seen years before in Ireland!

The other officials ignored the eccentric Englishman. They crowded into the lift and it began its laborious climb. Lord Dufferin meanwhile, went hunting for the manager's office. He had to know *who* the lift-attendant was and *where* he'd come from. But, before his Lordship reached the office, disaster struck. The lift's cable snapped and it plunged down the shaft to destruction. The passengers were killed outright—as was the ghastly lift-attendant—so he could never be questioned. The hotel manager could answer no questions either, for the attendant was a casual worker taken on for the day. He seemed to be a man without documents or records.

To add to the eeriness, no one ever came forward to claim or identify the lift-man's body. Lord Dufferin was baffled. Not even his money and influence could turn up a single fact about the man. The one certainty was that the hideous creature had saved Dufferin's life. But why only *his* life? Why not the others?

That, in its essentials, is the remarkable story that's been told many times before. These published accounts often vary in detail, but no one ever questions the basic truth of the tale. On the contrary, it's always asserted that the facts have been fully researched and investigated.

One writer, for example, states: "The evidence is incontrovertible . . . the details of this story have been carefully investigated . . . by the well-known French psychologist de Maratray, who brought them to the attention of the British Society for Psychical Research."

Another writer adds: "The accident was reported in the Press . . . but neither the management of the hotel, nor the accident investigators could find any record of the man's name or background."

So here we seem to have a case that can't be challenged. In truth, though, the whole account is nothing more than a grotesque patische of myths.

To begin with, this case was never investigated by the Society for Psychical Research. The Society was certainly in existence at the time of the alleged event, but its files prove that it heard and knew nothing about it. And no newspaper carried reports of the accident—for very good reasons. In fact, the first written account of the Dufferin case did not emerge until 1920—that is, eighteen years after the death of Lord

Dufferin and twenty-six years after the alleged "lift-crash."

The primary account was written by the French psychologist Monsieur R. de Maratray on July 18, 1920. He gave it to the French astronomer Flammarion who then included it in his book, *Death And Its Mystery.* De Maratray added force to his account by claiming that his wife was related to Lord Dufferin and his family had been kept informed of the events at the time. "The accident is historic," he wrote, "and its precise date could be easily verified."

Flammarion made no attempt to check the story for himself. He even neglected to ask why de Maratray had kept quiet for so long. He enthused that: "This fantastic adventure was an actual happening." Then he went on to conclude, "Warnings of this sort are certainly most strange! They prove to us the existence of the unknown world, the mysteries of which we hope to penetrate." Thus he took de Maratray's word for everything and published a document that is both false and ludicrous.

You see, the fatal accident in the lift of the Grand Hotel took place in 1878—some five years before the "vision in Ireland," and fifteen years before the date of Lord Dufferin's "miraculous escape." At the time of that genuine accident there wasn't a diplomatic reception at the hotel. In any case, Lord Dufferin wasn't even in Paris but was serving in Canada as the governor-general! On top of that, in the real accident only a young lady died—not a lift full of people—and certainly no unknown lift-attendant!

All these facts were firmly established shortly after Flammarion's book appeared. The intrepid investigator who nailed the story as a lie was Paul Heuze, a journalist with the Paris magazine *L'Opinion.* Heuze proved that, when it came to psychical research, Flammarion jettisoned all the logic and care that went into his astronomical work. As a result, his books were crammed full of unsubstantiated stories and hearsay. To his discredit, Flammarion made no attempt to revise these books, and the Dufferin story was given wide circulation and picked up by author after author. In fact, of all the tales vended by him, tall or otherwise, this is the *only one* which has achieved international fame.

But how did such a tale become linked with Lord Dufferin? Well, the files of the Society for Psychical Research provide part of the answer. They show that in November 1949, a Mr. Louis Wolfe of New York wrote to the SPR and asked for details of the Society's "Dufferin investigation." The SPR replied that it had never been asked to check the case. But, prompted by this enquiry, the Society's secretary then wrote to Lady Dufferin and asked for her help.

Lady Dufferin replied that the tale did not apply to the first Lord Dufferin himself. It was simply a new version of an old story her grandfather used to tell about *someone else!* In the original version, though, an unnamed man had taken his holiday in Scotland, at Glamis Castle. And the vision itself had involved a hearse driven by a man with an ugly and hateful face.

In that case, where did Lord Dufferin find the story in its original form? And was it in any way based on facts? These proved to be tricky questions, but a search through scores of books yielded up a passage that seems to clinch things. It appears in Marc Alexander's *Haunted Castles,* and it explains that the Glamis coach-story originated with the writer Augustus Hare. Marc Alexander also states that Hare was actually staying at Glamis when a fellow guest saw the coach and driver. Unfortunately, a check with Hare's journal showed that Alexander is quite mistaken.

The crucial testimony by Hare is printed as an appendix to *My Solitary Life.* It proves that, though he'd stayed at Glamis, he knew nothing about its frightful coachman until many years after his stay. Until July 29, 1902, to be exact. On that day he was told the full story by Eustace Cecil, but Cecil made it clear it wasn't based on *his* experience. He was simply repeating an account once given him by Lady F. Trevanion.

In Lady Trevanion's account, a guest at the castle saw a carriage (not a hearse) whose driver had a "marked and terrible face." Shortly afterwards, this unnamed guest stayed on the third floor of an unnamed hotel in Paris. He rang for the lift, but refused to take it when he saw the attendant's face. Seconds later the lift-cable snapped, and the cage hurtled down the shaft to destruction.

Now, Hare had already heard this story before, often in fact, but never before linked with Glamis. And it's plain that neither he, nor Cecil, nor Lady Trevanion had ever associated the tale with Lord Dufferin, nor with any other named individual.

This is not surprising, since further research showed that the yarn first appeared as an anonymous secondhand account in the spiritualist paper *Light* of April 16, 1892.

The editor of *Light,* at the time, was the Reverend Stainton Moses and his behavior paralleled that of Flammarion's, since he took the tale completely on trust. He wrote abut it: "It has been communicated to me by a personal friend, and is both authentic and trustworthy."

The anonymous lady wrote:

> I have just heard from a friend of a remarkable dream. She thought she heard a loud knock on the door, and on looking out she saw that a hearse had stopped at the house. Being greatly surprised, she rushed downstairs and herself opened the hall door. A strange-looking man was on top of the hearse; on seeing her, he said, "Are you not ready yet?" She said, "Oh, no; certainly not," and slammed the door. The sound seemed to have caused her to wake.
>
> She was much puzzled to know what could be the significance of such a very unusual dream. The face of the man haunted her, and for weeks she could not get the rememberance out of her head. All her family and friends were told about the dream, and all the circumstances of it had been discussed.
>
> Some weeks had passed when one day the young lady happened to be in a large warehouse in the City, and was just going to step into the lift, when she looked at the man who had charge of it, and immediately drew back, having recognized the face of the man she had seen in her dream. When she drew back her consternation was added to by the exclamation from the man of the very words she had heard in her dream, "What are you not ready yet, Miss?" Her determination not to ascend in the lift was confirmed, and she declined to go into it. It only reached the next floor, when the machinery gave way, the lift being smashed to pieces and the man killed.

From then on, the lift tale travelled to the United States and Europe, becoming constantly transmuted in its passage. Sixteen years later,it returned to England in a new guise, now posing as an authentic American happening! Ironically enough, it was promptly picked up and reprinted in the pages of *Light*. It seems the new editor and his staff had completely forgotten their earlier account furnished by a "personal friend" of the Rev. Moses. On February 9, 1907, it ran this story under the heading "Saved By A Vision."

> "The Progressive Thinker" gives an instance of a warning dream, as related by Miss Gray, "A young woman prominent in educational work" in Washington State. While staying in Chicago, where she had planned to visit "a new department store which had just opened, whose elevators were death-traps," she woke up in the middle of the night and saw an unknown face at the window, twenty feet above the

ground. On going to the window she saw a hearse standing in the street below, with her nocturnal visitant occupying the driver's box; he looked her squarely in the face and beckoned to her. The next day she visited the store, and on going to one of the crowded elevators the man in charge beckoned to her and said that there was room for one more. His features were those of the man on the hearse in her dream or vision of the night before. She refused to enter the elevator, which "started down, stuck, and dropped four storeys, killing two of its passengers and injuring everyone else in the car."

In the meantime, another variation of the story had been incorporated in Lord Dufferin's bag of after-dinner yarns. One day he related it to a young impressionable nephew and gave it special treatment. As it happened, adult wiles were not fully appreciated, the twinkle in Dufferin's eye was missed, and when he spun out the tale as his very own real-life adventure, the boy was awestruck and convinced. The boy grew up to become a diplomat and writer. Out of conviction he retold this "true story" frequently—possibly to the de Maratrays. The innocent culprit, the unwitting father of one branch of this tenacious myth, was none other than the late Harold Nicolson!

But *his* version still faithfully retained the coach and horses. The one featuring the coffin-bearer was Monsieur de Maratray's very own embellished handiwork!

13

ONCE MORE INTO THE LIFT, DEAR FRIENDS

As we have seen, the Dufferin version eclipsed all the other lift myths for over half a century. But, since 1950, two new interlopers have elbowed their way into the mythology. And what bounders they are!

The first story opens in Atlanta, Georgia in the 1950s. Elise Barnhardt from New York was making her visit to Georgia. She'd accepted an invitation from Ruthanne Reeves, a girl she'd met that summer in Greece. At the airport she was greeted by Ruthanne and her brother John. Then all three squeezed into John's tiny sportscar and they sped off into the country.

It was dusk and the drive took on a dream-like quality as they swept past the deserted cottonfields and countless little tin-roofed shacks. At last, they reached the Reeves' plantation, motored down its private entry-road and pulled up outside an immense, sprawling mansion. To Elise the mansion was the very essence of everything romantic. Tall columns supported the front and east and west wings, while its rear piazza overlooked a sleepy river that gleamed silver in the light of the full moon.

That evening friends arrived from the nearby towns and plantations for a dinner party and dance on the piazza. The lively party ended soon after twelve and by 1:30 A.M. the girls settled down to sleep. But Elise was so excited by the unexpected romance of the evening that she tossed from side to side in her four-poster bed, unable to sleep.

When she heard the grandfather clock in the hall strike two, she swung out of bed and opened the drapes to let in some cool air. At that very moment she heard the strange clatter of horses' hooves. She looked out with unbelieving eyes and saw a gold and black stagecoach drawn by four gleaming black stallions. It stood motionless on the circular drive beneath her window. Beside it stood a coachman dressed in a black coat and breeches. He held the door of the coach open, gestured towards the house with his free hand and called out "Room for one more!"

Elise stared down at his swarthy face. A long scar staggered irregularly across the man's left cheek, running from the corner of his eye to the top of his full lips. It was the sort of face hard to forget.

Before she could even recover from her surprise the coach and coachman seemed to ". . . literally dissolve into the darkness and disappear."

She was so frightened by this grotesque episode that she stayed awake for hours. At daybreak, she managed to snatch a short bout of sleep.

Next day, despite her fears, she was far too embarrassed to tell her friend about the eerie coach and its driver. But the memory haunted her all day. By evening Elise began to feel depressed and uneasy. Yet as soon as she eased herself into bed she fell asleep once more. An hour later, she woke up to the sound of horses' hooves. She hastened to the window and there, below, stood the coach and coachman.

"Room for one more!" she heard him shout and he looked up toward her window and smiled evilly. With that the coach vanished again and Elise sat back on her bed trembling with terror.

By the following morning she was so exhausted that it proved easy to convince Ruthanne that she was not well and needed to return home to New York. Unfortunately, she was not able to book a reservation on the flight she wanted, so she insisted on going on stand-by.

On arriving at the airport she bought a ticket and was told that, even though the plane was full, there was always the chance of a last minute vacancy and she was at the head of the stand-by queue. John and Ruthanne waited with her at the entrance gate and she chatted with them cheerfully now that she knew she was leaving the haunted plantation house behind. Then, her cheerfulness evaporated in an instant as she heard the cry, "There is room for one more!"

It came from the gate attendant who was walking toward them. Elise quivered with shock. She moved forward to inspect the attendant's face and, as she did, so he looked directly at her and called "Room for one more". She stared at him in terror. There was the swarthy face with its prominent scar. This was the ghastly coachman who'd twice summoned her in the night!

Almost hysterical, she begged her friends to take her back to the waiting room. Nothing would induce her to board that plane. But now she had to unburden herself to her friends. They listened with growing bewilderment as her story unravelled. They had never seen or even heard of a phantom coach and driver in the whole of their area. They agreed though, that Elise would be wise to wait for a later plane, for by then she might be more relaxed and fit to travel.

When the later plane was due to depart, the Reeves escorted Elise back to the departure gate. In attendance was a thin, blond young man—very different from the villainous creature all three had seen earlier.

"Where's the man with the scarred face," Elise asked, "the one who was here at 12:30?" The young attendant looked baffled.

"You surely must be mistaken?" he said. "I've been in attendance since early morning . . . and no one who looks like that even works here."

The young man was so convincing that argument was out of the question. So Elise said farewell to her friends and boarded her plane. A smooth take-off led to a pleasant, uneventful flight. Then, once back in New York, Elise felt too exhausted to ponder over the strange events of the past few days. Her sleep was deep and untroubled. But the headlines of the morning paper sent a shock through her.

"Plane Crashes on the Way to New York" it read. She shivered as she checked the details. The plane had set off from Atlanta. Its take-off time—12:30. It was the very plane she'd meant to take—the one that had "room for one more."

The second "true" story is much more precise. In it we encounter exact times, dates and locations—all the helpful features we need for a sound investigation.

It opens in Philadelphia in mid-June 1968, two weeks before schoolteacher Janice Metz was due to fly to Europe. She intended to take a vacation with 25-year-old, fellow-teacher Laura Shepherd. Their plans involved a ten-day stay in London before exploring Paris for a few days.

It should have been a time of growing excitement, but all Janice felt was a growing anxiety. Night after night she was disturbed by an odd, inexplicable dream. The dream involved a man's face. He had dark, piercing eyes, thin and bloodless lips and a long bony nose. On his head was a military-style cap with a badge and the letters H. F. encircled by braid. The man was quite unknown to her and the initials on the cap held no significance whatsoever.

Eventually, she told her friend Laura about the dream. Laura probed for the complete story but Janice explained that precious little happened in the dream. The man said nothing, he simply stared at her. Yet, at times it *seemed* that he wished to speak to her, but at that point iron bars moved in front his face—then swiftly disappeared.

Following this talk, Janice tried to concentrate her mind on the coming pleasures of the holiday, but the strange dream still visited her every night.

Two days before the start of her vacation she felt impelled to consult a psychiatrist. He questioned her at length and asked if she'd flown before.

"Only once," she answered.

The psychiatrist now felt that he understood her problem. He diagnosed her repeated dreams as a symptom of a subconscious anxiety about flying. The strange face was that of an airline pilot! Her worries about flying could be subdued by a mild sedative taken half-an-hour before boarding her plane.

On June 30, she and Laura flew to BOAC to England. They spent ten enjoyable days in and around London and, during this period, the unwelcome dream was absent.

While in London they bumped into several friends from back home. Among them was Mary Childress who'd been Janice's roommate at college.

Mary was due to get to Paris ahead of them. "Be sure to look me up when you arrive," she insisted. "I'm staying at the Hotel Fauborg. It's in the 2nd Arrondissement, near the Bourse-Opera."

On the night Janice and Laura arrived in Paris the dream returned with a difference. She told Laura about it at breakfast. This time the iron bars in front of the stranger were seen to be connected with wire mesh—like a cage. In this cage were several people, one of whom Janice recognized as Laura herself!

Laura was greatly amused by this.

"It's probably a prison cell. I'll have to watch my step," she joked.

The dream came again on the next night. This time it came with a growing terror, and Janice remembered crying out to Laura, imploring her to escape from the cage before it was too late. Janice woke up feeling that something terrible was about to happen. But what?

Later that morning they phoned Mary Childress at the Hotel Fauborg. She was excited to hear from them and suggested that they meet her that afternoon at two in her room.

The two girls arrived at the hotel shortly after two. Laura went ahead into the lobby while Janice paid off the taxi. By the time Janice reached the lobby Laura was already in the lift together with several other people. But as Janice walked toward this old-fashioned lift she felt a growing disquiet. There was something vaguely familiar about the scene. Then she caught sight of the lift operator. He gazed at her with penetrating eyes. His nose was long and bony, his lips thin and bloodless.

This was the face that had haunted her dreams. And on his head was a peaked cap with the initials H. F., the insignia of the Hotel Fauborg.

Janice screamed: "Laura, come back before it's too late!"

But it *was* too late. The door clanged shut and the crowded lift creaked upwards. Although two people got off at the third floor and one more left on the fourth, the ancient cables had already been weakened by the severe strain—"as the police pointed out later."

The cable snapped before the lift reached the fifth floor, and it plunged downwards. The exact words of the so-called original account tell us that:

"At 2:25 P.M. on July 13, 1968, all eight passengers crashed to their death at the bottom of the pit. Among them was Janice's friend Laura Shepherd. The ninth victim was Paul Routier, 47, the elevator operator."

Janice Metz never saw him in her dreams again. "Nor has any psychic investigator been able to explain the supernormal phenomena of his repeated warnings"—so concludes Emile Schurmacher in his book *More Strange Unsolved Mysteries*.

But are we really considering mysteries?

In the Atlanta, Georgia, tale, written by Nancy Roberts, the dates are too vague to make a newspaper check worthwhile. Tracing the Reeves would be equally difficult, since their plantation is located imprecisely, some miles out in the country from the airport at Atlanta. Still, these are not real problems. The account is unmistakably bogus. It is a modern update of the original coach and coachmen legend of 1892.

The precise Philadelphia/Paris story is equally bogus. All its exactness is just pure bluff designed to give it the air of authentic reporting.

There is no Hotel Fauborg in the 2nd Arrondissement in Paris and there never was. Enquiries with the police of the 2nd Arrondissement show that there was no lift crash in their area on July 13, 1968.

Neither was there such a lift crash in the whole of Paris on that day. Hardly surprising though, as here is the Dufferin story once again juggled around and modernized.

But stories don't write themselves. The choice of names, dates, locations and events results from deliberations. So, perhaps the inventors of these stories would like to stand up and receive a well-deserved brick-bat or two? After all, some people might resent being taken for a ride!

14

CRY "HALT" TO HITLER!

"The European War, which the Mars in Hitler's horoscopes tells us so much about, will not break out . . . An invisible power has written strange signs in the skies. Not everyone can decipher their meaning, but in flaming letters they cry 'HALT!' to Hitler."

With such enormously confident phrases, Leonardo Blake launched his book *Hitler's Last Year of Power*. Unfortunately for Mr. Blake, it rolled off the presses in August 1939. It was reviewed in the Spiritualist weekly *Two Words* on September 8, and the paper gave his views independent support. Its front page reported that the amazing trumpet-medium, Mrs. McCallum, had relayed spirit messages from a former editor named Ernest Marklew. Over in spirit land Marklew was very much concerned with the international situation. He actually said that he'd been in touch with General Foch, Earl Haig, Lord Roberts, and several others. These military gentlemen were doing all in their power to secure peace and overcome the war scare. So the deceased Mr. Marklew was of the opinion even then, "that there would be no war."

Alas, the eighth page of the paper had to be reset at the last moment to announce: "War! A Temporary Set-back to Our Ideals."

It was much more than that. For months, even years, the psychics had been reassuring the public that Hitler was overrated and misjudged. In *Prediction* of 1936 leading astrologer and mystic R. H. Naylor took up three pages to analyze Hitler's horoscope. He pronounced: "He personally would never be a willing party to war . . . this gloomy and idealistic careerist is at heart a kindly soul and a lover of little children."

The December issue of the same magazine revealed that Josef Ranald, the well-known palmist, had read Mussolini's hand and forecast that his career as a ruler would end at the age of fifty-four, giving him only two more years to throw his weight around.

Throughout the earlier part of 1939, spirit guides galore were lisping, whispering, and even bawling that there would be an age of peace. War was not in the cards, or in the stars, or in the offing.

There was such unanimity that Maurice Barbanell, editor of *Psychic News,* was able to write: "I am confident there is no possibility of error when the prophecy is so unanimous. From every well-known guide and from home circles all over the world there has come the assurance that never again will England be involved in war. While individual spirits are fallible when dealing with lesser issues, I refuse to believe in the possibility of a mistake in this particular instance." (July 22).

A cautionary tale certainly, and it poses the direct question: Can we *really* foretell the future? Can we do more than just guess at what *might* be possible? Many people are obviously convinced that we can. That's why every day millions of them read horoscopes or consult fortune-tellers of one type or another. But are they justified in their beliefs? Just what *does* the record show?

Consider those questions and you are bound to run up against difficulties. The claims are many and you could probably fill shelf after shelf with the great number of books which set out to provide the answers. Yet, for all that, the reliable evidence is, in my view, completely lacking. Let me give you some examples. Examples chosen, not because they're easy to demolish, but because they have been widely believed in—examples that, at first sight, seem most convincing.

First of all, we simply have to look at the French sage Nostradamus. He's rated as the greatest prophet of the past, and how can you ignore someone who's placed top of the bill? Surprisingly, although his books were written in 1555, they are still earnestly and painstakingly combed through in the search for clues to today's and tomorrow's events.

I first heard about this "seer" at school. The article I then read was breathtaking. It said that Nostradamus had correctly forecast the rise of Hitler and Napoleon and mentioned them *by name.* Now that was certainly staggering. But when I finally came to read the *original* I found that this was just untrue. The Hitler references are to a river called the Hister, not to a man. And the Napoleon forecasts are cleverly wangled by jumbling up the names of three French villages: Pau, Nay, and Loron.

In other instances, the striking forecasts have been deliberately faked or biased by adding words which are not found in the original French version. Here's a glaring example. It's supposed to forecast Napoleon's end.

The captive prince, conquered, is sent to Elba;
He will sail across the Gulf of Genoa to Marseilles;
By a great effort of the foreign forces he is overcome,
Though he escapes the fire, his bees yield blood by the barrel.

This translation of Quatrain, or Verse 24, of Nostradamus' "10th Century," appears in *Prediction and Prophecy* by Keith Ellis. Similar translations can be found in other books. And the verses do seem to contain an amazing hit. For Napoleon *was* conquered, captured, and sent in exile to the isle of Elba. Thus, at first sight we're presented with something that looks like a real glimpse of the future.

There's a catch though. The words ". . . and sent to Elba" were never written by Nostradamus. He simply mentioned a "captive prince conquered in Italy"—which is very different and could mean anyone!

For the record, Nostradamus interpreter Henry C. Roberts summarizes the authentic verse thus:

"A prince, captured in Italy, shall be brought back to France for trial in Marseilles. His friend shall obtain his release by bribing the city officials."

The truth is that playing around with the verses of Nostradamus is simply an engrossing game. That's why one interpreter can find Verse 40, Century 10, to be a forecast of the abdication of Edward VIII in 1936, while others mark it down as a prophecy relating to James I, first King of Scotland and England! This game is without rigid rules. That's why comparisons of the many interpreters show that, in scores of cases, the same verse has been attributed to the far past, the recent past, the present, the near future and the far distant future.

But what of our present-day prophets? Is it the same for them? I'd say yes. Perhaps an examination of the legend surrounding Jeane Dixon might

MICHEL NOSTRADAMUS.
Médecin,
Né à S.Remy, en Provence, le 14 Décemb. 1503
Mort le 2 juillet 1566.

Inventor of a game without rules.

underline why I feel that way. For Mrs. Dixon not only wears the mantle of the prophet, but has been described as "one of the most remarkable women who ever lived."

When Mrs. Dixon visited Britain every paper that mentioned her emphasized that she'd forecast the assassination of President Kennedy years before it had happened. This was repeated on radio programs and was even told to me by a lapel-grabbing and thoroughly convinced newspaper reporter—who was *sober*.

I decided to look into the claim. There was no shortage of references backing up the view that she *had* foreseen Kennedy's end. Many magazines and a stack of books said so. As well as that, it turned out that it was *this* particular prediction that won Mrs. Dixon her real fame.

Jeane Dixon's biography gives this account, ". . . reporters from *Parade* magazine were interviewing her . . . she declared 'A blue-eyed Democratic President elected in 1960 will be assassinated' . . . Her prediction appeared in the *Parade* issue of May 13, 1956. . . ."

But did it? Well, when I looked into the text of the article in *Parade,* I found a new twist to the story. It became clear that none of the commentators, writers, and reporters who enthuse over this story have ever taken the trouble to check it out. For the magazine report itself says something quite different. It reads, "As to the 1960 election, Mrs. Dixon thinks it will be . . . won by a Democrat. But he will be assassinated or die in office, though not necessarily in his first term."

So the man isn't identified in any way. There's no mention of blue eyes. And the assassination is only one of *two* possibilities—the other a mere death in office. Then, since the presidential term is four years, this death might occur any time during a span of eight years. So this "remarkably accurate" prophecy was nothing of the sort.

Yet even *if* Jeane Dixon had not been so vague and wooly—even if she'd firmly mentioned the assassination of the man elected in 1960—this would still have proved nothing at all.

At the time she made her prophecy, *every* president of the United States for almost a century had been sought after by assassins. One slaughtered President Lincoln. Another killed President McKinley. Yet another shot President Garfield. And Theodore Roosevelt was only saved from death by a wad of papers which deflected an assassin's bullet. His nephew President Franklin Roosevelt escaped death by an inch or two when the bullet meant for him killed the mayor of Chi-

cago, while President Harry Truman narrowly esc
the White House itself!

Unpleasant as it is, we have to face it that o
around the president keeps him alive. Take that
doubt if any president would last for six months
erful office acts as a veritable magnet for cranks, fanatics and the
mentally disturbed. And the United States has more than its fair share
of these. These misfits come to see the president as the *cause* of all
their problems. They dream that all will come right if only that evil
man at the top is eliminated. Their dreams often lead to action—even
if the ultimate deed is thwarted by the vigilance of the police or intelligence services.

So, put into context, Mrs. Dixon's famous forecast becomes trans-
figured. It's little more than a piece of lax reporting based on some
quite unremarkable guesswork—guesswork part-prompted by her
awareness of the then approaching centenary of Lincoln's assassination.

Other, even more impressive predictions wilt when placed in proper
context. Like the famous dream-prediction of Bishop de Lanyi. Brian
Inglis features this "strikingly prophetic dream" in his *Science and
Parascience*. He introduces it by saying: "Before the First World War
broke out, there had been countless portents of a coming Armageddon
from mediums in trances, in automatic writing, in dreams and in visions . . . Most were in similarly vague general terms; but a few contained more specific prophetic glimpses . . . most striking of all was the
nightmare when Richet was to recount in his thirty years of psychical
research, from the story which had appeared in 'Psychische Studien' in
1918. The facts, it was claimed had been checked."

The account used by Brian Inglis reads as follows:

Monsieur Joseph de Lanyi, Bishop of Grosswardin, dreamed on the
morning of June 28th, at 4 a.m. that he saw on his study table a
black-edged letter bearing the arms of the Archduke. M. de Lanyi
had been professor of the Hungarian language to the Archduke. In
his dream he opened the letter at its head saw a street into which an
alley opened. The Archduke was seated in a motorcar with his wife;
facing him was a general, and another officer by the side of the
chauffeur. There was a crowd about the car and from the crowd two
young men stepped forward and fired on the royal couple. The text
of the letter ran, "Your Eminence, dear Dr. Lanyi, my wife and I
have been victims of a political crime at Sarajevo. We committed

ourselves to your prayers. Sarajevo, June 18, 1914, 4 a.m."

"Then," says Mgr. de Lanyi, "I woke up trembling; I saw that the time was 4:30 a.m., and I wrote down my dream, reproducing the characters that had appeared to me in the Archduke's letter. At six, when my servant came, he found me seated at my table, much shaken and telling my rosary. I said at once to him, 'Call my mother and my host, that I may tell them the dreadful dream I have had.'"

In commenting on this dream, Brian Inglis assures us that, "During the day, a telegram arrived with the news of the assassination. It was not quite as the dream had forecast: the assassins threw bombs. But otherwise the dream had been accurate."

A correction is in order here. The Archduke and his wife were, in fact, shot. So, in that respect, the dream was more accurate than Mr. Inglis realized. But he seems blissfully unaware of the real problems surrounding this dream. In the first place, there are a number of conflicting versions. In the version quoted by Keith Ellis *(Prediction and Prophecy)* the dream telegram ends: "Cordial greetings from your Archduke Franz, Sarajevo, June 28th, 3:15 a.m." And when de Lanyi springs out of bed his clock shows 3:15.

The version printed in December 1967 *Journal Of The Society For Psychical Research* has the same telegram ending: "Cordial greetings from our Archduke Franz. Sarajevo, 1914, half past 3 a.m."

These differences in times (there are others as well) can't be dismissed as mere trivialities. If there is a master-statement made at the time by the Bishop there should be no divergences. Let us presume, though, that de Lanyi did have a dream broadly along the lines of the various versions. Is there anything in this dream that entitles us to regard it as paranormal—as a genuine glimpse into the future?

We can only do justice to ourselves and to the Bishop by now introducing the necessary context: the historical background that is so often and so conveniently missing from prediction accounts.

In 1914, Sarajevo was included in the province of the Austro-Hungarian Empire known as Bosnia-Hercegovina. It had been annexed in 1908, but the Bosnian people were still mentally wedded to their brothers over the border in Serbia. The day chosen for the Archduke's visit was the worst possible day in the eyes of the Serbians. Sunday, June 28, was the sacred anniversary of Vidovan or St. Vitus' day. It was a commemoration of the Serbian defeat at the battle of Cosovo in 1389.

Around this defeat at Cosovo the South Slavs had woven a starkly tragic tradition. The Sultan of the arrogant conquering Turks had been assassinated by a Serbian nobleman, Milos Obilic. From then on, the practice of tyrannicide was looked on as a sacred and patriotic act.

Patriotic anger and a desire to unite with Serbia led to the founding of the Young Bosnian Movement. On June 15, 1910, Bogdan Zerajic, one of the founders of this movement, trailed the Austrian emperor through the streets of Sarajevo. He was bent on an assassination attempt, but in the end he fired five shots at General Marijan Varesanin, the governor of the two provinces. This attempt was made on the same street in Sarajevo that witnessed the shootings in June 1914.

On June 8, 1912, the Obilic cult led student Luka Jukic to attempt to assassinate the governor of Croatia, Count Slavko Cuvaj. Cuvaj was again shot at by Ivan Pianinscak, four months later.

The unrest among Serbian patriots led to mass arrests. Then in the first four months of 1913, some two hundred high-treason trials were held. Yet, these trials did nothing to curb the assassins' zeal, for on August 18, 1913, the governor of Croatia, Baron Ivo Skerletz, was attacked by Stjepan Dojcic. Two months later, the Trieste police informed Vienna that a wide ranging conspiracy was being hatched, and the dissidents were planning to kill Archduke Ferdinand.

The fatal visit of the Archduke to Sarajevo was announced in the press as early as mid-march 1914. As soon as the announcement was made, fears for his safety grew. It was recalled that an earlier journey planned for 1911 had been postponed because of the fear of assassination. And it was recalled that in 1911, Father Galen had been sent in confidence to Sarajevo to sound out the city's possible reaction to a visit from the Heir Apparent. On his return Galen had produced an unfavorable report. Josip Sunaric had even told him "I know the Serbs. I know that they will wait for him in ambush as murderers."

Now, in 1914, Sunaric was still adamantly opposed to a visit. He dispatched a telegram to Joint Minister of Finance Bilinski, warning him that the Archduke and his wife would face great danger in Sarajevo. He was not alone.

Toso Zurunic, chief of the Department of the Interior of the Bosnian government, received many warnings that the Archduke was in danger. Similar warnings came from many sources in contact with Serbian nationalists. They came in from Vienna, from Budapest, from Berlin and even from the U.S. Minister of Foreign Affairs Berchtold even had a detailed dossier on the suspicious movements of Serbian students in Croatia. One of these students was quoted as saying: "The time for empty boasting is over, and now we must start working in earnest. Bombs and not merely loose tongues must go into action."

Despite all these warnings, and the dread fears amongst the people closest to him—people like Prince Montenuovo, his son Maximilian, and his doctor, Eisenmenger—the plans went ahead. On June 23, 1914, against the advice of the chief of police at Sarajevo, the exact route of the official procession was disclosed. Then, as June 28 approached, Chief of Police Gerde tried to warn General Potiorek and the military committee in charge of the visit about the menacing and dangerous atmosphere in town. He was ignored, but he covered himself by having the warnings entered into the official minutes.

When the Archduke and his wife set out for Sarajevo, they both were weighed down by morbid thoughts. They knew all too well that the Serbs were seething with resentment—that they regarded the visit as a calculated insult. The many warnings they had received had had their effect. Presentiments of disaster colored their outlook. So much so that on the twenty-third the Archduke himself said, after his special railway coach had been damaged by fire, "Our journey starts with an extremely promising omen. Here our car burns and down there they will throw bombs at us."

In the event, they escaped death by bombs only to fall victims to the bullets of a lone gunman, Gavrilio Prinsip. His shots were the opening shots of the First World War.

Now, Bishop de Lanyi had been close to the Archduke and was still an intimate member of the courtly circle surrounding the Austrian royal family. As such, he was acutely aware of the doubts and anxieties raised by the mistimed, provocative and crassy foolish visit. Like scores of the others in that privileged circle, and like many others outside it, he dreaded the outcome of the visit. The mood of the Serbs was known. Their violent traditions had been openly demonstrated—repeatedly. Their dark plots were all aimed at the hated monarchy and its adminstrators.

The Bishop's fears were, therefore, hardly surprising. He shared the same agonies of mind as many others. His agony culminated in a realistic dream that was right in parts. But only in parts—for example, only one gunman was involved, not a pair as featured in his dream. Still, my point is not to fault the gentleman's subconscious, but to show there was nothing of mystery in his mental tableau.

The Sarajevo visit was suicidal. As Tudor Edwards has put it: "Even a schoolboy would have foreseen the ambush, the rain of bombs and bullets."

Yet, if de Lanyi's faulty forecast fails our tests, how do the *many* predictions of Cheiro measure up? As I write, Cheiro's name is again being brought to the fore. The fiftieth anniversary of the abdication of King Edward VIII in 1936 has reminded journalists of Cheiro's amazing prevision of that emotional constitutional crisis. Cheiro, or Count Louis Hamon as he styled himself, wrote: ". . . the Prince who may be fond of a light flirtation with the fair sex . . . is determined not to 'settle down' until he feels a *grande passion,* but it is well within the range of possibility, owing to the peculiar planetary influences to which he is subjected, that he will in the end fall a victim of a devastating love affair. If he does, I predict that the Prince will give up everything, even the chance of being crowned, rather than lose the object of his affection."

I quote from *Cheiro's World Predictions*—1931 edition. But that text was actually in the hands of his publishers as early as 1925—years before Mrs. Wallis Simpson came on the scene, won Edward's heart, and precipitated the crisis. It's a direct hit by any standards, but, does it really display a paranormal content?

Decidedly not! I've talked with people who were deeply involved in the abdication turmoil—people who were intimates of the King, like Lord Carnarvon. What they disclosed showed me that Edward's aversion to the throne had been well-observed, long before 1936. He had emotional problems that made it pretty certain that the right, dominant, masterful woman would place him under her spell, to the exclusion of all other things—even to the point of abdication.

When you come to read everything that Cheiro says on this topic, you'll find that, despite his astrological flourishes, he actually reveals the real source of his knowledge. First of all, he draws parallels with the lives of earlier Princes of Wales. Then he records that "The present Prince of Wales has piqued curiosity many times by rumours of marriages that have faded into the air . . . Princesses from Italy, Russia, Sweden, Norway, Bulgaria and Greece have been confidently spoken of as future Princesses of Wales. Rumour says, that Queen Mary, and in a lesser degree, King George, have worried themselves seriously over this problem of the Prince. . ."

Cheiro further observes that: "At the present time the wide-spread impression gaining ground that the present Prince of Wales has no taste for the wearing of a crown has fixed increasing interest upon the studious attention of his brother, the Duke of York, to the exacting duties of the life ceremonial."

Cheiro's "society" contacts were many and close. He was party to all the tittle-tattle, rumors, and informed gossip that swirled around in those circles. Because of this, he knew more about the real problems faced by the Prince than many of the members of Parliament who were later to discuss Edward's fate in the Commons.

A nil score so far! How does it stand, though, with his predictions about the Second World War? These are often being quoted, and they're found again in the 1931 edition of *World Predictions*. In Charles Neilson Gattey's book *They Saw Tomorrow,* they're presented in this fashion: "England will be attacked in all her Mohammedan possessions. She will give India her freedom, but religious warfare will rend that country from end to end until it becomes equally divided between the Mohammedan and the followers of Buddha. Italy and Germany will at the same period be at war with France . . . The United States will be engaged in war with Japan and will not take part until later in the European carnage . . . In Ireland there will be civil war between the North and South."

A remarkably accurate set of forecasts most people feel. But this quotation has been doctored in a deplorable way. Its "accuracy" rests on chicanery. The proof lies in the real, unedited text in Cheiro's book. It reads:

England will be attacked in all her Mohammedan possessions. She will give India her freedom, but religious warfare will rend that country from end to end until it becomes equally divided between the Mohammedan and the followers of Buddha. All her colonies will again send large numbers of men to help "the Mother Country." Italy and Germany will at the same period be at war with France, and Spain under a Dictator will be engaged in a life and death struggle in North Africa. Germany and England will become allies and pour immense numbers of troops into Palestine and Egypt.

Russia will draw enormous masses of Chinese and Tartars with her and all Mohammedan races will be brought into the conflict.

The United States will be engaged in war with both Mexico and Japan and will not take part until later in the European carnage.

Great Britain will suffer terribly in the prolonged warfare, the most of London and Towns on the East Coast will be destroyed by fleets of aeroplanes from Russia.

In Ireland there will be Civil War between the North and South, and a new Irish Republic will inflict considerable damage by aeroplanes on such cities as Liverpool, Manchester, Birmingham, and the west of England.

Historians in particular will be puzzled to learn that in the Second World War Germany and England were allies and that most of London and the East Coast towns were destroyed by Russian aircraft. It will also be news to them that the Irish Republic used its miniscule air force to bomb Britain so dramatically. They will at once spot though, that the section involving war between the United States, and Mexico and Japan is simply based on the text of the notorious Zimmerman telegram of February 1917! At that time, the German government did its best to persuade Japan and Mexico to enter the war on their side and attack the United States.

Cheiro's original forecast was simply a meaningless mish-mash drawing on past history and a few current trends. Nothing can excuse the later falsification of his words in an attempt to make sense of them.

Having rescued Cheiro from the hands of his manipulators, let's look at the man himself. He has made many claims to spectacular successes. And one of his most famous successes dates back to the early part of his career in 1893. At the time he had had a breakdown in health and, after recovering, he decided to have a change of scene and visit the United States. On arrival in New York, he rented a fine apartment on Fifth Avenue and set up business as a palmist. For a while business was bleak, and then a woman journalist from the *New York World* called in and proposed a test. If he accepted and proved successful, the paper's Sunday edition would give him tremendous publicity.

The newspaper would collect a number of handprints on paper and keep the identities secret. Cheiro would then examine each one in turn and give a reading. His comments would be recorded and matched up against the lives lying behind the handprints.

Cheiro took up the challenge. The lady reporter bustled around collecting handprints, then returned to carry out the test. As each palm impression was handed to him, he studied it, pondering at length and then gave his verdict. Everything was taken down in shorthand.

When the test ended the exhausted palmist was told that he would have to wait for the following Sunday's edition of the *World* in order to know the results. Cheiro himself says: "It was then Tuesday. I lived under a very anxious strain for the following days. Saturday night I scarcely slept till morning. About nine o'clock my black servant knocked at the door and woke me. In the most matter-of-fact way he said, 'Get up, sir, there are over a hundred people sitting on the stairs waiting to see you.'

"I did not ask the reason; in his hand was the *New York World* with its entire front page devoted to the interview. I can still see the heading in big type, 'Cheiro reads successfully the Lives of the Mayor, the District Attorney, Nicoll Ward McAllister, Dr. Meyer,' etc."

According to Cheiro the most astonishing reading of all was the one which had involved the handprint of a murderer. The man was a Dr. Meyer from Chicago, aged forty-four, who at the time was actually in prison awaiting trial. Cheiro's reading brought all that to light. His account in his memoirs says:

> Then came the climax—it was about the fourth or fifth impression she put before me.
>
> "There is something in his hand so abnormal," I said, "that I shall refuse to read it until you can bring me the consent of the owner to tell what I see."
>
> "We have the consent of all these people," was the reply, and she showed me a letter from the *New York World* stating that the consent had been obtained from the various persons who had given these impressions.
>
> Under these conditions I agreed to proceed. The hand before me was that of a murderer, of that I was certain. I could make no mistake: . . . there was clear evidence that such a man had used his intelligence to obtain money by crime, and that a little over the middle of his life his very self-confidence would betray him into the hands of the law.
>
> "Whether this man has committed one murder or twenty," I remarked, "is not the question; at about his forty-fourth year he will be tried for murder and condemned. It will be found that for years he has used his intelligence, and whatever profession he has followed, to obtain money by crime, and that he has stopped at nothing to gain his ends. He will be condemned, will go under the greatest strain and anxiety, will live under the very shadow of death; but his life will not end in this manner, for he will pass the remainder of his life in prison."

A wealth of detail like that has to be impressive. But was it correct? Cheiro insisted it was. Once he knew the identity of the murderer he was able to check. Then he wrote: "What really did happen was this. This man, Dr. Meyer, was convicted of insuring people's lives in Chicago—he was either their doctor or managed later to attend them—and in exercising his profession it was believed he poisoned his patients, and later collected the insurance money. . . .

"When Dr. Meyer's case came on my prediction was fulfilled to the letter; after a long, sensational trial in which he fought every inch of the ground, he was condemned to death, but within a few days of the electrocution chair, on a technical point, the sentence was altered to imprisonment for life."

Little wonder then, that enthusiastic writers and broadcasters have jumped on this story to retell and expand on. Frank Edwards, for one, used the tale in his radio programs, in his books, and in his syndicated articles. Neilson Gattey features it as well. A great pity that not one of them opened the files of the *New York World!*

A copy of the *New York World* for Sunday, November 26, 1893, is in front of me. "I can still see the heading in big type," said Cheiro. So much for his memory. The heading in quite small type, at the top of only one column reads—"Character Read in the Hands." And the entire front page is not devoted to the interview—just two columns. However, the rest of the interview does take up a further three columns on page eighteen.

Let's allow him a little license—the really important things are all there in those five columns. Each palm print is shown in facsimile and each reading is printed in full. The alleged forecast claimed by Cheiro in his *Memoirs* and elsewhere, *is not there.* On the contrary, we find that he did not even attempt to read the palm print of Dr. Meyer but passed over it as the newspaper reporter testifies—in these words: "A sudden change passed over the face of Cheiro as he fixed his gaze upon the next imprint that I handed him. After a moment of apparent indecision he handed it back, saying, quietly, as he did so: 'I refuse to read that hand to any one but the owner.' I was speechless with astonishment. It was the hand of Dr. Henry W. Meyer, the man accused of wife-poisoning, and who is at present in the Tombs awaiting trial."

Cheiro was streets ahead of the people who set out to test him. The security around the test was ultra-sloppy. The young journalist even took a palm print from someone who'd already consulted Cheiro.

When the prints were handed to him, his experience gave him the edge over the trusting pressmen. He was able to gauge their moods, notice all their exchanged glances and subtle reactions.

The moment the Meyer print was extracted and handed over, he was able to spot the change in atmosphere. The extra air of anticipation and solemnity was enough to alert him that this was an extraordinary print. So he took no chance, refused to comment on it and handed it back.

He was able to fake his account because he knew all too well that his gullible readers would be unlikely to bother with anything as exacting as real truth. He was to continue faking stories for the rest of his life.

Yet one of his most grotesque stories still circulates without effective challenge. If it's true, then we have to reverse our verdict on the man. For even a liar sometimes tells the truth.

His story involves predictions made to a man named Douglas Murray. Murray called on Cheiro some time in 1887. He was a stranger and was in light-hearted mood. "Which of my hands are you going to take?" he laughed. Cheiro took the right hand and as he did an inexplicable feeling of horror and dread seemed to ooze from the palm.

Cheiro dropped the hand back onto the cushion and Murray, still amused, asked what was wrong. Cheiro found himself unable to explain but in his later account he said: "The hand *seemed to speak to me*. It was not that I attempted to read it, there was no need for me to make such an effort. It was as if I was taken possession of by some occult force of which I cannot give any explanation. Without any regard to the effect my words might have, and with the feeling of listening to myself speaking without the power of preventing the words coming, I blurted out rapidly, 'I feel this right hand of yours will not be yours for long. A picture forms in my mind of a gun of some kind bursting and shattering it to pieces. This is followed by terrible suffering and finally the entire arm will have to be amputated,' and I added quickly, 'Your hand, sir, seems to be calling to me to try and save it from this impending disaster.'"

At this point, Murray burst into laughter, completely unconvinced, then Cheiro continued: "Your hand shows me another picture. It draws a number out of a lottery, the number gives you a prize that you do not want to have. Out of obstinacy and fatalism you take it, and from that moment on commences a series of misfortunes, beginning with the loss of your right arm."

His client still stayed amused and said that he'd never won a thing in a lottery ever. What's more he didn't believe he ever would. Still he asked, "Does this wonderful hand of mine tell you what this extraordinary prize is likely to be?"

A picture began to form in Cheiro's mind. First the shape of an oblong object. Then strange hieroglyphics appeared and the shape became revealed as an Egyptian sarcophagus with a carved figure on the lid. He described what he saw to Murray and begged him not to touch it. If Murray did, it would bring misfortune to him and anyone else involved with it.

But his warnings failed to overturn Murray's cheerfulnes. He left smiling, handing his card to the palmist.

A year later, Douglas Murray went to Egypt on a shooting expedition with two friends. They planned a trip up the Nile but before leaving Cairo they learnt of a mummy case of rare beauty that was up for sale. In those days, Egyptology was all the rage, so Murray went along to see the case and found that it had once housed a priestess of the Temple of Amen-Ra.

Her image was depicted in superb colors on the case. It was vivid and impressive. Even though it dated from 1,600 B.C., time had been kind to it. His two friends admired the mummy case as much as he did, and the all-round admiration was so great that in the end, they decided to draw lots to see which one of them should end up owning it. The lots were drawn and Murray won the case.

He arranged for the precious antique to be crated and dispatched to London. Then he set off on his shooting expedition. Tragically, a few days later the gun Murray was carrying exploded in his right hand. Immediately his boat headed back for Cairo but unusually strong headwinds made their progress gruellingly slow. It took ten days to reach the hospital. By this time gangrene had set in and despite the efforts of the doctors he was in danger of losing his life. They saved him by amputating the right arm above the elbow.

Misfortune followed Murray on his voyage back to England. Both his companions were taken ill, died and were buried at sea. On arrival at Tilbury two trunks containing valuable scarabs and curiosities were stolen. From then on misfortune after misfortune hit Murray, his family, and anyone who came into close contact with the mummy case. Finally Douglas Murray gave the case to the British Museum, hoping that in some way this would negate its malignant influence.

Now the mummy case story doesn't end there, though it does for us, because we now have to look at the evidence for Cheiro's reading. When Cheiro told this story he believed, like most people, that Douglas Murray had bought the mummy case in 1888 and lost his arm in the same year. What he didn't know, however, was that Douglas-Murray (correct form) had given a complete account of his expedition and his diaries to Mrs. H. Spoer. Another account had also been provided by the sister of A. F. Wheeler—the man who'd actually brought the mummy case to England.

Both accounts show that the history of the mummy case had become garbled. But more importantly, they prove that the 1888 date is absurd. The visit to Egypt, the purchase of the mummy case and the loss of the arm, took place *twenty years earlier,* in 1868.

Though Cheiro was a charming fellow and a honey-tongued re-conteur—he was beautifully bogus. He wasn't a count, his name wasn't Hamon. He was plain William John Warner, born at Bray, County Wicklow, Ireland. His birthdate? November 1, 1866. Which means that at the time of Douglas-Murray's tragic Egyptian excursion, Cheiro was a tiny tot, aged two!

If anything, that proves that the surest way of predicting the future lies in cultivating the faculty of one hundred percent hindsight. By comparison, all other approaches are dismal non-starters!

15

DR. SOAL'S MR. HYDE

A musical box tinkled away in the background while a dead man spoke freely about his past. The university lecturer sat enthralled as he listened. The voice was that of an old school acquaintance. He'd died a soldier's death. And yet here were his familiar tones issuing from the end of a fiber megaphone held to a woman's lips.

The woman was the British "direct voice" medium, Blanche Cooper. The message that came through her lips that night marked the first stage in the unfolding of a strange case that has baffled psychical researchers ever since 1925. It became known as the "Gordon Davis Case" and Muriel Hankey has said it ". . . posed a problem to which there has been no conclusive explanation . . . it is the classic of its kind. So far as I know it has never been repeated." Many other commentators agree with her. Conan Shaw has devoted a sixteen-page study to it and Gracia-Fay Ellwood has published an eighteen-page analysis. So what made this case so special?

At the start, we have to consider the lecturer, Mr. (later Doctor) S. G. Soal. His specialty was mathematics, but during the First World War he began to consider the question of survival. In April 1919, he joined the London Spiritualist Alliance and a month later received his first puzzling message. At one of their meetings, medium Annie Brittain had turned to him and asked if he knew of "Canuter" or "Canuder"— she wasn't sure if it was a place or person.

Soal was highly impressed. She was aiming at *Canewdon,* a tiny village just two miles away from his one-time home. At the age of six he'd walked to Canewdon every day to attend classes held at the rectory. Later, other mediums offered him the name of this "obscure village" from his past. Mr. Soal became hooked. This was surely an exhibition of "supernormal faculty."

But on me, this incident had a very different effect. As soon as I read of it I developed a wariness where Soal was concerned. Did he want to believe *so much* that he could blot out so many significant memories? You see, tiny Canewdon is the one village in all Essex that is justly famous in occult circles. It is in the very heart of an area still known as "Witch Country." Within recent memory children of Canewdon danced seven times around its church to ward off witchcraft. Its history is full of legends of ghosts and uncanny events. And, when Soal was a boy in the 1900s, Master of Witches, George Pickingale, still skulked around its lanes browbeating the superstitious villagers.

Now, the mediums knew Soal's address in South East Essex; it was on their register. So the Canewdon connection, conscious or otherwise, was an obvious one to them. And it should have been to Soal—yet he blocked out the thought. Very odd indeed. But then, Soal was a very odd fish, as I went on to discover!

On September 1, 1921, he embarked on a series of sittings with Mrs. Blanche Cooper. They were to last until June 1922 but were not published until late 1925 in the *Proceedings of the Society for Psychical Research*, vol. 35. Following publication the furor began.

All the reports raised many interesting questions, but the Gordon Davis report was unique. For Soal had recently discovered that the dead man was very much alive. The recorded messages had been checked and verified. And a strange new set of problems had emerged.

These problems centered around the description of Davis's house. At the sitting of January 9, 1922, the "dead" Davis had not spoken directly but had passed these details through the medium, ". . . about his house. He says something about a funny dark tunnel . . . there's five or six steps and a half . . . think it's the front."

When asked to describe the inside, the medium replied, "He says there's a very large mirror and lots of pictures . . . these pictures are all scenes . . . Glorious mountains and the sea—there's one picture where a road or something seems to go between two hills . . . Some vases—very big ones with such funny tops and saucers, but not to drink out of . . . Oh downstairs there's two funny brass candlesticks . . . think they are on a shelf . . . there's something right in front of his house—not a veranda—something that's not in front of the other houses."

Soal asked if the house was in a street, if so, what was the street name? The medium described the house as: "Joined up to others—don't think it's a proper street—like half a street . . . Get the letter 'E's'." The Gordon Davis message ended at that point.

Soal had earlier found that he was impressed by the "life-like reproduction of Davis's mannerisms of speech, tone of voice and accent." This helped give the messages an extra-convincing air, even if

Soal didn't understand why Davis was bothering to make contact.

Following that, for two-and-a-half years, the Davis messages were forgotten. They seemed to be pointless. Then, in February 1925, Soal learned that Gordon Davis was happily running a flourishing estate agency in Southend-on-Sea. Soal explained, "I live, however, in Prittle-well and do not frequently visit Southend and in this fact is to be found an explanation of my continued belief that Gordon Davis was dead."

Over six weeks later he made the journey from "far-off Prittlewell" to Southend and visited Gordon Davis in his house at number 54 Eastern Esplanade. He noticed that to reach the front door he had to ascend six steps, one of which, the bottom, was thinner than the others. This is what the message had forecast!

The house was a part of a single, long stretch facing the sea "like half a street." At the side of the house was a curious tunnel leading from the street to the back yard—obviously the "funny dark tunnel" of the sitting.

On entering Soal examined the front drawing room. There were seven pictures hanging on the walls. Every one was a picture of scenery. Apart from two desert scenes, each one contained mountains or was a seascape. In two or three pictures mountains and sea were combined— the mountains in every case were in the foreground. One picture featured a road and a stream passing between two high hills. Even the two desert scenes could easily be mistaken for seascapes, since the empty expanses on them had a bluish coloring.

Over the mantelpiece was a single large mirror extending from the ceiling right down to the mantelpiece. And there were two large saucer-shaped china plaques hanging on the north wall, and there were five fairly large vases in evidence—one a Japanese piece with a curious top.

Downstairs in the basement dining-room Soal found two brass candlesticks—one at each end of the mantelshelf. While looking through the drawing-room window he saw that opposite the house on the other side of the street was a seaside shelter with seats all round it, giving the impression of a veranda. This was sited exactly oppsite the gate of number 54.

That the details matched so well was astounding. More arresting still were some dates provided by Gordon Davis. In 1922, at the time of the sitting, he did not live in that house but in a London flat. His move to 54 Eastern Esplanade only took place on December 13, 1922. He'd certainly inspected that house as early as January 6, 1922, but it was then already tenanted, needing repairs, in a dirty condition, and with quite different pictures—mainly cheap prints—on its walls.

In 1925, researchers noted these anomalies and debated their implications. Rivalries in the bustling world of the spiritualists led to an attack on the report by H. Dennis Bradley—a writer who imagined that he had a near monopoly on secret interpretations of messages from spirit land.

Bradley derided the Gordon Davis case. It was merely a number of commonplace coincidences, in his eyes. Soal challenged Bradley to find another house in the whole of England which corresponded to every item of the description given by the supposed spirit of Davis. Bradley ignored the challenge, and Soal triumphantly said, "I was able to demonstrate that the odds were of the order of millions to one against such a group of correct items being the result of chance coincidence."

Soal's reasoning won the day. It became accepted that for some unaccountable reason the spirit of a living man had posed as dead and had spoken about events that hadn't even happened. Psychical researchers have pondered and stayed perplexed ever since. And yet, the answers have been there in front of their eyes, all along. Regrettably the vital primary sources were neglected.

Let's rectify that right now. But first, a closer look at Soal's personality. Was he naive? Did he understand the necessity for accuracy? Did he understand the importance of witnessed accounts and the need for a full revelation of his working conditions? In his *My Thirty Years of Psychical Research* he says, "As a mathematician I've always disliked vagueness of every kind." Then in his review of Dunne's *An Experiment With Time* he wrote:

> Mr. Dunne is very chary throughout his narrative of giving us the exact dates and times of the various occurrences described . . . it is a matter for regret that Mr. Dunne, who has such a keen sense of experimentation, and who seems fully alive to the psychological possibilities of his subject, should have omitted to take the simple precaution of getting his dream records witnessed and posted immediately to some responsible scientific man. Cases of prevision, in which the evidence is unimpeachable, are at present as rare as lunar rainbows, and it is a pity that such good cases as Mr. Dunne presents may possibly have to be discounted on the grounds of insufficient corroboration.

So he does know how to act responsibly. But in practice Soal violated *all* the rules.

In mid-February 1922, he's told Gordon Davis is alive. His records now assume a new importance. Yet no "responsible scientific man" is allowed to examine and witness them. No copies are sent posthaste to the SPR or any other body. Instead, he sits on these potentially exciting documents for over six weeks—until *after* his visit to see Gordon Davis.

And why this extraordinary delay in visiting Davis? He could have been with him in under ten minutes any time he chose. For the nebulous, vaguely located Prittlewell is, in fact, part of Southend! Soal's house was a mere mile down a straight main road from Gordon Davis's offices. You'd never guess this though from reading Soal's account. He's free and exact with distances that don't matter—but Prittlewell?

But as we'll see Mr. Soal was a devious character. And it's clear that in the six weeks at his disposal he had plenty of chance to find out things about number 54. I've visited the house myself and noted that all Soal had to do was walk past the place, then ride past on the double-decker bus and record everything that could be spotted through the plain glass windows.

Let's not mince words. I'm asserting that the house forecasts were faked. The original exercise books he used to record his sittings were easily falsified. The metal staples only had to be sprung and the pages would lift out, allowing newly written accounts to be inserted. In that matter he was able to create a cunning enigma.

Here I should emphasize that there were genuine "messages" in the accounts that needed no doctoring, but these were the parts dealing with schooldays and other trivia. These did not exhibit precognition or anything vaguely startling, and Soal could have learned of all the bits and pieces involved by quite normal means. Only the house forecasts were destined to make this affair noteworthy and extraordinary. So only those passages needed to be re-jigged or invented.

Is this just a wild, spiteful theory? Or is there any proof to back it up? Yes, there is proof. Even though Soal carefully covered his tracks, he blundered.

Initially, he was clever. When he called on Gordon Davis he took with him a typed copy of the handwritten accounts of the relevant sessions. The typed and written accounts naturally had to be identical, since Soal wanted Davis to comment on each item and sign a statement of either dissent or agreement. Up to that point everything looked foolproof.

His blunder came after leaving number 54 on the night of his visit. He walked with Gordon Davis up to the Davis & Hollins Agency offices, some five minutes away. At the offices Soal became too elated by his success and overreached himself. He suddenly "remembered" something that fell outside the scope of the typed records. He called it a "curious oversight." As he later put it: "I entirely overlooked the statement concerning 'black dicky bird on piano' . . . I remembered to mention it. Mr. Davis then informed me that he had in his possession a small ornament in the form of a kingfisher which stood on a black china pedestal. At the time of my visit it was actually standing in a plant-pot on the piano, and owing to its being almost hidden inside the plant-pot, had escaped my notice."

A nice, little extra touch, so it seemed. And Soal made the most of it—devoting almost three columns of comment on it in his published paper. Naturally he had to locate this new information somewhere. So he claimed that this delightful dicky bird had popped up in a message found toward the middle of the sitting on Monday, January 30, 1922.

But this is pure fiction. His knowledge of the bird came from his observation of Davis's kingfisher ornament—not from any séance. When he spontaneously invented this morsel, he'd forgotten one vital factor. He'd forgotten that a complete record of the essential sitting had been in private hands for the past three years.

In January and February 1922 the Reverend A. T. Fryer of Bath had helped Soal investigate some Cooper messages concerning James Miles, a young boy who'd drowned. In the end it was accepted that the messages were based on newspaper reports. But, as an aid to his investigations, Reverend Fryer had been sent copies of all the sittings involved. Luckily for truth, one of these copies was of the sitting of January 30, 1922. It survives.

This copy is in Soal's own handwriting. It lists, stage by stage, every statement made that day and it even lists every pause during the sitting. Nothing is omitted—even when the message is as slight as a single letter. Yet there is no mention of Gordon Davis on any page of this record. The dicky-bird message simply *does not exist*.

So, fittingly, the faker stands betrayed by his own heady enthusiasm.

But why should a gifted academic want to deceive and bemuse

people in this way? There we really have a problem. The search for motives can often prove unrewarding and highly frustrating. In Soal's case we can only make inspired guesses—and stay frustrated.

We know that Soal was first attracted to spiritualism following the death of his brother Frank, who was killed on the Somme in September 1918. He recalls: "I argued that if Sir Oliver Lodge could get in touch with the surviving spirit of his son Raymond through the intermediary of (medium) Mrs. Leonard, then surely I ought to be able to make contact with my brother Frank through the powers of this same Mrs. Leonard or some other medium."

Initially, then, he was sincere. He proved this by diligently sitting week after week with Blanche Cooper, recording everything that he heard. Or rather *thought* he heard. In the end he admitted, "The net result of my thirty odd sittings with Mrs. Cooper was to weaken seriously any belief I had in the spiritistic interpretation of these phenomena." As he saw it, the messages were either telepathic or just scraps of knowledge obtained from normal sources.

By 1925, he had developed strong suspicions that he, himself, may have played an *active* part in creating the séance messages—though he didn't make these doubts public until years later. So, at a time of semi-disillusionment, he was suddenly presented with new possibilities in the Gordon Davis case.

On learning that Davis lived, he understandably wished to make contact. His nearby library had (and still has) a shelf of local street directories going back many years. In the then current directory for 1924, he found the home and office addresses for Davis. At the same time, he would naturally wonder why he'd missed seeing Davis around for all these years. Perhaps, he'd not been in Southend long? A glance at the earlier directories would show him that Davis's home address had only come in with the 1924 edition.

Now the original, unaltered Cooper record may have contained references to a house. Out of excited curiosity, Soal would be drawn to take a quick look at Eastern Esplanade, to see if they coincided. A 1922 glimpse of a 1924 home would set the psychic world reeling. But the details didn't coincide—after all, why should they? This discovery must have been specially galling for Soal. The one case that promised to be so very different was now drastically diminished in interest.

Back home, he may have had a battle with his conscience, but in the end his bizarre side conquered. And he faked the records. The

Davis case became the locomotive that hauled all his other cases into public view. It brought him his first brush with national fame. And it created a long-lasting puzzle.

The results were more than gratifying for him, as he wrote: "The Blanche Cooper report received very favourable notice in the better newspapers. The 'Observer' devoted a column and a half to it and I had the distinction of being one of the few persons who have been according a leading article in the 'Morning Post'."

Soal was cast in the strangest of molds. As Betty Markwick observes, he was ". . . obsessive, absorbed, secretive and subject to bouts of dissociation."

Under certain conditions, with one hand held by a woman, he would write automatically and fluently at the reported rate of 3,000 words an hour. In this fashion he delivered whole chapters obstensively from Oscar Wilde. Soal later discovered that many of the Wildean descriptions came from the assorted literature he'd read, while other people discovered that a secret, well-hidden, poetic side of Soal was involved, for some of the Wildean flourishes were actually "borrowed" from letters Soal had earlier written while in the Army.

As well as this, he was dogged by involuntary whispering. And here the implications for his Blanche Cooper sittings are enormous. Blanche used to hold one of Soal's hands and she hummed incessantly when she wasn't struggling with hardly audible words. Under those conditions, Soal most likely went on to semi-automatic pilot, vocalized away, and, with the lady's humming acting like a carrier-wave, ended up by listening to his own voice!

Years after his first triumph the doctorer was doctored. Weighty ESP experiments brought Dr. Soal fame once more. A fame that teetered unsteadily along until 1978, when statistician Betty Markwick revealed that his marvelous, significant results rested on "data manipulation." In other words, this was fakery. Dr. Soal's Mr. Hyde had struck once more.

So, it was goodbye to one of the most impressive series in experimental parapsychology. But a few questions still remained—perhaps some always will. However, the most important of all these is now answered, allowing us to wave goodbye to Gordon Davis—whose time is truly up!

16

THE WORLD SHALL HEAR FROM ME AGAIN!

"WHO WERE YOU IN 1432? Joan of Arc had just been burnt at the stake, the Hundred Years' War dragged on and an infant was King of England. You may have had a hand in those events that shaped history. Now you can see for yourself. You can explore your own past lives, see who you have been and learn who you can become. . . ."

That's an advertisement for a Past Life and Future Freedom Hypnotic Regression Seminar. It may seem funny to some, but for many thousands in the Western World hypnotic regressions are alluring. For them, these sessions are able to lift heavy veils from their memories. And now, the domestic tape recorder has become the invaluable ally of truth—as it captures the "authentic" accounts of long-hidden, life-cycles.

It all began with the Bridey Murphy case of 1952. An American housewife apparently regressed back to an earlier life in nineteenth century Ireland. The book about the case topped the U.S. best-seller list and was translated into five other languages. The book spawned a motion picture; a disc from one of the recorded sessions sold tens of thousands of copies; and all over the United States tape recorders began purring away at innumerable regression sessions.

Twenty years after the Bridey Murphy sensation a much more impressive group of "past-lives" startled the public. The Bloxham tapes were first presented as a BBC Television documentary produced by Jeffrey Iverson. Then they were included and enlarged on in Iverson's book *More Lives Than One?* They were regarded as ". . . the most staggering evidence for reincarnation ever recorded . . . amazingly detailed accounts of past lives—accounts so authentic that they can only be explained by the certainty of reincarnation." Inevitably, they achieved international renown.

The tapes themselves had been accumulated for years by an elderly Cardiff-based hypnotherapist, Arnall Bloxham. Bloxham had been unable to study as a doctor and turned to hypnotherapy as a second best. He was a life-long believer in reincarnation, but his "past-life" regressions only emerged quite late in his career. Despite that, he managed to collect a cupboard full of "past-life" tapes drawn from his experiments with over four hundred people.

Jeffrey Iverson first heard about his collection casually at a party. As a producer with the BBC in Cardiff he was constantly on the lookout for program ideas, so in October 1974, he called at Bloxham's house. After listening to the calm old man's claims Iverson concluded that, if these claims were true, then the recordings were possibly the largest investigation ever undertaken into this type of regression. If true, Iverson thought, "then that single famous case . . . The Search For Bridey Murphy was just a tune on an Irish fiddle compared to his symphony of voices."

Iverson began with a weeding out process, discarding those tapes which he felt could not be researched and proven. Gradually, he came to concentrate on a limited number of the tapes where it seemed to him that the details "coincided remarkably with known but quite obscure periods of history . . . in which people talked about cities and countries they had apparently never visited in their present lives."

Two outstanding cases resulted from all this weeding. In one, Graham Huxtable, a Swansea man, regressed to a squalid life aboard a Royal Navy frigate engaged in action against the French, some two hundred years ago. But the most important case involved a Welsh housewife, Jane Evans.

Mrs. Evans produced a remarkable set of six "past-lives." They were remarkable not so much for their number and diversity as for the sheer, almost overwhelming, amount of detail packed into three of them. In her minor "lives," she was first a London sewing girl named Anne Tasker living about 1702; then a lady-in-waiting to Catherine of Aragon two centuries earlier; and finally Sister Grace, an American nun living in Des Moines, Iowa, up until the 1920s.

Of the three major "lives" two center around the town of York. The earliest was set up in the third century B.C. at the time of the rebellion of Carausius, the Roman admiral who seized power in Britain and declared himself emperor. Jane Evans was then Livonia, the wife of Titus, tutor to the youngest son of Constantius (governor of Britain) and his wife Helena.

As Livonia, she describes how Constantius had to return to Rome and how the rebellion is engineered in his absence. As a consequence she and her husband and the rest of Constantius' household flee from

Eboracum (York) to Verulam (St. Albans) where they live apprehensively until the rebel regime is overthrown by an army led by Constantius. Yet, her husband's triumphant return only brings sadness for the Lady Helena. Roman power struggles have dictated that her husband has had to divorce her and contract a new marriage with Theodora, daughter of the Emperor Maximianus.

Helena, therefore, decides to stay in Verulam. There they are influenced by a Christian woodcarver, Albanus, and Titus becomes so zealous that he volunteers for the priesthood. On the eve of Titus' induction as a priest, Roman troops swoop on Christian houses and burn them. Titus dies in the melee and Livonia apparently dies in some terror, a short while afterwards.

Her next life in York also ended tragically. It unfolded at the year 1189 in the north of the city, where "most of the wealthy Jews live." Then, she was Rebecca, wife of Joseph, a rich Jewish moneylender. For her and the rest of the Jews, the times were troubled. Anti-Jewish risings had occurred in "Lincoln, London, and Chester." In York they were subject to abuse and threats. One of their community, Isaac of Coney Street, was even murdered by a mob.

By the spring of the next year it was obvious that violence was inevitable. So Rebecca and her family prepared their flight from the city, but they left their move too late. An armed band broke into the next-door house, killed the inhabitants, looted the place, then set fire to it. Joseph, Rebecca and her two children were only able to run as far as the castle of York. But even there they were unable to reach safe shelter. They finally found refuge of a sort when they entered a church, took the priest and his clerk captive and hid down in the cellars.

Later, from the safety of the church roof, they could see flames and hear distant mobs screaming, "Burn the Jews, burn the Jews!"

Their respite turned out to be short-lived. Their captives escaped and alerted the mob and the soldiers came into the church to deal with the family. At this high point in the story Jane Evans became "almost incoherent with terror" as the soldiers took her daughter; then, whispering "dark . . . dark" she presumably died.

Her other major "life" was lived in medieval France around about 1450. At that time, she was apparently a young Egyptian servant, named Alison, in the household of Jacques Coeur—the outstanding merchant prince of that period. She was able to talk at length and knowledgeably about Coeur's intrigues, about the king's mistress, Agnes Sorel, and about the clash between the Dauphin Louis and King Charles VII. She knew a great deal about Coeur's possessions and his extraordinary house at Bourges. Her knowledge of the clothes worn by her master is accurate—"tunic edged with miniver, red hose . . . shoes of red Cordovan leather . . . a jewelled belt around his waist and a chain around his neck."

She is again accurate when she tells of Jacques Coeur's fall from favor. He was once close to the King, but after the death of Agnes Sorel, rumors spread at the Court hinting that Coeur had poisoned Agnes. Coeur was arrested, tried on a number of charges and imprisoned. But Alison knew only of the arrest. According to her, when the soldiers came for her master he gave her a poisoned draught to drink and she ended her life by accepting it.

Whenever televison viewers saw Jane Evans under hypnosis and heard the astonishing stories come naturally from her, they were rightly impressed. Her narratives seemed completely free from any attempts at acting a part. When fear and anguish came into her voice, it was clear that she was racked with real emotions. And her easy grasp of often difficult names of people and places made it seem that she was indeed remembering things that she'd only known about intimately. But Jane Evans in her unhypnotized state was adamant that she knew nothing of Jacques Coeur, nothing of Carausius and his times and nothing of the massacre of the Jews at New York.

Iverson's conclusion was that: "The Bloxham Tapes have been researched and there is no evidence that they are fantasies. In our present state of knowledge about them, they appear to convey exactly what they claim: a genuine knowledge and experience of the past." But were these tapes ever researched as painstakingly as they should have been? And was the search for Bridey Murphy ever thorough enough? And is it possible that quite another phenomenon, rather than reincarnation, can account for these rich narratives?

17

THE DARK VAULTS OF THE MIND

Are "past-life" regressions really evidence for reincarnation? Or could they be glimpses of ancestral memories? Both theories have their followers. Yet, rigorous research provides a distinctly different answer. These regressions are identified as fascinating examples of cryptomnesia.

To understand what cryptomnesia is, we have to think of the subconscious mind as a vast, muddled storehouse of information. This information comes from books, newspapers and magazines; from lectures, television and radio; from direct observation; and even from overheard scraps of conversation.

Under everyday circumstances much of this knowledge is not subject to normal recall, but there are times when some of these deeply buried memories are spontaneously revived. Some of these revived memories re-emerge in a baffling form, since their origins are completely forgotten. This is cryptomnesia proper.

Because the origins are forgotten, the information can seem to have no ancestry and can be mistaken for something newly created. The late Helen Keller was tragically deceived by such a cryptomnesic caprice. In 1892, she wrote a charming tale called "The Frost King." It was published and applauded, but within a few months it was revealed that Helen's piece was simply a modified verison of Margaret Canby's story, "The Frost Fairies," published twenty-nine years earlier.

Helen Keller had no conscious memory of ever having been told the story. She was blind and deaf—completely dependent on others for her knowledge. But enquiries revealed that a friend had, in fact, read a batch of Miss Canby's stories to her by touch, in 1888. "The Frost Fairies" was among them.

When this was made plain, Helen was devastated. She wrote: "Joy deserted my heart. . . . I had disgraced myself . . . yet how could it possibly have happened? I racked my brain until I was weary to recall anything about the frost that I had read before I wrote 'The Frost King'; but I could remember nothing."

Other authors have been trapped in the same way—as Samuel Rosenberg has testified. Rosenberg worked for Warner Brothers Pictures as a literary consultant on plagiarism cases. He records the valuable advice given him by his legal supervisor who said: "Don't be fooled by the sometimes astonishing resemblances you will find when you compare *any two* films, plays, stories, books, or film scripts. During the past twenty-five years we have made hundreds of such comparisons in parparation for court trials, and in a great many cases we have found that *both* of the quarreling authors—each convinced that *he* was honest and the other writer was an idea-thief—had copied their plots, ideas, sequences from an *earlier* literary classic or from the Bible or some 'forgotten' childhood story."

In a similar fashion a number of cases of automatic writings, supposed to be from discarnate spirits, have been traced to published works. For example, the famous "Oscar Wilde" scripts of the 1920s were gradually shown to be derived from many printed sources, including Wilde's own *De Profundis* and "The Decay of Lying."

Dr. S. G. Soal, one of the writers of these automatic scripts, was led to remark: "the variety of sources from which the script is drawn is as amazing as the adroitness with which the knowledge is worked up into sentences conveying impressions of the different mannerisms of Wilde's literary style."

This is a significant verdict, but even so, could such unconscious plagiarism account for Bridey Murphy and her offspring? Were the "past-existences" nothing but subconscious fantasies yielded up in order to please the hypnotists? Were they simply a pastiche of buried memories made gripping by the sincerity that accompanies cryptomnesia? In 1956, Dr. Edwin Zolik of Marquette University, set out to answer these questions.

Once he'd hypnotized his subjects he instructed them to "remember previous existences," and his subjects obliged by providing convincing accounts of "past-lives". Everything was tape-recorded—preserving every subtlety and nuance in the voice as the tales unfolded. The recordings were listened to by the subjects in their waking states. Their verdicts were clear—they knew nothing about these "past-lifetimes".

Their disclaimers were obviously sincere. But, when he rehypnotized and re-examined his subjects they were able to remember the fictitious sources they'd used in constructing their "past-life" adventures. In brief, Zolik's detailed analysis showed that "past-life" memories could easily be nothing but a mixture of remembered tales and strong, symbolically colored emotions.

Zolik's method of probing for the real-life origins of reincarnationist material was something he recommended to anyone seriously interested in the truth. Unfortunately, few if any, of the enthusiastic hypno-regressionists took any notice of his advice, and session after session was committed to tape and marvelled over without any effort being made to verify the origins or meaning of this material. Hypnotherapist Arnall Bloxham, for one, recorded over four hundred "past-life" regressions without ever once digging for the possibly mundane origins of these alleged "lives." On the other hand, the Finnish psychiatrist, Dr. Reima Kampman, devoted years to the systematic investigation of the cryptomnesic origins of "past-life" accounts.

Arnall Bloxham—hypnotherapist. The face that launched a thousand slips!

Dr. Kampman of the Department of Psychiatry at the University of Oulu, Finland, began his work in the 1960s. He found his subjects among large groups of volunteers drawn from the three highest grades of the secondary schools of Oulu. All those who could enter a deep hypnotic state were selected for closer study. Kampman found it relatively easy to induce "past-life" recall as a response to his instruction: "Go back to an age before your birth, when you are somebody else, somewhere else."

His most amazing subject proved to be a girl who conjured up eight "past-lives." In one "life" she lived in Ancient Babylonia, her next "life" began in Nanking, then followed a "life" in Paris, another in England, and a final existence in revolutionary Russia.

One of her "past-lives" was as Karin Bergstrom, a seven-year-old girl who had died in an air-raid back in 1939. She was able to supply an address for her old home, and she knew the names and occupations of her former parents. Enquiries showed that, indeed, there had been an air-raid on the exact date she'd given. What's more, the addresses she'd given had actually been hit. But the population records showed that neither a real Karin Bergstrom nor her relatives had died in the raid.

So the girl was asked to age-regress to the time when she'd first heard of the Bergstroms or the bombing, and she soon remembered herself as a little girl turning over the pages of a patriotic book. In that book were photographs of the streets and houses hit by the bombs, and something about the people made homeless. The exact date of the raid was given and one picture showed two of the victims killed that day—significantly, a mother and her seven-year-old daughter. So, the complete regression was assembled from nothing more than the disjointed material found in this one book.

But the really exciting adventure involved her thirteenth century "English life"—as Dorothy, an inn-keeper's daughter. This brought to light "a very explicit account of contemporary happenings." And she astonished everyone by singing a song that none of the listeners were familiar with. She called it "the summer song."

The unusual language used in the song was later studied by a student "with high honours in the English language." He had no difficulty in identifying the words as examples of an old-style English—possibly Middle English. But this meant nothing to the girl, who had no memory of ever having heard the words or music of the song before.

The solution to this riddle came during a later experiment. She was asked to go back to a time when she might have seen the words and music of the song—or even heard it sung. She then regressed to the age of thirteen and remembered taking a book from the shelves of a library.

This was a casual choice. She made no attempt to read and absorb its contents. She merely flicked through its pages. Yet, she not only remembered its title, but was able to state just where in the book her "summer song" could be found.

The crucial book was *Musiikin Vaiheet*—a Finnish translation of *The History of Music* written by Benjamin Britten and Imogen Holst. And the mystery music was, of all things, the famous round—"Summer Is Icumen In"—with words rendered in a simplified medieval English.

A spate of similar successes led Kampman to conclude that he had demonstrated "that the experiences of the present personality were reflected in the secondary personalities, both in the form of realistic details and as emotional experiencess. The recording of a song from a book simply by turning over the leaves of a book at the age of 13 is an outstanding example of how very detailed information can be stored in our brain without any idea whatever of it in the conscious mind, and how it can be retrieved in deep hypnosis."

These cases allow us to look at the Bridey Murphy and Bloxham cases with extra understanding.

18

SOLVING THE BLOXHAM MYSTERY

When the Bridey Murphy case first surfaced it was greeted with naive enthusiasm, and this inevitably provoked a sour reaction. The *Chicago American* published a stinging "exposure" claiming that Ruth Simmons' Bridey-knowledge came from her relatives and acquaintances in Chicago. The *Denver Post* countered by sending their man, William J. Barker, to Ireland in search of supporting material. The rival papers fought fiercely for their totally opposed viewpoints. Yet, neither side produced a conclusive answer.

But, in the end, the onus of proof must always lie with the side which makes the positive claims. Regrettably, Morey Bernstein, author of *The Search for Bridey Murphy,* and his friends were far too quick to make claims on the basis of slender research. And even this slender research is marred by flaws.

Let's note how they marvelled over Ruth's knowledge of the old custom of kissing the Blarney Stone, yet failed to spot a complete work on the custom, written by John Hewlett and called *The Blarney Stone.* It was published in New York, of all places, in 1951. They were equally overawed by her knowing about the Irish Uillean pipes, about Irish jigs and about Irish customs and geography. She had never set foot in Ireland, they reasoned, and yet she knew all this fine detail concerning last century Erin. But their skimpy research failed to uncover the fact that Americans had twice had the chance of delving deeply into Irish life and customs, without moving a single inch out of the United States.

In 1893, The World's Columbian Exposition was staged in *Chicago.* Among the exhibits at this giant fair was an Irish village—the brainchild of Lady Aberdeen. Her original idea was modest—just a single Irish cabin. Yet, by the opening day this had grown into a complete village of fifteen cottages. They were grouped around a green facing a full-sized replica of the tower of Blarney Castle.

To give the exhibit life, Ishbel Aberdeen travelled to the farthest corners of Kerry, Connemara, and Donegal and chose girls who could spin, sing, make butter, and dance jigs. The rose-cheeked colleens were then shipped, suitably chaperoned, over to the States to live and work in the Chicago village.

Every day, for the six months of the fair, visitors could hear the burbling Uillean pipes, listen to the songs of old Ireland, and see the traditional jigs danced on the green. A huge relief-map of Ireland could be viewed from on high; books and souvenirs could be bought; and to crown it all, a replica Blarney Stone could be kissed in the traditional manner at the summit of the massive Blarney Castle tower.

On opening day, some 20,000 visitors paid their 25 cents to enter the Irish village. After that the crowd grew, the sales mounted, and the village became one of the three shows that made money. So, by the end of the fair over three and a half-million people had been brought into contact with all things Irish. And it did not end there! The whole venture was so wildly successful that an Irish village, complete with the full-size tower of Blarney Castle, was erected once more for the St. Louis Fair of 1904.

Now Ruth Simmons, (or rather Virginia Tighe) was born in 1923, so during her formative years there was still a veritable army of people around who had first-hand experiences of these Irish villages. The possibilities for gaining knowledge of Ireland, in her home town of Chicago, were obviously enormous.

Just as the possible sources were neglected, so was the tried and proven method of probing, under hypnosis, for the real-life origins of the Bridey saga. Perhaps it's still not too late. An independent hypnotist could still put the crucial questions to Virginia. Until she consents to this the case can only reasonably qualify as a famous curiosity—and no more.

It is very different, though, with the Bloxham Tapes. The extravagant claims made for these tapes impelled me to investigate them, even with the limited amount of time and funds at my disposal. The snags were great. Graham Huxtable proved unable to help in any constructive way, while Jane Evans flatly refused to cooperate. As a result, the only course left open lay in a scrutiny of the texts, and a laborious search for the probable origins of the previous "lives."

Upon investigation, the Huxtable naval regression proved empty. Its verifiable content was nil. Even its period flavor was grossly overrated. I carefully listed every archaic and little-used word in this regression and found that there were only two of them that were not known to me *as a schoolboy*. And my schoolboy memories reminded me that there were large numbers of historical novels and boys' adventures based on the Royal Navy of the relevant period. A check with publishers' lists showed that there were, indeed, scores of books falling into this category. Apart from that, there were innumerable magazine stories along the same lines.

The ship that the "seaman" Huxtable sailed in is clearly fictional. He calls it the "Aggie." It has thirty-two guns. No ship of that description served in the Royal Navy at that period. Remember, we're not talking about an obscure period in British history, but one which is extremely well documented. For example, Captain Manning and Commander C. F. Walker's book *British Warship Names* (Putnam, 1959) lists the name of every warship of importance for centuries. A thirty-two gun frigate is automatically in this category. But you will not find an "Aggie," or any name resembling this in their listings.

Some people, as a last-ditch attempt to salvage this story, have nominated the "Agamemnon" as a possibility. But this is out of the question. The "Agamemnon" was a sixty-four gun giant.

Little need be said about Huxtable's voice transformation. It has been described as having ". . . a much deeper tone and a strong South of England accent." In other words, a real-life character from the past has emerged. In reality, however, what we encounter is simply the easily assumed pantomime-style "Treasure Island" accent, with all its unsubtlety. As such it has no evidential value.

The six "past-lives" of Jane Evans were obviously the real challenge. Iverson himself considers this to be—"the most consistently astonishing case in Bloxham's collection." I agreed—hers was the case to concentrate on.

My reinvestigation soon showed that the claims made for the tapes were false and the result of misdirected and inadequate research. For example, one of Jane Evans' minor "lives" as a handmaiden to Catherine of Aragon could easily have been based, sequence for sequence, on Jean Plaidy's historical novel *Katherine, The Virgin Widow*.

But the three major "lives" proved to have the most illuminating ancestries. Her recital as Alison, a teenage servant to Jacques Coeur—the fifteenth century French merchant prince—was said to prove that she ". . . knew a remarkable amount about medieval French history." Yet, in her waking state she said, "I have never read about Jacques Coeur, I have never heard the name."

Jeffrey Iverson even concluded that she could not have picked up her many facts through the standard sources. After all, she knew so much, including inside-knowledge of the intrigues surrounding the

King's mistress, Agnes Sorel. Among other things, she was able to describe fully the exteriors and interiors of Coeur's magnificent house—even giving details of the carvings over the fireplace in his main banqueting hall. More surprisingly, she spoke of the carved tomb of Agnes Sorel that was housed in a church. According to Iverson, this tomb ". . . had been cast away by French revolutionaries and spent a hundred and sixty-five years, until its rediscovery in 1970, out of sight in a cellar." But, like a number of observations in the book *More Lives Than One?*, this does not stand up to scrutiny.

The truth is that the Sorel tomb was placed in its present setting in 1809. It has been a tourist attraction for the whole of this century and it is described in detail in H. D. Sedgwick's *A Short History Of France* published in 1930—a book popular for decades and often found in public and school libraries. Apart from that, the tomb has been referred to in many other books and photographed frequently.

It is very much the same with Jacques Coeur's house. In fact, this is one of the most photographed and filmed houses in all of France. Fine, explicit photographs are included in Dame Joan Evans' book *Life in Medieval France*. There, one can see the stone carvings over the fireplace and gain a sound idea of how the place looked—both inside and out. There is now little doubt that Jane Evans has seen these or similar pictures.

There is overwhelmingly strong evidences that the rest of Jane's material was drawn from a source not known to Iverson—a 1948 novel, *The Moneyman* by T. B. Costain. This is based on Coeur's life and provides almost all of the flourishes and authentic-sounding touches included in her "past-life" memory.

In particular, the novel very neatly answers an important question raised by Iverson and other commentators—a question prompted by the curious fact that Alison does not know that her master is married! As Iverson puts it: "How is it that this girl can know Coeur had an Egyptian bodyslave and not be aware that he was married with five children?—a fact published in every historical account of Coeur's life? . . . If the explanation for the entire regression is a reading of history books in the twentieth century, then I cannot explain how Bloxham's subject would not know of the marriage."

Thomas Costain's short introduction to his novel clears up the mystery. He writes: "I have made no mention of Jacques Coeur's family for the reason that they played no real parts in the events which brought his career to its climax . . . When I attempted to introduce them into the story they got so much in the way that I decided finally it would be better to do without them."

Yet the view that her tapes were simply the result of cryptomnesia could still be contested, if it were not for the confirmation provided by the vetting of her remaining two major "lives."

As Rebecca, the Jewess of York, she was supposed to have met her death during the massacre of 1190. At that time, most of the Jewish community died in the York Castle Keep, but Rebecca's death came in the cellar of a church where she had taken refuge. Around this cellar episode a formidable legend has grown up. It is now asserted that the church was positively identified as St. Mary's, Castlegate, and that a crypt was actually discovered there *after* Jane's regression. The truth is that the original TV program script stated that there were *three* possible churches that could qualify as the place of refuge.

St. Mary's was chosen to film in simply because it was the most convenient, since it was being converted into a museum. And it was this conversion which led to the uncovering of an aperture under the chancel. For believers, this was naturally a *medieval* crypt and proof of Rebecca's story.

For many of them, it was joyfully received, almost as if it were some sign from heaven! It gave a fillip to their beliefs or yearnings—so it had to be true.

Writer after writer gloried in unravelling the tale of the wonderful evidential crypt. "This really makes the skeptics' doubts stick in their throats," wrote one. While Brian Inglis wrote: "It is little touches of this kind which rule out cryptomnesia . . . It is no longer possible, therefore, to maintain that cryptomnesia (or, for that matter, deliberate fraud; the pretence of remembering a past life) is an adequate explanation."

To add strength to their assertions the believers constantly cited Professor Barrie Dobson of the Department of History, University of New York, as if he were a supporter and ally. In doing so they drew on phrases found in Iverson's book. But the point needs to be made, and made as strongly as possible, that some of the references to Professor Dobson in that book are misleading. They are based on informal correspondence *never intended for publication*. As such, they are easily open to misinterpretation.

It is significant, though, and predictable, that not one of the believers ever took the trouble to check things out with Professor Dobson. Had they done so, they would have found that his views on the crypt are as follows: (I quote with his full permission from his helpful letter to me dated January 15, 1986.)

> There remains the issue of whether the "cellars under the church" in which Rebecca alleges she is sheltering at the time of the massacre of the Jews at the castle of York can be proved to have existed in 1190. The answer to this can only be a definite negative, for it now seems overwhelmingly most likely that the chamber which workmen reported encountering when renovating St. Mary's Castelgate in 1975 was not an early medieval crypt at all but a post-medieval charnel vault. The Royal Commission on Historical Monuments Survey of *York,* Vol. V *(The Central Area)* 1981, says of it on page 31: "Beneath the E. end of the chancel is a charnel vault with a barrel vault of stone rubble, probably a later insertion and now inaccessible."
>
> The fact that this vault or chamber remains inaccessible in January 1986 must not, in my opinion, persuade anyone into believing that Rebecca's reference to cellars under a church adds any authenticity to her story. The evidence available is now revealed as so weak in this instance that it fails to support any thesis which suggests that Rebecca's regression contains within it genuine and direct memories of late twelfth-century York.

For all that, the furor over "the crypt" is meaningless, since the Rebecca regression is clearly a fantasy. It is an amalgamation of at least two different stories of persecution taken from widely separated centuries.

The proof that we are dealing with a fantasy lies in the historical absurdities found in the tale. Rebecca repeats four times that the Jewish community in York was forced to wear yellow badges, "circles over our hearts." But the Jewish badge was *not introduced* until the following century and even then the English pattern consisted of two oblong white strips of cloth, representing the tablets of Moses. The yellow circle was, in fact, the badge worn in France and Germany after 1215. This is one aspect of Jewish history over which there are no legitimate doubts whatsoever.

A group of further absurdities was discovered in passages from the tapes that were *excluded* from both the book and the film. In these revealing passages Rebecca repeatedly speaks of living in the ghetto in the north of York. This ghetto was a quarter without street names, where only the rich Jews lived and she pointedly mentioned a poor Jew who could only afford to live in ". . . the middle of York in a street called Coney Street."

Now there was never a special Jewish quarter in York. The Jews lived scattered among the Christians in places like Mickelgate, Fosgate, Bretgate, Feltergayle and near the center in Jewbury. And the idea that a Jew would live in Coney Street because of his poverty is ludicrous. Coney Street was, in truth, the choice place for many of the rich Jews to settle—including Josce, the wealthy head of the Jewish community!

As for the notion of the ghetto itself, this involved a leap in time of over 300 years—since the first ghetto was not set up until 1516 in Venice. It was established on an old foundry site and the very name is derived from the Italian *geto* or foundry.

This means, inevitably, that Jane Evans has the ability to subconsciously store vivid accounts and combine and edit these creatively—to the point where she becomes one of the characters involved. The clinching proof that this is so is provided by the Roman wife, or Livonia regression, for this is the purest of all, based on one source only.

This particular life involves a turbulent period in Britain's history: a time of rebellion and instability. At the opening of this period the name of the Roman governor in Britain is unrecorded in existing historical records. The "past-life" memories seem to fill this gap for us by stating that Constantius, father of Constantine the Great, was in charge. After consulting his reference books Iverson was happy to conclude that: "Nor can the regression be dismissed as a fiction built around a blank area of history. Livonia knows a considerable number of verifiable historical facts that fit perfectly into her vision of the missing years. No modern student of history could contradict the names and events she describes . . ."

After hearing the tape, Professor Brian Hartley, an authority on Roman Britain, seemed to agree since he commented: "She knew some quite remarkable historical facts, and numerous published works would have to be consulted if anyone tried to prepare the outline of such a story."

Professor Hartley was right, much painstaking research went into the making of Jane's story, but the research was undertaken by the late Louis De Wohl. In 1947, he wrote a best-selling novel *The Living Wood,* and Jane's life as Livonia is taken directly from that novel. Brief comparisons will show just how.

Livonia's tale opens in Britain during A.D. 286. She describes the garden of a house owned by the Legate Constantius. His wife is named as Lady Helena, his son as Constantine. The son is pictured being taught the use of shield, sword and armour by his military tutor Marcus Favonius Facilis. This entire sequence is taken from chapter 2, Book II of the novel, where Constantine trains in the use of arms and armor under his military tutor Marcus Favonius, called "Facilis . . . because everything was easy to him". De Wohl based this character on a real-life centurion whose tombstone is now in Colchester Castle Museum. But his account of this centurion's life is pure fiction—since Facilis died in the first century A.D.

Livonia then describes a visit by the historical character Allectus. He brings Constantius an urgent message from Rome, but despite the urgency he had "stopped at Gessoriacum to see Carausius who is in charge of the fleet." This section is drawn from the same section of the novel, where the visit leads up to the take-over of rule in Britain by the rebellious Carausius aided by Allectus. Iverson writes: "Livonia gives a basically accurate picture of this quite obscure historical event." Quite so, but only because the whole of the material rests on De Wohl's research.

In the same way *every single piece of information* given out by Jane Evans can be traced to De Wohl's fictional account. She uses his fictional sequences in exactly the same order and even speaks of his fictional characters—such as Curio and Valerius—as if they were real people.

There are two minor differences worth noticing, since these involve her editing faculty. In the first instance, she takes the slight character, Titus Albus, a Christian soldier willing to die for his faith, and recasts him as a tutor to Constantine. But only the name itself is taken, for all of Titus' feelings and actions are those of De Wohl's character, Hilary. Hilary is converted to Christianity by Albanus, ordained as a priest by Osius, and killed during a violent campaign against his faith. All these things happen in turn to be Jane Evans's Titus!

In the second instance, she takes another insignificant character, Livonia, described as "a charming creature with pouting lips and smouldering eyes," and amalgamates her with Helena. A composite character recast as the wife of Titus emerges. This new character is able to act as both an observer and as someone who voices Helena's senti-

The novel from which Jane Evans's life as Livonia was taken.

Engraving shows the style of dress and the Ullean pipes that could be seen at the Irish village of the 1893 World's Columbian Exposition in Chicago.

ments—thus making the story that much fuller and far easier to relate.

This feat of editing reveals a little of the psychology behind these fantasies. For Hilary is the eminently desirable male in the novel, described as having "a beautiful honest face with eyes of a dreamer." He is also secretly in love with Helena. As Titus, he becomes the lover of Livonia of the pouting lips and smouldering eyes—in other words of Jane Evans herself. And there we have all the combustible material that warmed a young girl's daydreams. And all inspired by an exciting historical novel.

Now if the subconscious can engineer *all that,* why bother to drag in the extravagant notion of reincarnation? By all means let us study the mind's strange abilities through regressions—but in the direction that cryptomnesia points. The other way leads to chasing antique moonbeams. And that's a sport best left to nimble, grass-green leprechauns.

19

A LEVER CAN MOVE THE WORLD!

People have long toyed with the idea that physical laws can be set aside by willpower or by specially developed forces within the body. This age-old dream has inspired the publicity behind a number of stage acts, so much so, that less than a century ago audiences were convinced that they were actually witnessing "the negation of the iron laws of nature."

First to succeed with this deception was the "amazing magnetic girl," Lulu Hurst, also known as the "Georgia Wonder." She was the fourteen-year-old daughter of a Baptist deacon of tiny Cedartown, Tennessee. The public were told that her strange powers emerged after a severe electrical storm and a spate of poltergeist-style happenings. Her public demonstrations, however, at no time involved the activities of unseen entities. In full light, using nothing but her hands, Lulu made strong, burly men look like puny weaklings. She presented them with a broom-handle or long pole and calmly defied them to control it against her wishes.

In one of her feats, two men grasped the pole at its center using both their hands. Lulu then simply placed the open palms on either end of the pole, and after a few slight movements the pole began to twist vigorously up and down, and the men found themselves staggering around the platform guided by the tiny laughing girl.

Another, visually more spectacular, feat, involved an attempt by two men to force the pole down onto the stage. The men held the pole vertically while Lulu stood away from them, nonchalantly stretched out her arm and encircled the pole with her open palm. When the word was given the men pushed downwards with all their strength. They struggled away until the sweat rolled from their faces, but the pole stayed in the air with Lulu looking on amused and unruffled!

There were many other feats. For example, one that involved the tipping up of a chair laden with four men. And another where she defied anyone to lift her by the elbows. Although they were different, it was claimed that they all had a common factor. They were proof positive of unique "magnetic-electrical powers" inherent in Lulu's body and under her control.

It was soon shown, however, that her powers were far from unique, for a crop of imitators suddenly arose and began to match Lulu's act. And for some years theaters and music-halls of the United States were entertained by "electric" or "magnetic" females. The most famous of these imitators was Mrs. Abbott, who later performed in Britain and France in the 1890s.

For a while Mrs. Abbott convinced French scientist Dr. Henri Goudard that her powers were indeed paranormal. Fortunately, her visit gave J. N. Maskelyne, Nelson W. Perry, and Sir Oliver Lodge the chance to independently study "the magnetic phenomena" at close quarters.

Maskelyne published his analysis in Dr. Lionel Weatherly's *The Supernatural?;* Perry's appeared in *The Electrician;* while Professor Lodge's was published by the SPR in its *Journal.* The three reports drew the same conclusion; all the feats were the result of the clever use of well-known physical laws. The astonishing behavior on stage arose from nothing more than the controlled deflection of muscular forces by the use of efficient leverage!

FIG. 1.—THE ELECTRIC GIRL.   FIG. 3.—THE ELECTRIC GIRL.

Paranormal? Or parlor tricks?

This can be well-demonstrated by considering the second of the two pole feats. When the two men tried to push downward, the magnetic girl simply deflected the pole toward her. Since her hand was placed as far down the pole as possible, she had an enormous advantage in leverage. As a consequence, the men's strength was deflected flected upward in a horizontal direction, so they ended up struggling to keep the pole vertical and most of their energy was effectively used *against* them.

In a similar fashion, when she placed her hands at the end of the horizontal pole, she gained immense leverage. With only very slight pressure on the ends, she could move, not only the stick, but the arms of her challengers. They in turn tried hard to resist but she had only to relax and change the direction of her movements in order to use the men's strength against them and throw them off balance. This was repeated often, until the men were virtually staggering around, helplessly, trying to combat an "unseen force."

An understanding of the natural forces used in such acts should have put researchers on their guard against future extravagant claims. Yet, just two decades later another stage act was being hailed as even more magnificent and inexplicable. Only this time, it featured a man who used no apparatus whatsoever but could successfully "reverse the force of gravity."

The man was Johnny Coulon, a tiny figure just five feet tall and weighing under eight stone. For all that, he was a tough athletic character. In fact, before the First World War he had reigned for a time as the American bantamweight boxing champion.

After his retirement from the ring little was heard of him; then, in the autumn of 1920, he turned up in Paris with a stupendous stage act. He would appear stripped to the waist and challenge anyone in the audience to lift him off his feet. It seemed a rather empty challenge, for it looked so simple. After all, he was smaller than many schoolboys, and on a large stage he must have looked like a midget.

As can be guessed, he was never short of volunteers. But each of these eager volunteers soon left the stage baffled and frustrated. A newspaper of the time, the New York *Times,* explains why: "When Johnny consents, men of normal physique can toss him aloft and twirl him in mid-air; but when he places one finger on the opponent's right arm at the radial artery, Yves le Boulanger and a dozen other strong men have failed to budge him from the floor. They tug, they twist, until Johnny is bruised and sore, but there he sticks!" (Dec. 26, 1920)

In an earlier report the same newspaper proclaimed: "Paris Puts Coulon Second to Newton. Scientists Aclaim Him as a Discoverer of New Physiological Phenomena."

It was only natural that many attempts were made to explain Coulon's powers. Some said that he was a brilliant hypnotist and could *instantly* rob his challengers of their strength. Others suggested that he had metal plates glued to the soles of his feet and huge electro-magnets hidden under the stage. These magnets were switched on when he said "No," and would hold him down firmly to the boards. This last suggestion was clearly nonsensical, since magnets of such strength would have wrenched the very trouser-buttons off his opponents. In any case, he showed that he could work as well with his plimsolls kicked off and with his bare feet inspected just a second before the act began.

For most people, though, these theories were far too commonplace—they yearned for something much more spectacular. Indeed a section of these sensation-seekers *insisted* on a supernormal explanation. They asserted that Coulon was a medium with unique powers, and these came to his aid when needed. And many believed this.

There were other sensationalists who would not touch these ideas. In thier case, they put forward what they thought of as a "scientific theory"—though, to be objective, it looks more like science-fiction. In their view, Coulon had discovered a way of *reversing* the force of gravity itself. Unfortunately, this science-fiction group included some well-qualified scientists who should have known better.

To his credit, it must be pointed out that Coulon himself never made any extravagant claims. He never once said that he was able to violate natural laws. He was content just to present a baffling stage act and make a living doing this. If others wanted to make wild statements—well, that was up to them.

It remained exactly like that when Coulon appeared in New York in mid-1921. The press wrote about his "supernormal" powers, but Johnny said nothing. These press notices naturally intrigued Houdini. He talked to his fellow magicians, but none of them had any experience of Coulon's act. Since Houdini hated a mystery, he decided to see the act for himself.

Before the act began Coulon's manager appeared and made a declaration on the stage in which he said: "Johnny makes no claims being unable to explain the basis of his unusual powers. For many months he has mystified the doctors and scientists of Europe by performing feats before them that seemed to violate natural law and for which they had no explanation. We shall require a committee of ten or twelve gentlemen to come on the stage to test Coulon."

At that point, Houdini nudged his friend Joseph Rinn, and Rinn hastened to the platform to make up the dozen challengers. Now, Joe Rinn naturally had the better view, but both men were satisfied that there was no hidden apparatus in use. As for Johnny Coulon, he did nothing that was in the least suspicious. In fact, the only thing he did was to powder himself liberally with talcum powder, but then, every stage athlete did that. There was nothing out of place in that.

As soon as the performance began Rinn watched every move closely, yet as challenger after challenger failed to lift Johnny, so Rinn grew more and more puzzled. It was proving impossible to spot just *how* the trick was worked. Then came Joe Rinn's turn to try.

From about a foot away he had to place a palm on each side of Coulon's waist and try to lift when the word was given. Coulon in turn stretched his right hand and pressed a finger lightly on Rinn's throat. Then Johnny shook his head and said that he could not be lifted, and indeed, Rinn found it impossible to get any leverage. He tried as hard as he could, but it felt like trying to lift a marble column. So he gave up. Then Johnny smiled and asked him to try again, saying that, this time, he'd allow himself to be lifted. And in a trice Rinn found that he could lift him just like a bundle of feathers.

When Rinn left the stage he said nothing to the audience, yet he knew *exactly* how Johnny worked his act. All along it had rested on an incredibly simple piece of trickery. So ultra-simple, in fact, that when he first gave the details to Houdini, the escapologist found it hard to believe—so hard that Houdini had to rush home and experiment at once.

Aided by his secretary Oscar Teall, Houdini tried out the trick over fifty times and accepted that Rinn had hit on the right solution. Yet, they kept their knowledge to themselves. As they saw it, Coulon was not making false claims, so there was no possible reason to prevent him from staging his act. In fact, they wished him well and admired his audacity.

So what *was* Johnny's secret? Well, remember that he powdered himself with talcum—now Rinn noticed that he did this even when he wasn't perspiring. So Rinn slyly dipped is fingers into the powder bowl and found that it was not filled with composite talcum. The white powder was, in fact, pure powdered soapstone. When Johnny tensed his powerful stomach muscles, his powdered waist became as smooth as glass and it was impossible to grip it and gain leverage. Yet, when he wished to be lifted, he simply relaxed his muscles, leaned forward slightly and in a split-second the lifter's hands would sink in under the ribs and provide all the leverage needed to throw his lightweight frame into the air! And that, believe it or not, was *all* there was to it!

Yet, despite our present state of knowledge, there are stil people who cling to the idea that Coulon was a scientific freak, or a medium. Just as there are people who still assert that "magnetic" girls had mastered secret powers. But then as magician Maskelyne often used to say—"Give a lie a twenty-four hour start and the truth will never overtake it."

20

O FABULOUS FLIGHTS OF FANCY!

The fire was sudden, violent, and heart-stopping. No one in France had ever witnessed such an enormous, solitary funeral pyre before. When the flames scaled down to mere tongues, only a tangle of metal girders remained. The 800-foot-long tangle was all that was left of British airship R-101.

It should have been the pride of Britain's planned air service to India. Its destruction, in October 1930, marked the end of British airship dreams for the next fifty years.

The fate of the R-101 baffled the world. Unanswerable questions seemed to bedevil the enquiries and the theoreticians. Feverish conjectures were rife—ranging from the mild to the wild. But the strangest questions of all rose out of the séances of medium Eileen Garrett.

Mrs. Garrett was a remarkable woman who ruled queen-like over her teahouse in London's Hampstead. She had little formal education, but had developed a ready tongue, a sparkling wit and an enviable capacity for enchanting people and making friends. Perhaps being Irish helped!

Her circle of friends reads like an illustrious publisher's list. George Bernard Shaw, H. G. Wells, James Joyce, Robert Graves, Aldous Huxley, Conan Doyle, W. B. Yeats, D. H. Lawrence, Katherine Mansfield—all these were part of her circle. And I've only mentioned some of the most famous.

In the 1920s, while still in her thirties, she began to see full-color visions. Some of these, she felt, were previsions of coming events. These visions troubled her, and she turned to Hewat McKenzie for guidance. McKenzie had founded a body called "The British College of Psychic Science." His BCPS premises provided a meeting place for psychics of all categories, and there they trained and sat for clients. At this "college" Eileen now attmepted to develop and understand her strange faculties.

In 1928, on the way to the BCPS building, Eileen Garrett saw a brilliant silver airship sailing across the sky. Suddenly its flight became erratic, it plunged down toward the ground, and smoke began to billow out of its envelope. Unmistakably on fire and in distress, it dived into a thick cloudbank and disappeared from sight.

Eileen was left numb, for just two years earlier she'd seen something almost identical. On that occasion she'd accepted it as a vision. Yet, this time it felt different so she checked the papers for a week, just in case she'd witnessed a real air disaster. No such disaster was reported. So she realized that, for the second time, a visionary ship had invaded her mind. But why?

Meanwhile, two rival, giant British airships were under construction. The decision to commission them had been taken in 1924. The R-100 was to be built by the private Airship Guarantee Company of Howden in Yorkshire. The R-101 was allotted to the state owned Royal Airship Works at Cardington, Bedford. The vital hangars and mooring-towers were to be erected at Cardington, Ismailia and Karachi—along the India route—by the Air Ministry direct.

By January 1930, R-100 was displaying its sleek lines and its championship of the air, while R-101 was airborne but bumbling by comparison. Then on July 29, 1930, R-100's Condor gasoline engines roared into life, and she slipped into the skies and headed off for Canada. Seventy-eight hours later she moored at St. Hubert Airport in Montreal.

Its return trip in triumph was little noticed, but it was certain that R-100 was a thoroughly healthy beast. R-101, by contrast, was beset by troubles. Her much heavier diesel engines and equipment gave her all the grace of an overweight and ailing elephant. She was sluggish in the air and could hardly lift her own bulk. Drastic surgery was employed. The R-101 was cut in half and a new 45-foot-long section was fixed between the halves. She at once gained an extra 500,000 cubic feet of gas capacity. With her other bags overinflated she was at last blessed with the extra lift she needed.

Now buoyant, she was proclaimed ready for the great flight to Karachi. But her India expedition ended after she'd journeyed a mere 216 miles!

The R-101 met her end on October 5, 1930. Two days later, séance messages involving the crash came through Eileen Garrett's lips and created a sensation, when the newspapers pounced on them. Yet these messages weren't the first to be picked up by Eileen. As early as 1928, some fragmentary doubts about R-101 had been voiced by an entity supposed to be the dead aviator, Captain Walter Hinchcliffe. These doubts recurred in later sessions. Eileen's mind was troubled. First, there were the visions of burning airships. Next came hints from séances of possible disaster.

In mid-September 1930, her concern led her to warn Sir William Sefton Brancker. For years Air Vice-Marshall Brancker had been a be-monocled, bristling-moustached, caricature of a military man. Now clean shaven and looking quite urbane, he was the dynamic Director of Civil Aviation. All along he'd been driven by semi-religious fervor to place Britain first in airline development. The R-101 was to be the pinnacle of achievement. First India and next Australia would be served by her and her successors. He was proud to be one of those due to fly on the first major flight to India. But just a week or so before, he attended a dinner-party whose guests included Eileen Garrett.

At first, Eileen was hesitant about button-holing Sir Sefton. Instead, she confided in actress Auriol Lee, hoping that Auriol would then gently alert him. But Auriol went further than that. She brought Sir Sefton over to meet Eileen and in a quiet corner they discussed the visions and the séance hints.

Brancker, however, could do no more than insist that they were committed to the flight. And in further conversation he suggested that the omens might be no more than memories of earlier disasters, like the one involving the R-38 in 1921. To that suggestion Eileen had no conclusive answer. She had revealed all there was to reveal. She could go no further.

Three days before the R-101 was due to fly, Harry Price received a strange phone call from Australian journalist Ian Coster. Price had built up a reputation as an energetic and independent psychical researcher. He had a flare for publicity and was the natural choice for a journalist seeking headlines. Coster wanted an interview with a dead author, and Price was just the man to nominate the medium most likely to succeed. Price thought at once of Eileen, for this dead author was none other than Sir Arthur Conan Doyle, an old friend of hers. A sitting was then arranged for the afternoon of October 7, 1930—exactly three months after Sir Arthur's death.

On that day, Coster arrived hopeful. Perhaps he *could* please the editors of *Nash's* magazine, who'd given him the freak assignment. At first, he felt disappointed. After her "guide," Uvani, had taken Eileen over, the messages that came through were about a man called Irving or Irwin. No trace of Doyle. But as he listened, he began to realize that the urgent speech involved the airship crash of two days earlier.

The stenographer worked at full speed to take down the torrent of words. Some of them seemed quite technical. She didn't recognize them but they were faithfully recorded. These messages took up the greater part of the session. Doyle did, in fact, come through later, but everyone felt that in a way, he'd been over-shadowed by the airship man.

In his book *The Airman Who Would Not Die,* John G. Fuller comments: "Price and Coster were spellbound. There was one clear thought in Price's mind, as he wrote later: No one could *invent* a story at this speed. No one could fabricate such a stream of technical terms. . . . Coster had not forgotten his assignment to try to get Conan Doyle. But he was stunned by the impact of the alleged Captain Irwin message. He found himself trying to explain. It was incredible. Along with Price, he was convinced that Eileen Garrett was not consciously cheating. He was also convinced that she, as a layman, was totally incapable of framing that stream of information."

John Fuller sums up Harry Price's bewilderment by saying: "He almost became paranoid; Could there be espionage here? Only scanty details of the R-101's technical problems had appeared in the press. . . . Eileen had spoken fluently of engines, grosslift, air screws, bore capacity, and in almost desperate haste. There was never any groping or hesitation for phrases that Price himself couldn't replicate in a million years—and he was technically minded."

In the aftermath of the séance, Coster agreed to hang on to the R-101 story until the official hearings were over. In the meantime, Price would seek out an airship expert to appraise the séance record and give a verdict.

It wasn't too easy to find such an expert. Few people wanted to be involved with something as controversial and suspect as a séance record. In addition, "still tongues" was the official attitude. The correct place for comment and judgment was a Court of Inquiry.

The required Court of Inquiry opened hearings on October 28. Present at the hearings was Major Oliver G. Villiers, a senior intelligence officer at the Air Ministry. Villiers had worked with and suffered under Brancker. He was deeply moved by the tragedy. And in that state of mind he had already had a "psychic experience." Before the hearings, he had inwardly heard the voice of the R-101's captain, Irwin. The voice had urged "For God's sake, let me talk to you. It's all so ghastly. I must speak to you. I must. We're all bloody murders. For god's sake, help me speak with you."

Now Villiers had been a spiritualist since 1925, but a passive one. In fact, he'd only visited a medium once, ever. Yet after hearing the "voice" he felt impelled to sit with the most powerful medium in Britain. According to Villiers, his friend Julian Sorsby recommended Garrett. An appointment was quicky arranged for the evening of the thirty-first—four days after the start of the inquiry.

Unlike Coster, Villiers turned up for his sittings without a stenographer. He intended to rely on pencilled notes and his excellent memory. He had total recall—a claim that some regard as doubtful. Nevertheless, he sat with Mrs. Garrett and later produced pages of detailed records, which he stated were accurate and evidential. These records supplemented the original Coster séances. They were also distinguished by a grasp of "airship technicalities." As such, they were to Villiers valuable insights into the real reasons for the disaster as well as proof of survival.

These are powerful claims. The spirits are rarely noted for their grasp of technical terms. And was Villiers the best man to evaluate the technicalities of the messages? We have to note though, that Villiers was not alone.

An article on Conan Doyle's return, written by Price and Coster, appeared in Britain and the United States. It briefly, almost as an aside, mentioned the R-101 message. Following its publication in December 1930, and January 1931, Price received a letter from Will Charlton, supply officer of the R-101. He wrote that he "was familiar with all parts of the ship and its equipment and personnel." At last, here seemed to be the expert Price had been looking for. Charlton was sent a confidential copy of the séance record and he wrote back, "If Mrs. Garrett was completely ignorant of these technical matters concerning R-101, then the document is an extremely wonderful one."

Charlton was eager to be of aid, provided his identity was kept secret. Price readily agreed to this. In all documents or minutes Charlton would become Mr. X. This suited Charlton who hinted darkly that near-secret information was involved.

When Charlton brought his report to London, Price was ill. So on April 14, 1931, Mrs. K. M. Goldney stood in for Price and painstakingly combed through Charlton's comments. According to Charlton, these represented the views of staff at Cardington who'd been consulted.

His considered verdict was that about 70 percent of the information was absolutely correct. A further 20 percent was "most likely." The remainder was either confused or wrong. In short, Mrs. Garrett had provided a startling document. One that even included knowledge of secret documents!

So, did Airship Captain Irwin speak through Eileen Garrett? Spiritualists have no doubt that he did. They've even claimed that: "Air tragedy happened because seance messages were ignored" (*Psychic News,* October 13, 1979).

John Fuller's book is certainly wedded to the proposition that Irwin did indeed speak throgh Garrett. Writers Michael Hardwick and David Beaty concur, while Peter Underwood is convinced that: "'Irwin' made many . . . observations and statements concerning highly technical tests which it is difficult to believe were in the normal knowledge of anyone living." Many other writers have been taken in by these scripts, which are worthless and little more than flights of fancy.

On examination, the alleged technicalities involved are either commonplace, easily absorbed bits and pieces, or plain gobbledegook. The so-called secret information just doesn't exist. Now, Charlton is to a great extent responsible for the initial false belief in these scripts. But later writers must also take responsibility. They've failed to check the empty vaporizings with proven experts.

One man who did check was the late Archie Jarman. He was a friend of Eileen's and accepted her statements that she was oblivious to the things said and done at her séances. So, in 1962, at her suggestion, he began a detailed search into the R-101 séance and its background. He interviewed witnesses in England and France and drew up an exhaustive 80,000 word report. He turned down the handsome fee offered for this report, since he wished to have a free hand. Fortunately, he was wealthy enough to be able to finance the investigation out of his own pocket. His findings were devastating. But before considering them, let's look at the results of my own independent survey.

Two pieces of information in the scripts greatly excited Charlton. One involved an obscure German warship. The other involved a "secret test." These secrets were alleged to be contained in the medium's puzzling words: "This exorbitant scheme of carbon and hydrogen is entirely and absolutely wrong."

Charlton was dogmatically certain that he'd solved this puzzle. Garrett had been talking about projected engine and fuel tests. In detail he explained: "At the time of the R-101 flight, a series of experiments was contemplated with the idea of burning a mixture of hydrogen and oil fuel (i.e., of carbon and hydrogen; commonly known as hydrocarbon). This was to form the basis of proposed experiments. The hydrogen would have been obtained from the gas bags, and the carbon from the oil fuel of the ship. For the purpose of this experiment at Cardington, a special gas main had been installed from the gas plant to the engine test house, to be utilized there in conjunction with oil fuel. No experiment had actually taken place at the time of the flight, but preparations were in process. This would have consisted in a highly technical and important experiment—and would be unlikely to be known of outside official circles."

Later commentators have made much of this. John Fuller states: "To Charlton the most remarkable reference was to the mixture of hydrogen and oil. This was a hush-hush experiment that only a handful of technicians knew about. It had not even been put into practical use yet."

Incredible as it may seem, this "hush-hush experiment" did not exist! It was a pure fantasy invented by Charlton's over-eager mind. There had been airship experiments involving hydrogen and kerosene fuel, but these were never secret. They had, in fact, been fully carried out and abandoned *three years earlier*. What's more, this fuel scheme was never considered in respect of the R-101, which was saddled with deisel engines, working on compression-ignition. These fuel tests were only feasible with the R-100 which used spark-ignition, gasoline engines.

The tried and abandoned plan for the R-100 was to use a kerosene and gas fuel in Bristol Jupiter engines. But "In 1927, after suitable experiment, Barnes Wallis decided that the proposed power units of paraffin-hydrogen engines was inadequate" (Prof. J. E. Morpuego, *The Life Of Barnes Wallis*, 1972). So the whole scheme was dropped. The Jupiter engines were put to one side and Rolls Royce Condor engines were fitted instead.

Charlton's second marvelous find, involving the German airship, lay in the sentences, "Load too great for long flight. Same with S.L.8.— tell Eckner." Eckner was easily identified as the Zeppelin constructor. The real problem surrounded the designation "S.L.8."

Charlton wrote: "The S.L.8 has been verified as the number of a German airship—S.L. standing for Schutte Lanz. This verified only after X. had been through complete records of German airships (i.e., it was not known to him offhand.)—But it would be known to Irwin."

In commenting on this, Fuller asserts that: "Charlton and his colleagues of Cardington had been strongy impressed with the reference to *'S.L.8.'* No one on the staff of Cardington could confirm this designation and number until they looked it up in the complete records of German airships. The *'S.L.'* stood for a designer named Schutte Lanz. The designation was for the eighth ship in the series."

This statement by Charlton, echoed by Fuller, is so absurd that it simply has to be yet another invention. For the personnel at Cardington were by no means ignoramuses—as we'll see.

We should first note that Schutte Lanz wasn't the name of a designer, but a company. But this is a minor point. The S.L. airships, designed by Dr. Johann Schutte of Danzig University, had been world famous just over ten years earlier. Even as early as 1909, the Schutte designs were illustrated in British publications. Then, when the First War broke out, millions of people in Britain came to know of the S.L. airships. They even knew the names Schutte-Lanz, even if they couldn't pronounce them properly. For almost every pub, railway station, factory, theater, barn, and spare billboard came to display a large black and red poster showing the different shapes of the British and German aircraft.

Under the dramatic heading "Public Warning," the text read: "The public are advised to familarise themselves with the appearance of British and German Airships and Aeroplanes, so that they may not be alarmed by British aircraft, and may take shelter if German appear . . . In the event of HOSTILE aircraft being seen in country districts, the nearest Naval, Military or Police authorities should, if possible, be advised immediately . . . ."

It was the sort of warning that made people sit up and take notice of the German airships shown on the poster. They were three in number—a Parseval, a Zeppelin and a Schutte-Lanz.

In addition to that, on September 2, 1916, the brand-new airship *S.L.11* was shot down at Coffley, north of London. Its destruction made national news. Ironically, at the end of the war, the Schutte-Lanz building principles, using Russian fir-wood, were actually applied to the construciton of British rigid airship R-31.

So, if we were to believe Charlton, we would have to imagine that people had suffered total amnesia about the warning posters and the newspaper references. As well as that, we would have to accept that the Cardington research and design staff had started off with completely blank minds, ignoring the lessons of early design successes and failures, thus ignoring the previous British use of Schutte-Lanz techniques. It's all so preposterous. Part of the Cardington brief involved the considerations of the lessons of all previous designs, good or bad. The S.L.s were therefore inescapable.

So, what was Charlton up to—and why? Here Archie Jarman's research proves invaluable. He was able to glean that Charlton had a much inflated idea of his own importance. He was a competent steward of stores and supplies but was lacking in aeronautical knowledge. His expertise was imaginary. But, significantly, he was a spiritualist, and the séance report most likely gave him the jubilant feeling that he could play an important role in advancing his beliefs. It certainly pleased him to have "top psychical researchers" dependent on him—hanging on his every word. He was determined not to disappoint them.

Tragically, John Fuller has allowed himself to ride along with Charlton's follies. Fuller claims that Charlton "had discussed and reviewed Price's transcript with the entire executive technical staff at Cardington. Almost without exception, they were amazed and puzzled. They agreed that it was an astounding document."

This popular claim is without backing of any sort. It's in direct conflict with the real content of the scripts. And it's in conflict with the testimony of expert Cave-Browne-Cave, who was intimately involved with airship technology from 1913 to 1931.

Fuller goes on to amplify his claims by stating that the technical staff were not only amazed and puzzled but that "together they found over forty references to highly technical and confidential details." Really? Then where are they? When undisputed experts considered the same séance scripts they were unanimous in rejecting them as valueless.

One such expert was the veteran airshipman Wing Commander R. S. Booth—the man who'd flown R-100 to Canada and back. He found the scripts technically empty. As for the view that they threw light on the reasons for the disaster, he wrote: "I have read the description of the Price/Irwin séance with great care and am of the opinion that the messages received do not assist in any way in determining why the airship R-101 crashed on October 5th, 1930."

Wing Commander Cave-Browne-Cave, highly qualified in airship design and involved with the R-101 planning, backed up Booth, stating:

"I entirely agree and I do suggest that if the communication is to have value as a contribution to psychic knowledge by comparing it with known facts, the observations of Mr. Charlton should be totally disregarded."

The moment you totally disregard Mr. Charlton, the séance record loses its phony authority. It becomes an odd collection of unremarkable facts and sparks of imagination. It reads like the notes for a possible yarn for a boy's magazine. Even so, where did Mrs. Garrett pick up all the odd bits of airship jargon and this message of agony? What made it all accumulate in her subconscious?

It probably began with her war-time experiences in London, when she'd witnessed bombing raids by Zeppelins. From then on, airships were associated with danger and menace. With the war over, a series of airship tragedies only served to strengthen the association with danger.

British airship R-34 hit a hillside and later had to be destroyed. Her predecessor R-33 was badly damaged. And Airship R-38 broke in two while flying over Hull. In the same period, the French *Dixmude* had crashed into the Mediterranean, and the American airships *Roma* and *Shenandoah* had been destroyed with heavy loss of life.

With all these thoughts in mind, Eileen Garrett began to pick up the gossip surrounding the R-101. The problems it faced—its lack of lift, its unwieldiness, the multiple leaks from its gas bags, were never kept secret.

In total, she would form an unhappy picture of the Cardington enterprise. We have to remind ourselves as well of the implications of her busy social life. As a hostess figure, she was constantly surrounded by a welter of conversation. She enjoyed her position and, naturally, had to keep abreast of affairs. As a result, all topics of current interest, from the important to mere tittle-tattle, were of interest to her. And the airship program was one of the big talking points of the late twenties.

It was all so easy to absorb information about the state-backed R-101. Nevil Shute, part of the rival R-100 team, has testified in his *Slide Rule* to the "incessant publicity of the competing (R-101) staff." He expands on this by saying: "At times it seemed that every newspaper we picked up had a column describing the wonders of R-101, ending up with a brief sentence that R-100 was also being built at Howden . . . We gleaned our technical knowledge of R-101 from patent specifications, from popular articles in the press, and from hearsay."

Rifling through the popular press of the day, we notice that the stories are often illustrated by photographs and line drawings. In one case, there are even thirteen detailed artist's impressions of the R-101 superstructure, inside and out. The newspapers were lucky. The Air Ministry was bountiful with its publicity. For example, its press hand-out dated September 19, 1930, comprises twenty-four large pages listing everything one could possibly wish to know about dimensions, engines, air screws, framework, gas bags, ballast and fuel systems, ground organization, mooring arrangements, and the airship's many novel features.

To supplement all this, there were seven lectures on the progress of R-101 delivered to the Royal Aeronautical Society. They were later published. With so much material around, the surprising thing is not that Mrs. Garrett soaked up information, but that she made such a mess of the facts she took in!

But does that include the seemingly amazing hit she made? She had "Irwin" say that the airship "almost scraped the rooftops at Achy." Harry Price thought this fragment astounding, since he couldn't trace Achy on the French motoring and road maps. After a morning's search he finally found it on a large-scale railway map. It was a small village on the main line between Amiens and Beauvais.

Now Beauvais had figured in the press reports, but not Achy. So how did she alight on this unmemorable place that even map makers ignored? Archie Jarman was easily able to dispose of this enigma. He discovered that Eileen had frequently motored from Calais to Paris in the twenties. The road she had taken carried her past Achy, which was vividly signposted. So the mysterious reference depended on nothing more than holday memories triggered off by the Beauvais connection.

There were, of course, the later set of airship sittings. The ones with Major Villiers. But the least said about these the better. In many ways they are even more muddled. And technically considered, they are absurd. Indeed, after considering them, Wing Commander Booth wrote: "I am in complete disagreement with almost every paragraph . . . the conversations are completely out of character, the atmosphere at Cardington is completely wrong and the technical and handling explanation could not possibly have been messages from anyone with airship experience."

Booth cites as an example, the statement allegedly from Irwin, "I noticed the gas indicator was going up and down, which showed there was a leakage or escape." Booth comments tersely: "No such instruments were fitted."

Wing Commander Cave-Browne-Cave considered the same records, gave his own thumbs down and wrote to Jarman saying: "Booth and I have been able to tell you how impossible most of the suggestions are."

After completing his 80,000 word investigation, Archie Jarman had no hesitation in dismissing the séance material as valueless. Regrettably, he died the week before I was due to meet him, and go through his research material. But before he died he had asked for one thing to be clarified and emphasized. At no time did he ever come "to the conclusion that the Harry Price session was almost foolproof and indicated strong evidence of communication with Captain Irwin." This statement appears in John Fuller's book (p. 293). It completely misrepresents Archie Jarman's views. In fact on November 3, 1977, Jarman wrote to Fuller saying, "The less said about the alleged psychic side the better."

So perhaps we'll let Archie have the last word on this affair, for he has written: "Best forget the psychic side of R-101; it's a dead duck—absolutely!"

21

THE JUDGE WHO JUGGLED WITH FACTS

London's Whitechapel murders were at their peak on the night of September 30, 1888. Two hours after the second murder of that night, Police Constable Spicer came across a likely suspect. The man looked out of place in the squalid court. He was well dressed, yet he sat on a filthy brick-built dustbin with a sluttish prostitute at his side. His shirt cuffs were blood-stained and he carried an ominous-looking black bag. When questioned, the man proved evasive, so P.C. Spicer put him under arrest and hauled him off to the local police station.

At the station the man stated that he was a doctor from Brixton— whereupon he was promptly released. No one even asked for his bag to be opened. P.C. Spicer then received a reprimand for bringing in a *respectable* citizen.

During that period respectability and position in society were paramount. If you were in the right social strata, then it was almost a guarantee of your honesty and reliability. And the higher up the scale, the more certain it was these virtues would be cherished.

When the Society for Psychical Research (SPR) was formed in 1883, it naturally absorbed this prevailing view of society and its various strata. And when the Society was still in its infancy it received a most remarkable communication from a gentleman who was eminently respectable. In February 1884, a letter arrived written by a retired judge.

This judge was Sir Edmund Hornby, formerly with the Consular Court at Shanghai. His letter described his encounter and dealings with a very solid-looking phantom! What's more, his account was backed up by the testimony of his wife and mother-in-law.

The SPR investigators were more than impressed by this letter. They regarded it of great importance. The judge's training and experience made it certain that *anything* he had written would be carefully considered and accurate in every detail.

The judge's story was set in Shanghai some nine years earlier. On the day in question, he'd spent a whole evening writing out details of a

183

judgment he was due to give the next morning. He had taken longer than usual, for this was quite an important Admiralty case. When he'd finished, the time was eleven-thirty. He then put the judgment in an envelope and left it with his butler. This was his regular practice and part of his arrangement with the local newspaper editors and reporters. They all knew that they were welcome to call at the house and make an advance copy of any report that they wanted to set up in print.

Shortly before twelve, the Judge retired to bed and in a short while fell fast asleep. He was soon roused, though, by the sound of someone knocking on the door along the corridor—the door leading to the study. In his fuddled state, he assumed it was the butler and took no notice. Then, there came a tap at the bedroom door and this time he was certain it *was* the butler, so he called out "Come in!". Yet, when the door opened, in walked the chief journalist and editor of a local newspaper.

Now this journalist was well-known to the judge and quite unmistakable, since his head seemed to lie sideways on one shoulder, giving him the appearance of being deformed. So the judge wasn't startled. He simply took it that the man had come looking for the judgment paper, and he said, "You've mistaken the door—but the butler has the judgment, so go and get it." The reporter though, made no attempt to leave. He just stood there looking sad and deathly pale. Then he asked to be told details of the judgment, then and there.

At this, the Judge grew angry and ordered him from the room. In fact, he felt like leaping out of bed and throwing him out! But there was something so tragic about the man that Judge Hornby finally relented, got out of bed and dictated a brief summary. He then ended by saying, "This is the last time I will allow a reporter in my house." The journalist looked at him wistfully and replied, "This is the *last* time I shall ever see you—anywhere." Then he left. With that the Judge went back to bed, noticing that the time was exactly 1:30 A.M.; so, in all, the whole encounter had taken up just ten minutes.

Sir Edmund's wife was a heavy sleeper; but, even so, she'd been vaguely aware of something going on. When he returned to bed she woke up fully and asked what the fuss was all about. She was told what happened, then they both went to sleep, without any further discussion. But the next morning, the Judge went over the events again with her. He explained that, "The poor fellow looked awfully ill." But he also made it clear that he was due for a reprimand when he saw him next in the courtroom.

When Judge Hornby reached his courtroom and looked for the journalist he found him missing, and at ten o'clock he discovered why. As he wrote:

> The usher came into my room to robe me when he said, "A sad thing happened last night, sir. Poor ——— was found dead in his room." I said, "Bless my soul! What did he die of, and when?" "Well, sir, it appears he went up to his room as usual at ten to work on his papers. His wife went up about twelve to ask him when he would be ready for bed. He said, 'I have only the judge's judgment to get ready, and then I have finished.' As he did not come, she went up again, about a quarter to one, to his room and peeped in, and thought she saw him writing, but she did not disturb him. At half-past one she again went to him and spoke to him at the door. As he did not answer she thought he had fallen asleep, so she went up to rouse him. To her horror he was dead. On the floor was his notebook, which I have brought away. She sent for the doctor, who arrived a little after two, and said he had been dead, he concluded, about an hour." I looked at the notebook. There was the usual heading:
>
> "In the Supreme Court, before the Chief Judge.
>
> "The Chief Judge gave judgment this morning in the case to the following effect"—and then followed a few lines of undecipherable shorthand.

At this point, pause and mark up the evidence that seems to back up his statement: His wife had been informed. His Court Usher has already gathered in an almost complete account from the reporter's wife. And the quoted notebook seems to confirm the story, since the judgment could *only* be obtained from Hornby's house. So far, the support seems extremely strong. And in fact, Hornby goes on to add even more support when he writes:

> I sent for the magistrate who would act as coroner, and desired him to examine Mr. ———'s wife and servants as to whether Mr. ——— had left his home, or could possibly have left it without their knowledge, between eleven and one the previous night. The result of the inquest showed he died of some form of heart disease, and had not and could not have left his house without the knowledge of at least his wife, if not of his servants. Not wishing to air "my spiritual experience" for the benefit of the Press or the public, I kept the matter at the time to myself, only mentioning it to my Puisne judge

and to one or two of my friends; but when I got home to tiffin I asked my wife to tell me as nearly as she could remember what I had said to her during the night, and I made a brief note of her replies and of the facts.

When he reached England, the fact that he'd discussed the weird events with his wife and made notes, while their memories were fresh, gave him enough confidence to write: "As I say then, so I say now—I was not asleep but wide awake. After a lapse of nine years my memory is quite clear on the subject. I have not the slightest doubt I saw the man—have not the least doubt that the conversation took place between us."

The Judge's story first appeared in print in the *Journal* of the SPR. So at first it was only known to a very small circle. But the SPR's secretary was so excited and delighted with the case that he arranged for it to be republished in the *Nineteenth Century* magazine. His excitement was understandable since the story seemed to be unshakable evidence for the paranormal. Indeed, Edmund Gurney of the SPR had diligently checked out the account with Lady Hornby and her mother and found them "model witnesses." In his report he wrote: "Lady Hornby *absolutely positive* of getting the note from Court telling her of the death . . . her mother, whom I also saw, remembered being told the same day."

It was fortunate that the story appeared in magazine form—otherwise it might have remained unchallenged and been repeated over and over again as an impregnable, true event. But as it was, a copy of the magazine reached Shanghai, where it was read by a Mr. Frederick Balfour, who reacted with amusement and amazement.

Balfour was a newspaper editor who'd known Sir Edmund well. He'd also known the dead newspaperman—Mr. Hugh Lang, and he promptly wrote a piece challenging the story. It then emerged that Hugh Lang had not died at 1:30 A.M., but at his office, about nine in the morning—following a good night's sleep. And there was no inquest, since it wasn't needed. Apart from that, the death had occurred on January 19, 1875, and on that date there was no Lady Hornby! At that time, Sir Edmund was a long-time widower—in fact, he didn't remarry until three months *after* Hugh Lang's death.

Once Balfour's letter appeared, obituaries were checked and Sir Edmund's whole story fell to pieces. He sadly agreed that, on the day of Lang's death, he wasn't wed—he even added that, at the time, he only knew his future wife just well enough "to bow and to exchange civilities." So those three vital discussions with his wife just couldn't have taken place—the main evidence to back up the tale simply vanished.

But what on earth had prompted the Judge to make up such a vivid and compelling story? To that there is no full answer. All we know is that the Judge did admit that he'd been ill that year and sometimes delirious as well. That might possibly acocunt for a lurid dream, or hallucination, becoming confused with the real-life event. Even so, this cannot in any way explain why his wife and mother-in-law were prepared to support his fiction. The reason for their endorsements still remains a mystery.

Edmund Gurney, himself, could offer no explanation—he simply repeated Hornby's words that "his memory must have played him the most extraordinary trick." And Gurney blamed himself for failing to check the Chinese newspapers before accepting the tale as true. The case itself was ignominiously deleted from the records of the SPR.

And on that note, the Hornby saga usually ends—but not now. The full story has never yet been told. There are intriguing sequels to be considered.

We start in 1962 when the Hornby case was dealt with in the spiritualist magazine *Light*. A protest letter was then received by the publishers. It came from none other than Judge Hornby's daughter, Mrs. Constance Drummond. The letter was incredible and most revealing.

Mrs. Drummond now furnished a totally different version of her father's Shanghai experience. She made it clear that she wanted her version made public. Very well, her wish is granted. On March 7, 1962, Judge Hornby's daughter wrote this:

My father was Chief Justice in China. . . . The story as he told it to me is the following:

My father had given judgment in a case where a *Chinese* (not a reporter) was accused of murder and my father had sentenced him to death. That night when reading over the evidence in bed he began to wonder if his judgment had been right and was greatly worried. Then through the window of his room came a figure whom he saw was the Chinaman whom he had sentenced. The man came up to his bed and in pigeon English said he was not to worry as he *had* committed the murder and his sentence was justified. He then walked out. My father rang for his Boy and sent him down to the jail thinking the man had escaped. He was found dead hanging in his cell.

That is the *true* story. My father's *first* wife was with him and he *was* married. But now comes the sequel.

The "gentleman" in Shanghai who exposed the story as untrue had just lost a case in Court (a civil case) and my father had convicted him. Out of malice he apparently put this story round and saying that my father was not married at the time, the dates had somehow been changed. No one who knew my father believed that the story was untrue but this man in Shanghai had the garbled account sent home and I believe the Psychic Investigation Society printed it. Years ago I wrote them the true story but evidently this false account is still believed.

I feel we have to accept her story as true. She's obviously repeating the gist of her father's words. For it's just unimaginable that she would be foolish enough to invent such an easily demolished collection of absurdities. But, since Hornby had fabricated this nonsense, what does that tell us about his state of mind? Well, this farrago of lies could only come from a mind completely out of touch with reality. For it put his unwitting daughter in an impossible position. Through believing in her father's words, she was condemned to go around making a fool of herself for the rest of her life!

So when did Hornby start losing touch with reality? I suggest shortly after his retirement. It's certain that the tale he unravelled in England has no touch point with the real events in Shanghai. At one time, I was inclined to think that this was a one-off aberration, but his daughter's words rule that out. And these findings also negate the apology he made to Gurney at the time. After talking of his illness he wrote "If ever there was an unconscious or unintentional liar I am the man."

Strangely enough, a second attempt was made to save the Hornby story as recently as 1969. This time, the rescue attempt came from the late Guy Lambert of the SPR. In the SPR *Journal* of June 1969, he analyzed the affair and speaking of Hornby said: ". . . he would not withdraw any detail of his account of the experience, of which he had a vivid memory . . . The solution of this 'imbroglio' is relatively simple." And what was Lambert's solution? It involved the following line of reasoning:

The certain date is that of the death of the journalist Hugh Lang, whose apparition the Judge saw . . . that was on 19th January, 1875 . . . But the correspondent from Shanghai said they (the Hornbys) were not married until 29th April 1875. The Judge's bride was an American lady, and the couple presented themselves for marriage both to the British Consul and to the U.S. Consul, presumably sometime in 1874, and considered themselves married, no doubt setting up house together accordingly. They were both eligible, he being a widower since December 1873 and she a spinster. But they had not reckoned with "red tape," and overlooked the fact that, each party being a foreigner in relation to the other, neither the British Consul nor the U.S. Consul could complete the arrangement, and it was some months before they could get married in Church ("North China Herald," etc. 1st May, 1875). The disclosure of this nine years later in England was naturally inconvenient, and of course Gurney did all in his power to stop *further* circulation of the story, and took more than his fair share of the blame for what had occurred, in the interests of the Judge and his wife.

Thus, the story was stopped, not because it proved untrue, but because it proved socially embarrassing.

This attempted defense is ingenious but quite unacceptable. The Judge's account does not stand or fall on the backing given by his relations. He claimed that the time and place of Lang's death had been confirmed by the court usher, a magistrate, Lang's family and a coroner's inquest. He claimed that he'd seen Lang's notebook, with the beginnings of the evidential judgment. Yet, all of these claims were found to be false.

But the most unpleasant thing of all about this defense is that Guy Lambert knew it to be untrue. On May 22, 1962, he wrote to Dr. Eric Dingwall, saying, "I then went to the G.R.O. (General Register Office) and obtained the enclosed marriage certificate which is of interest.

"It shows that Hornby married his third wife before the Consul on the same day (29th April 1875) that he was married in church there. This knocks on the head my surmise that the civil marriage might have preceded the church marriage by some weeks."

So it looks as if illusion breeds illusion which again breeds illusion!

Perhaps the happiest way to wind up this whole unsavory affair is to allow Hornby to have his longed-for epitaph. For back in 1884, he wrote: "Please see that on my tomb-stone is graven:

HERE LIES A LIAR
UNCONSCIOUS OF UNTRUTH
SHOULD HE BECOME A BRIAR
ITS TANGLED TWIGS
WILL TYPIFY HIS MIND."

22

MEET ME AT MIDNIGHT!

Could a coffin develop a homing instinct? That's a problem worth considering. For strangely enough, there's such a case in the super-normal archives. It rests alongside a group of allied tales. They're all about the drive of the dead to return to a loved one, a close friend, or even a precious place.

One of the best known is that of Lord Brougham. It involves a youthful friendship that defied death, time and place. In 1799, when he was twenty-one, Brougham was travelling through Sweden. He reached an inn on the road to Gothenburg, hired a room and tired and cold, sank into a hot bath. By then, it was about one in the morning. As he soaked and relaxed, he idly glanced at the chair where he'd dumped his clothes. He was then severely shocked to see an old school and college friend sitting silently on the chair, calmly looking at him.

Brougham next found himself out of the bath sprawled on the floor, as if he'd fallen into a faint. The apparition, or whatever it was, had vanished. Later Brougham reflected on the unnerving event. At college his friend and he had often discussed the immortality of the soul. What did the future state have in store? Could the dead appear to the living? At one time they'd gone beyond speculation and drawn up an agreement written in their own blood. In this pact, they vowed that who ever died first should appear to the other. In that way the problem of survival would be resolved.

After leaving college, their two paths diverged. His friend joined the Indian Civil Service, while Brougham stayed put in Europe.

This unique vision seemed to mark the fulfilment of the blood-pact. His friend must have died far off in India, and his sudden appearance had to be seen as a proof of an after-life. All this happened, according to Brougham's *Memoirs,* on Deember 19, 1799.

When drafting his memoirs, in October 1862, Brougham added this: "I have just been copying out from my journal the account of this strange event . . . And now to finish the story begun about sixty years since. Soon after my return to Edinburgh there arrived a letter from

India announcing G . . .s death, and stating that he died on December 19th."

This story has often been repeated. It seems a clear case of an apparition appearing at the exact time of death. An apparition motivated to fulfill a solemn promise. And yet there isn't the slightest reason for accepting it as truthful.

The journal Brougham quotes from is always taken to refer to as a record made at the time of the event. But careful examination shows that it was written sometime *afterwards*. Its wording is in the past tense, for example: "One day I had taken a hot bath . . . I had no inclination to talk about it, or to speak about it . . ."

Then, since the story was "begun about sixty years since", that would put the journal account at roughly three years after the event. Still, is there any independent proof of any sort?

Well, Brougham didn't tell his companion Stewart, at the time, neither did he tell anyone else. Then he constantly referred to his friend as G——, even as late as 1862. There was no possible reason for keeping this cloak of anonymity. But by concealing the name Brougham prevented any accurate check on his story taking place.

But then, Brougham was that kind of man. Lord John Russell observed that Brougham had an obstinate disregard for the truth. Chambers' biography went further, speaking of his; ". . . arrogance, self-confidence and eccentricities which sometimes verged on insanity . . ." As for his memoirs, well that: "was written in extreme old age and is very untrustworthy." His untrustworthiness is never disputed by modern historians.

A rather different problem surrounds the celebrated story of John Donne and the vision of his dead child. It is related by his biographer Walton, who says that he was told it by a close friend of Donne's. Oddly enough, it doesn't appear until the *fourth* edition of his *Lives* in 1675. It has been surmised that the delay was the result of time taken to check that the details were correct.

The account involves Donne's reluctant visit to France in 1612. He'd been asked to accompany the new ambassador, Lord Hay, on his visit of appointment to the French Court. Sir Robert Drury strongly urged him to agree. But Donne's wife was in bad health and heavily pregnant, so at first he refused to consider the idea. Sir Robert continued to press his point and Donne eventually agreed, providing the visit was limited to two months.

It took twelve days to reach Paris from London. Two days later, Sir Robert found Donne in a completely altered state of mind. He sat silently in his room, his face changed, seemingly in a state of shock. Sir Robert was understandably shaken. Yet at first, Donne was unable to speak. He stayed like that for some time, then said, "I have seen a dreadful vision since I saw you: I have seen my dear wife pass twice by me through this room with her hair hanging about her shoulders, and a dead child in her arms."

Sir Robert hastened to comfort him by suggesting that this had been nothing but a melancholy dream. But Donne remained firm. He had not slept and he was sure that at his wife's second appearance, she had stopped and looked him in the face before vanishing.

His stout confidence troubled Sir Robert, who then sent a servant over to England to visit Mrs. Donne and report on her health. Twelve days later the servant returned. He brought sad news. Mrs. Donne was in low spirits and confined to bed. After a dangerous labor her child had been born dead. This death had occurred on the very day and at the very time of the vision witnessed in Paris.

This poignant story was a favorite of W. T. Stead's. It appears in Brian Inglis's *Natural and Supernatural* and in June 1962, it was featured in a piece sent by Professor Ian Stevenson to the *Journal of the SPR*.

I'm grateful to Professor Stevenson for saving me the time and trouble of checking out this story. For in the June 1984 *Journal of the SPR*, he provided a sequel to his earlier piece. He wrote:

> It is almost certain that Donne never had any such vision, and on the grounds that it should never be too late to correct a mistake, I should like to have this noted in the Society's record.
>
> Walton wrote incorrectly about several of the background facts pertinent to Donne's visit to France in 1612. For example, he described the English embassy as being sent to King Henry IV of France; but Henry IV was assassinated in 1610. He said that the English Ambassador was Lord Hay; but Hay was not in fact sent on to an embassy to France until 1616.
>
> These errors weaken confidence in Walton's account of Donne's vision. It receives, however, a more decisive blow from letters that Donne actually wrote from France in April 1612, more than two months after the expected (and actual) date of his wife's delivery. He complained in these of having no news of his wife's delivery, specifically "whether I be increased by childe or diminished by the loss

of a wife". These letters are incompatible with Walton's claim that Donne's vision had been verified almost immediately after it occurred by a messenger sent back to England. . .

Perhaps we'll have more luck with the wonderful wandering coffin. Its history seems to be well backed up by research. Frank Edwards even describes it as "one of the best documented."

Its astounding history first reached international fame round about 1928, after Robert Ripley included it in his syndicated "Believe It Or Not!" series. Headed by the drawing of a coffin, his brief text read— "Charles Coghlan Comes Home! He died in 1899 and was buried in Galveston. When the tragic flood came his coffin was washed out to sea—and the Gulf Stream carried him around Florida and up the coast to Prince Edward Island—2,000 miles distant—where he lived."

The tragic flood he mentions followed the great hurricane which struck Galveston Island on September 8, 1900. Over six thousand people died in the disaster and thousands of buildings were reduced to rubble. The flood waters hammered into the cemeteries, shattered vaults and wrenched coffins out of the earth. Some of the coffins sank, others floated out into the Gulf of Mexico and were scattered in all directions by the waves.

According to the story given to Ripley, actor Charles Coghlan's coffin was one of these. It was caught up by the West Indian currents, carried into the Gulf Stream, drifted around the tip of Florida and began moving northwards. It was presumably buffeted about for years, but its northward progress never ceased. Finally, in October 1908, following a series of gales, it came to rest on the shores of Prince Edward Island. There it was spotted by fishermen who dragged it on to the beach and scraped away the thick crust of barnacles. Under the barnacles they discovered a silver plate screwed to the casket. It was engraved with the words "Charles Francis Coghlan—born 1841, Prince Edward Island, Canada. Died 1899, Galveston, Texas." Charles Coghlan had come home to rest, and with full honors he was buried near the church where he'd been baptized.

When Ripley's potted version appeared in the *Evening Post* (U.S.), it was read by Charles Coghlan's daughter—wife of Augustus Pitou, who was once Coghlan's manager. She was more than intrigued. She had hired men for long periods and spent thousands of dollars on a twenty-seven-year-long search for her father's body.

The Pitous made contact with Robert Ripley and asked him where his information came from. He supplied them with references in books published by Sir Johnston Forbes-Robertson and Lily Langtry.

In Forbes-Robertson's book, *A Play Under Three Reigns* he relates how he took Coghlan from his home on Prince Edward Island to play Mercutio in *Romeo and Juliet* in London. He later adds: "In about a year, I think he died at Galveston. Shortly after his burial there was a great storm come up from the Gulf which swept his coffin, with others, into the sea. The Gulf Stream bore him around Florida, up the coast, about 1,500 miles to Prince Edward Island and he came ashore not far from his home."

Having read the accounts, the Pitous asked Sir Johnston Forbes-Robertson for more clarification. Who gave him the story? Forbes-Robertson then grew rather vague but suggested that they ask George Tyler, who'd been Coghlan's manager at one time. When Tyler was approached he said: "I've heard that story . . . not once but many times . . . close friends of his have told me since of his coffin having been found on Prince Edward Island. It was washed ashore, as I heard it, at Fortune Bridge. . ."

And there the Pitous's involvement seems to melt away. Though logically, it should have led to a grand finale.

The story retreated into limbo for a while, then it was resurrected by the notoriously-inaccurate American broadcaster, the late Frank Edwards. He made it into a piece for radio, and a chapter of a book. It was picked up and enlarged on by Vincent Gaddis. It then became embraced by the strange breed of "Bermuda Triangle" word-spinners.

Richard Winer uses it in his *The Devil's Triangle 2,* and wangles it into the strait-jacket of "Triangle" theory. Then in 1979, Alan Vaughan wove the story into his book *Incredible Coincidence.* From there it crept into the *Daily Express* columns.

It all looks so good and wholesome. Yet something is missing. Where are the newspaper columns reporting the coffin's recovery in October 1908? Where are the records of the reburial? Where are the photographs of the church where he was reinterred? And what does his new tombstone say?

Amazingly, none of these things exist. It's the same pattern all over again. None of the believers, Ripley included, have ever searched the newspaper files and public records of Prince Edward Island.

Had they done so, they would found that the whole story is a fantasy. The fate of Coghlan's coffin is unknown to this very day!

Our last case is in some ways the strangest of all. It was recounted in 1892 by freelance journalist Mr. R. D'Onston. He'd supplied articles to the spiritualist and editor, W. T. Stead, and when he knew that Stead was looking for true ghost stories, he gave him, free of charge, the following convincing account:

To those instances of ghosts who have kept promises made in life to appear to those dear to them, may I add my own experience? The incident occurred to me some years ago, and all the details can be substantiated. The date was August 26th, 1867, at midnight. I was then residing in the neighbourhood of Hull, and held an appointment under the Crown which necessitated my repairing thither every day for a few hours' duty. My berth was almost a sinecure.

I had a love affair with a girl at Hull. I will call her Louise. She was young, beautiful, and devoted to me. On the night of the 26th of August we took our last walk together, and a few minutes before midnight paused on a wooden bridge running across a kind of canal, locally termed a "drain."

We paused on the bridge, listening to the swirling of the current against the wooden piles, and waiting for the stroke of midnight to part for ever. In the few minutes' interval she repeated sotto voce, Longfellow's Bridge, the words of which, "I stood on the bridge at midnight," seemed terribly appropriate. After nearly twenty-five years I can never hear that piece recited without feeling a deathly chill and the whole scene of two souls in agony again arising before me.

Well! midnight struck, and we parted; but Louise said: "Grant me one favour, the only one that I shall ever ask you on this earth: promise to meet me here twelve months tonight at this same hour." I demurred at first, thinking it would be bad for both of us, and only reopen partially healed wounds. At last, however, I consented, saying: "Well, I will come if I am alive!" but she said: "Say alive or dead!" I said: "Very well then, we will meet dead or alive."

The next year I was on the spot a few minutes before the time, and punctual to the stroke of midnight Louise arrived. By this time I had begun to regret the arrangement I had made; but it was of too solemn a nature to be put aside. I therefore kept the appointment, but said that I did not care to renew the compact. Louise, however, persuaded me to renew it for one more year, and I consented, much against my will; and we again left each other, repeating the same formula: "Dead or alive."

The next year after that passed rapidly for me until the first week in July, when I was shot dangerously in the thigh. . .

As soon as I was able to be removed (two or three weeks) I was taken home, where Dr. Kelburne King, of Hull, attended me. The day—and *the* night—(the 26th August) came. I was then unable to walk without crutches, and that for only a short distance, so had to be wheeled about in a Bath chair. The distance to the trysting place being rather long, and the time and circumstances being very peculiar, I did not avail myself of the services of my usual attendant, but specially retained an old servant of the family, who frequently did confidential commissions for me, and who knew Miss Louise very well.

We set forth "without beat of drum," and arrived at the bridge about a few minutes to midnight. I remember that it was a brilliant starlight night, but I did not think that there was any moon . . . "Old Bob," as he was always affectionately called, wheeled me to the bridge, helped me out of the Bath chair, and gave me my crutch. I walked on to the bridge, and leaned my back against the white painted top rail, then lighted my briar-root, and had a comfortable smoke.

I was very much annoyed that I had allowed myself to be persuaded to come a second time, and determined to tell "Louise" positively that this should be the last meeting. So, if anything, it was in rather a sulky frame of mind that I awaited Louise. Just as the quarter before the hour began to chime I distinctly heard the "clink, clink" of the little brass heels, which she always wore, sounding on the long flagged causeway, leading for 200 yards up to the bridge. As she got nearer I could see her pass lamp after lamp in rapid succession, while the strokes of the large clock at Hull resounded through the stilly night.

At last the patter, patter of the tiny feet sounded on the wood-work of the bridge, and I saw her distinctly pass under the lamp at the farther end—it was only twenty yards wide, and I stood under the lamp at my side. When she got close to me I saw that she had neither hat nor cape on, and concluded that she had taken a cab to the farther end of the flagged causeway, and (it being a very warm night) had left her wraps in the cab, and for purposes of effect had come the short distance in evening dress.

"Clink, clink," went the brass heels, and she seemed about passing me, when I, suddenly urged by an impulse of affection, stretched out my arms to receive her. She passed *through* them, intangible, impalpable, and as she looked at me distinctly I saw her lips move, and form the words: "Dead or alive." I even *heard* the words, but not with my outward ears, with something else, some other sense—what I know not. I felt startled, but not afraid, until a moment afterwards, then my blood seemed turned to ice.

Recovering myself with an effort, I shouted out to "Old Bob," who was safely ensconced with the Bath chair in a nook out of sight round the corner: "Bob, who passed you just now?" In an instant the old Yorkshireman was by my side. "Ne'er a one passed me, sir!" "Nonsense, Bob," I replied. "I told you that I was coming to meet Miss Louise, and she just passed me on the bridge, and *must* have passed you, because there's nowhere else she *could* go! You don't mean to tell me you didn't see her?" The old man replied solemnly: "Maister Ros, there's something uncanny about it. I heerd her come on the bridge, and off it, I'd knaw them clickety heels onywhere; but I'm henged, sir, if she passed me. I'm thinking we'd better gang." And "gang" we did; and it was the small hours of the morning (getting daylight) before we left off talking over the affair and went to bed.

The next day I made inquiries from Louise's family about her, and ascertained that she had died in Liverpool three months previously, being apparently delirious for a few hours before her death, and our parting compact evidently weighing on her mind, as she kept repeating "Dead or alive! Shall I be there?" to the utter bewilderment of her friends, who could not divine her meaning, being of course entirely unaware of our agreement.

As it stands, this is a story of considerable charm, probably the best of its kind. But true? Well, Stead and his daughter believed it to be. Indeed, Estelle Stead gave a copy of ths narrative to the Reverend C. L. Tweedale for inclusion in his book *Man's Survival After Death*. Its publication by Tweedale ensured a wide readership for the tale. And over the past ninety or so years, not a breath of suspicion has surrounded it. And then, I started probing!

There was something vaguely familiar about D'Onston's story and about D'Onston himself. Yet I knew this familiarity had nothing to do with my research into the paranormal. My files were raked through systematically and two distinctly different paths interlocked.

In 1930, Fleet Street crime-reporter Bernard O'Donnell began looking back at the crimes of Jack the Ripper. He'd been given a tip that an old lady in Balham had something new to add to the saga. The lady was a Baroness Vittoria Cremers, a theosophist and a former friend and companion of writer Mabel Collins.

O'Donnell called on her and wrote down her revelations. They centered around a man who'd once written for the *Pall Mall Gazette*— Stead's paper. This journalist's name was Stephenson, but he wrote under the name *Tautriadelta*—a name which had links with black magic cults. Stephenson lived in a lively swirl of fantasy. He'd claimed he'd studied magic with Sir Edward Bulwer Lytton, studied chemistry at the University of Giessen, then carried out successful Doppelganger experiments! After that, he'd joined Garibaldi's army as a medical officer and visited India to observe the methods of the fakirs.

In 1888, he became so obsessed by the Jack the Ripper murders that he became an object of suspicion. When he roomed with Cremers and Collins he talked about the murders so often and in such detail that they became convinced that he *was* the Ripper. Oddly, even W. T. Stead thought so for a while. It was this suspicion that made the two ladies acutely conscious of everything he said and did. In his dealings with them, though, he dropped the commonplace name Stevenson and used a more exotic aristocratic-looking name—he called himself Dr. Roslyn D'Onston!

One of the curious tales that stayed in their memory involved his shattered romance with a young lady called Ada. In 1930, Vittoria Cremers revealed that story:

As a young man D'Onston held a commission in the army. He came from a fairly well off yeoman family, and it was generally understood that he would marry the daughter of a wealthy neighbouring family who was very much in love with him. However, on one of his jaunts to town with some of his brother officers, he met a woman of the streets named Ada. He began to visit her regularly, fell in love with her and, Gissing-like, determined to marry her and take her away from her miserable life.

Understandably, his family was appalled. His father cut off his allowance. Always a gambler, D'Onston lost a lot of money at the tables one night, and, unable to pay his debts, was forced to seek his father's help. His father agreed to discharge those debts—on one condition. That he undertook to end his association with Ada and marry the heiress. Reluctantly, D'Onston agreed.

And so D'Onston and Ada parted, but not before they had made a solemn pledge that, whatever happened, dead or alive, they would meet at midnight on the anniversary of their parting at the place where they had first met—the middle of Westminster Bridge.

Then—tragedy. Within an hour of D'Onston's departure, Ada walked to Westminster Bridge and threw herself into the river.

True to his vow, D'Onston kept his tryst with the dead woman on Westminster Bridge. He leant over the parapet where Ada had flung herself to her death twelve months before. As the chimes of Big Ben sounded, he heard the click-clack of heels coming towards him. He saw nothing, no one, but he knew that Ada, too, had kept her promise.

And there we have it. The touching tryst at midnight resolves itself into a tear-jerking fantasy dreamed up by a man whose whole life was make-believe. His background was a humble one, not the well-off one he'd boasted about. His medical qualifications were bogus. Even his claims to know the identity of Jack the Ripper were derisively rejected by the police.

To the Steads he offered the gentle version of his tryst tale; while Cremers and Collins were entertained by the more earthly version.

And as those imaginary heels click off into fairyland, I'll bet that someone, somewhere, is at this very moment cooking up a brand new hoax to keep peoples' spines a-tingling. In the meantime—have you heard the one about the man who got stuck in a treacle-mine?

NOTES

Chapter 1

1. I first exposed "The Amityville Horror" in the former magazine *Alpha.* When the film of the book was launched in Britain, Fleet Street journalist Dan Slater learned of my work and invited me to meet the publicity people boosting the film. We met at lunch. The Lutzes' publicity agent considered what I had to say and declared that the Lutzes would be quite happy to meet me when they reached Britain. As it turned out, this was a rather naive view, for I'd made it clear that I wished to meet the Lutzes face-to-face on radio and TV programs and present them with the accumulated evidence of their complete unreliability. In the meantime, Dan Slater considered the case I had presented against the Lutzes and in the *Sunday People,* January 1980, he wrote an article debunking the film.

When the Lutzes reached London, they read my article and Dan's and decided that it would be far too dangerous to meet someone who knew the background of their story. My invitation to attend the movie premiere was withdrawn. My phone calls to the publicity agents were not replied to. And the Lutzes hopped around from place to place making sure that they spoke to no one who was well informed! In this shabby way they escaped—but only for a while.

In 1982, the sequel, *Amityville II,* was published and I received a review copy. Here again was the same old tiresome nonsense and the same old cynical disregard for impressionable readers. But they went too far. Their twenty-fifth chapter gave a lying account of their appearance on the "Tonight" program of the BBC. On that program they were interviewed by my friend, the now deceased Dr. Anita Gregory. The account of the interview in this chapter was an arrogant and gross libel on Anita. It bore no relationship whatsoever to the real interview—which fortunately, was preserved on videotape. Everything in the chapter was rigged to make George Lutz look like some sort of saintly hero confronted by a vicious, back-biting creature, described as a vulture.

They even dragged in the representative of Pan Books as an alleged witness to the interview, writing of her—"Bravo, she thought. George and I may have some friction of our own, but he does know how to handle these vultures in close combat."

Dr. Gregory brought an action against the Lutzes. Pan Books backed her up by repudiating the alleged role played by their representative. The

BBC ran the tapes of the interview and provided a transcript. As a result, the Lutzes apologized for the libel, paid damages to Dr. Gregory, and the book was withdrawn.

Since then, this flagrantly dishonest book has been reissued with a new chapter 25 minus the invented interview. For no matter what happens, the pursuit of cash is more important to such people than any pangs of conscience—but then, I doubt if the Lutzes worry too much about anything as trivial as that.

2. In the United States the Lutzes have also run into trouble. They have tried their best to avoid exposure by refusing to meet intelligent investigators. Peter Jordan and Rick Moran, who actually made revealing on-the-spot checks, have repeatedly tried to interview the Lutzes. But their letters were never answered, neither were their phone calls. However, the Lutzes were not able to avoid the legal action brought against them by Jim and Barbara Cromarty, present owners of the Ocean Avenue house. Their action charged that the book was a hoax which had damaged their lives because of the sensation-hungry creatures who'd been drawn to the place by the Lutzes' fiction. The suits were settled in the Cromartys' favour. According to Clarence Peterson (*Chicago Tribune,* September 23, 1982), they received a six-figure sum in settlement. Peterson goes on to say, "The Cromartys are happy at home; the imaginary demons are long gone; and as Ed Lowe puts it, the Wackos, the card-carrying certifiable organised lunatics who descended upon Amityville in 1976, finally have dwindled to a precious few—at least until *Amityville II* comes out."

And Ed Lowe, *Newsday* columnist, adds this: "It had to have been a setup since Day One. The day after the Lutzes fled, supposedly in terror, they returned to hold a garage sale—just lots of junk. It was obvious they hadn't moved in there with anything worth anything. And during the entire 28-day siege that drove them from the house, they never once called the police."

Chapter 4

1. A cool appraisal of psychic detectives shows that they often make use of an artful dodge. They make claims about events that have happened in far-off places. This makes it extra-difficult to check on newspaper and other reports. Interviewing people is often out of the question. For example, Doris Stokes in Britain has claimed that she was able to help the Baltimore County Police in a case involving the disappearance of teenager Jamie Griffin. But a statement by Colonel Joseph A. Shaw, chief of Field Operations of the Baltimore County Police Department in Towson, Maryland, U.S., refutes her claims. It reads:

Ms. Stokes was making an appearance in Baltimore and attracted the attention of Mrs. Griffin, whose 17 year old son, Jamie, has been missing under suspicious circumstances since April 2, 1982. Mrs. Griffin made contact with Ms. Stokes and discussed her son's disappearance. The next day we made contact with Ms. Stokes in company with and at the request of Mrs. Griffin. Ms. Stokes did not go to the Gunpowder State Park. We had earlier dug up 24 acres of the park in search of the missing person's body. Ms. Stokes was aware of this. She was never at the park. She visualized the empty grave. We dug numerous acres with negative results. Ms. Stokes was given maps by our Department. Ms. Stokes did not contribute any useful or informative information nor did she supply any new information which could not have been given her by the Griffin family or by newspaper articles printed prior to her visit. Everything she told us was after she had extensive conversations with Griffin relatives and had access to newspaper files collected by the Griffin family.

In Britain itself her claims are just as suspect. In her book *Voices In My Ear,* chapter eleven, she describes at length how she was involved usefully in the police investigation of the murder of a girl at Kirkham, in Lancashire, and the murders of three youngsters found dead in the children's ward of Blackpool's Victoria Hospital. If you believe her, she actually told the detectives who the ward murderer was and told them that if they acted fast they'd find him in the hospital's operating theater. The murderer, in fact, was a surgeon at the hospital. But was he identified by Mrs. Stokes?

This is what Detective Chief Superintendent Brian Woods of the Lancashire Constabulary Headquarters at Preston has to say: "I can confirm that Mrs. Stokes made no contribution whatever to the detection of either the murder of the children at Blackpool or the girl at Kirkham."

2. In Australia psychic detective Zandra-Marie is approaching newspapers with claims of her marvelous successes with crime cases in Britain. Among her absurd assertions is one which involves the Yorkshire Ripper. She says that eleven days before the police arrested Peter Sutcliffe she had visited the graves of his victims and drawn an exact sketch of the murderer. She gave this sketch to the police and as a result they were able to make their arrest. The facts are, that no portrait—whether artist's impression, psychically-inspired, or photo-fit, played the slightest part in the arrest of Peter Sutcliffe. His arrest came after police had been monitoring motorists who took on board prostitutes. His parked car was spotted. The police observers checked his license plates with their national computer records and discovered that he was using false license plates. He was taken to the police station for questioning and, later, the grounds near his parked car were searched and his murder weapons came to light. Following that, Sutcliffe confessed.

3. An illuminating, "successful" psychic detective story appeared in the May 1983 issue of *Fate* magazine. An eighty-two-year-old psychic, Ann Hunt, led searchers along the banks of the San Joaquin river looking for missing

nine-year-old Steven Brown. He'd disappeared over six weeks before on August 23, 1982. The body was found on the river bank, but, strangely enough, the psychic messages that led to the discovery were not picked up by Ann Hunt. They were intercepted, so it seems, by Jackie Skeels, the girlfriend of the boy's father.

The search party had dug in several spots unsuccessfuly and searched through bushes in vain. Jackie, in the meantime, went along the bank making her own search. In about fifteen minutes she returned, crying hysterically. She said that she'd heard Steven's voice crying: "Daddy, find me. Daddy, I'm here." She then led the party along the river and every now and again stopped as if listening. Eventually Steven's body was found partly hidden under vines. And that, it seemed, was a successful conclusion to a tragic hunt.

It turned out, though, that there was much more to it. The November issue of *Fate* published a letter from Helen McCay, of Fresno, California. She pointed out that Jackie Skeels hardly had a psychic experience. She knew exactly where the dead boy's body would be located. That's why she'd been found guilty of first-degree murder. Steven had been drowned by her.

Chapter 6

1. Some readers might feel that my unravelling of Nella Jones's thought processes is far-fetched. After all, I can't see into her mind. Agreed. But we do know enough of the workings and vagaries of the mind to make worthwhile judgments.

In considering her claims I started by asking just what *was* available to her in the form of books, photographs, newspaper, television and radio reports. Having located this material, I then examined it just as she had. Some of her pronouncements were traced to their common-knowledge sources at once. The more obscure pieces—things like the "Ainsworth" name became clear after a second, slower examination.

It is indisputable that mediums do find "future forecasts" by examining the patterns of the past and present. Cheiro did it often—I've given some examples.

If anything, I've understated my case. The tortured wanglings they indulge in are even more convoluted and grotesque than I've shown. Consider this excellent example of the way that psychic Alan Vaughan has tried to hijack the past in the interest of soothsaying.

After the assassination of Robert Kennedy in June 1968, Vaughan began thinking about the assassin, Sirhan Sirhan. He sets down his chain of reasoning in his *Patterns of Prophecy*. He begins: "'What will be Sirhan's fate? Could it be foretold by synchronistic links with annother assassin?' Those were questions I asked myself as Sirhan's trial for the assassination of Robert Kennedy began. I looked through the records of assassination: Charles Guiteau, assassin of President Garfield . . . no; Leon Czolgosz, assassin of President McKinley . . . no; but then, there he was—John Schrank, who attempted to assassinate another presidential candidate of another famous family, Theodore Roosevelt. . . ."

The attempted assassination of Theodore Roosevelt took place on October 24, 1912. Roosevelt was saved by the bulky folded speech in his breast pocket, together with the cover of his metal spectacle case. These absorbed the energy of the bullet leaving him shaken, and with a fractured rib. For Vaughan, time is swept to one side. The radical differences between this event and the Kennedy shooting are ignored and he goes on to say:

> Synchronistic parallels seem to link Schrank and Sirhan in an archetypal pattern of assassination:
> • Both shootings took place at night at a hotel during campaigning for the presidency.
> • In both shootings the weapon was a revolver.
> • Both victims made a speech the night of their shooting.
> • Both assailants were immigrants, Schrank from Germany, Sirhan from Jordan.
> • Both Schrank and Sirhan were unusually short, and both were bachelors.
> • Both Schrank and Sirhan were loners. Schrank said: "I never had a friend in my life." Sirhan said: "Sirhan means wolf, and I became more and more of a lone wolf."
> • Both Schrank and Sirhan were tackled by football players immediately after the shooting, narrowly escaping being lynched. Provocatively, one of Sirhan's tacklers was *Roosevelt* Grier.
> Even the very names of Schrank and Sirhan are similar having five common letters. But already credulity is strained by the search for synchronisities—if indeed these coincidental parallels are. The test for that lies in the future, in the final fate of Sirhan Sirhan. If this pattern of assassination is prophetic, then his fate should correspond to Schrank's. . . . If the parallel goes further, it may even be shown that like Schrank, whose bullets were nonfatal, Sirhan's too were nonfatal—that is, the fatal bullet fired from behind Kennedy's head was fired by someone else.

All this is enough to leave one speechless—so I rest my case!

2. Another factor needs to be underlined. Two or more unrelated events, words, or pictures may be perceived on different occasions and yet all of them will lead to just one resting point in the brain. In the case of the odd name from nowhere—"Ainsworth"—I have shown the strongest leads to that name. There might well have been others that helped reinforce the name. For example, at the time when Nella Jones was involved with the Genette Tate case, there was a book on sale and display called *The Phantom Cyclist*. It was a book of ghost stories and its eerie cover depicts a wraithlike figure in shorts on a bicycle. The cyclist could be either a young boy or a tomboy.

In the story a young boy cycles along a country lane, passes two other boys, then disappears completely. Later on his abandoned, wrecked bicycle is found. In the Tate case something very similar happened. Genette cycled past two of her friends, then disappeared completely, leaving her bike sprawled in the hedge of a country lane.

This eye-catching book with its prompting title was written by—Ruth Ainsworth!

Mrs. Jones could also have picked up a link from her very involvement with the *Yorkshire Post*. For, strangely enough (something that's not even hinted at in her book), one of the *Yorkshire Post Group* reporters was named Richard Hainsworth. Believe it or not, he is the son of Magistrate Peter Hainsworth, in whose grounds Sutcliffe strangled Marguerite Walls!

3. Though a great deal of mediumship involves conscious planning, I accept that often mediums are deceived by the caprices of their own sub-conscious minds. At those times they honestly don't know where their visions, words, or forebodings come from. This happens to Nella Jones. She records that at one point she saw a sneering face hovering in front of her eyes and the word "Dudley" written underneath. "Even now" she says, "I am unable to explain the significance of that one word."

Yet, there's an obvious significance. She starts off with Bradford in mind. In 1976, enormous publicity surrounded the trial of *another* Bradford murderer. This was Donald Neilson, who'd been dubbed the "Black Panther." For almost a year before Neilson's arrest, his murderous exploits were common knowledge. In that year he shot Gerald Smith at the Freightliner Terminal at Dudley, and kidnapped Lesley Whittle. Later the kidnap car was found abandoned in Dudley. Dudley then became the center for the police search headquarters. The bizarre kidnapping, imprisonment and tragic death of Lesley Whittle kept the name of Dudley constantly before the public eye.

4. After hearing the tape sent by the hoax "Ripper," Nella phoned Shirley Davenport of the *Yorkshire Post*. Nella had woken up with a strong sense of foreboding. She felt the Ripper had traveled south of Manchester and some-thing was about to happen. Nothing did happen. Nella had failed to realize that her subconscious had fed her false clues. For on the tape she'd listened to, the hoaxer had boasted: "I will strike again . . . I am not sure where, maybe Manchester."

A similar thing happened when she was thinking over the Genette Tate case. She records that she heard a voice, ". . . saying clearly over and over: 'Find Genette'." This psychic message however, was simply a repetition of the exact wording of the car stickers issued in their thousands by the police force.

These examples show, again, how already existing knowledge can be imagined as psychically inspired and as a forewarning.

5. I have asserted that, in the case of Jacqueline Hill, pure coincidence has helped make Mrs. Jones's predictions look sensational. It could be thought that my introduction of the element of coincidence is simply an

easy solution to a vexing problem. On the contrary, coincidences can be found in so many cases of crime that this is just one of the many factors one has to be on guard against. Some examples from the Ripper case will make this clear.

For those who see significance in everything, note that the same Ripper story appears on page 115 of Nella Jones's book and page 115 of Michael Nicholson's book. Meaningless? Of course. Next note that Ripper victim, Yvonne Parson, had shared a flat just a few hundred yards away from Sutcliffe's house in Heaton, Bradford.

His next victim, Helen Rytka, was murdered in Huddersfield, over ten miles south of Bradford. Yet, she had not only once lived in Bradford, but had frequently visited Tanton Crescent at the time when Ripper Sutcliffe was living there. Even stranger, she'd actually been a guest at the house *next door* to the Sutcliffes. This incredible state of affairs all came about because she'd made friends with a girl who happened to be related to Ronnie Barker, Sutcliffe's neighbor.

Coincidences abound but have no meaning or significance. This can be demonstrated by the Victorian Jack the Ripper murders, where strings of such coincidences have led to some dozen or more people being branded as *the* culprit.

Chapter 7

1. Many spiritualists will undoubtedly protest that Lees was a saintly creature who'd never indulge in fantasies or lies—so it's worth noting that he never publicly repudiated the false claims made in the Chicago article. In that way he gained himself a false renown and gave respectability to blatant untruths. And it must be recorded that he made false claims himself about his involvement in police investigations.

He told his daughter Eva that, in 1883, when ". . . acting as a guide for some American visitors, taking them around places of interest in London, he heard a voice telling him to report them to the Yard. He did so several times before the police would listen. Then he was seen by Sir John (sic) Anderson who knew him. He told Sir John they were staying in Villiers Street. They were arrested. One of them was the notorious Irish Revolutionary, Dr. Gallagher." (Interview with Dr. D. J. West of SPR 10 November 1948.) In checking out his claim we find that Dr. Gallagher arrived in London on Easter Monday, March 26, 1883 and booked into room 312 of the Charing Cross Hotel under the alias "Fletcher." He toured Westminster—on his own—on the twenty-seventh to finalize plans for a Fenian bombing campaign. Prior to his arrival a member of his team, James Murphy, had opened a paint shop at 128 Ledsam Street, Ladywood, Birmingham on February 6. He used the alias "Alfred George Whitehead."

A third member of the team, calling himself Wilson, rented a room at 17 Nelson Square, Blackfriars. From there he wrote to Whitehead in Birmingham on April 2.

Whitehead busied himself buying large quantities of chemically pure glycerine—a necessary plus for the nitroglycerine bombs he had in mind. These uncommon purchases aroused the suspicion of George Pritchard—a storeman with the suppliers. He shrewdly guessed that the glycerine wasn't being used to make hair-oil, Whitehead's bluff. He began checking up on Whitehead and found enough incongruities to go to the police.

The police used skeleton keys to enter and search the shop at 2 A.M. on April 2. They left knowing that they'd found a bomb factory, but since they wanted to capture the whole gang, they simply posted men to watch the place.

The gang began to move the nitro on April 4. For a while the police lost track of the member who was carting 200 pounds of the stuff. So they swooped down on Whitehead and found Wilson's letter with its address in Blackfriars.

The London police were informed and they waited at Nelson Square for Wilson to return. When he turned up, Dr. Gallagher was with him, and both were arrested. Finally, the complete team was brought to trial and imprisoned.

So, the arrests were due to the alertness of the storeman, George Pritchard and owed nothing to Lees's "supernormal insights." And the assertion that Lees had assisted Anderson five years prior to the Whitechapel murders is exposed as sheer bunkum. If it had been true, then Lees would have had an impeccable reputation among the police and would have had no trouble in winning a hearing in 1888.

2. In June 1981, I gave the late Maurice Barbanell a sporting chance to repudiate this story if he wished—but he was quite happy to stick with it. When I asked him if he'd ever seen the famous "document" he replied: "I do not know what happened to the document dictated by R. J. Lees. It was in the possession of his daughter for some time, but she has now passed on. I never saw it, but one of my colleagues, Arthur Findlay, did so. He said it confirmed all we had written in *Psychic News.*" (Letter July 1, 1981)

Yet, as I've shown, there never was such a document. (Even Eva Lees, herself, said so.) That explains why Maurice Barbanell's most lengthy account (in *Cavalcade*) was little more than a reworded version of the *Express* articles.

So, Findlay and Barbanell, two of the outstanding leaders in British Spiritualism, both endorsed this spurious history without making any precautionary checks. They then used it to add luster to their movement.

3. The Lees story was inevitably resurrected in *Psychic News* and tied in with "psychic information" about the Yorkshire Ripper. And it's been given a further boost by being incorporated in the 1979 film *Murder By Decree*—a Sherlock Holmes adventure in which Lees is a vital character!

4. All the evidence points to the mischievious *Chicago Times-Herald*

article as being one of the products of two American Bohemian Clubs. The introduction came from William Greer Harrison of the San Francisco Bohemian Club, while the bulk of the article was concocted in Chicago's own Bohemian Club—a club so infatuated with the Ripper murders that it even called itself "The Whitechapel Club." James Milne writes of it:

> In Chicago, I was taken to a Whitechapel Club, which the literary and artistic Bohemians had so christened, because it sported an atmosphere of the "horrible and awful," as well as kindly hospitality. In particular it invited "all stories" from its members, and then it shouted them down with a weird chorus, of which one verse ran:
>
> > In the days of old Rameses; are you on?
> > They told the same thing, they told the same thing
> > In the days of old Rameses; the story had paresis—
> > Are you on, are you on, are you on?
> > [*A Window in Fleet Street,* 1931]

Chapter 10

1. Among supplementary "evidence" brought forward in 1915, was a tale which plainly had no connection with Machen's fiction. This spoke of a "Comrade in White" who roamed the Front bringing succour to the dying and wounded. The Comrade was immune to shell and bullet alike—clearly a supernatural being.

Two different versions of this tale were included in *On The Side Of The Angels,* one alleged by Begbie to have been sent home ". . . by a distinguished British officer, who took it down from the soldier's own lips, a man named Casey." The basic story was a moving one that ended with George Casey saying to the Comrade, "'You are wounded too,' . . . he answered gently: 'This is an old wound, but it has troubled me of late.' And then I noticed sorrowfully that the same cruel mark was on his feet. You will wonder that I did not know sooner. I wonder myself. But it was only when I saw His feet that I knew Him." So Christ himself had been there, on the pitiless battlefields. The testimony was inescapable.

But the full truth was revealed in October 1915, when the British publishers, H. R. Allenson, brought out a volume of stories by W. H. Leathem. It was called, *The Comrade In White,* and included the full text of George Casey's statement. This was the origin of all the subsequent versions and, once again, it was simply dramatic fiction—a short story which had first appeared in the June number of *Life and Work.* In his book's preface, Leathem showed how the story was being misrepresented and wrote: "It is essential therefore, to say that the contents of this little book are of no evidential value whatsoever."

Regrettably, the American public never had the chance to know of this warning. When Leathem's book was published in the U.S. in 1916—by the Fleming H. Revell Co.—his disclaimer was not included in the text.

2. There's one seamy aspect of this affair which it would be dishonest to conceal. The fact is that the legend was often *forced* on wounded soldiers by sensation-seeking women. These haunted the hospital wards in search of strange thrills and satisfactions. They were a peculiar breed whose deep, hidden frustrations had been brought out by the tensions of war.

Vera Brittain, for one, observed their behavior at close quarters: "Sister J. came in and told us about some very bad cases of wounded from Neuve Chapelle . . . After that the ladies seemed to try to outdo one another in telling of war horrors . . . In those days I knew, of course, nothing of psychology . . . I was still too young to realise how much vicarious excitement the War provided for frustrated women cut off from vision and opportunity in small provincial towns, or to understand that the deliberate contemplation of horror and agony might strangely compensate a thwarted nature for the very real grief of having no one at the Front for whom to grieve" (*Testament of Youth,* p. 103).

Such women were quick to press the wounded for tales of supernatural signs and portents. All too often semiliterate men from rough backgrounds found that they could become the focus of "posh" female interest simply by confirming or repeating the yarns that these ladies eagerly thrust at them.

3. Twelve years after the end of the war the inventive were still churning out fresh legends about Mons. For in February 1930, Colonel Friedrich Herzenwirth, described as an ex-officer of the Imperial German Intelligence Service, wrote a newspaper article which claimed that the Angels had definitely appeared at Mons. But they had been nothing but motion-picture images beamed onto the cloudbanks by German aircraft equipped with enormously powerful Zeiss projectors. The initial idea was to create panic among the British, but it had misfired and brought hope instead. However, this scheme *had* worked well against the Allies on the Russian Front. And there ". . . entire regiments who had beheld the vision fell on their knees and flung away their rifles." Within days of this claim, a spokesman from the German War Ministry declared that the story was a hoax—what's more, there was no such person as ex-Colonel Herzenwirth of Army Intelligence, either!

4. One remarkable statement, published in the *Evening News* on September 14, 1915, was taken by some as providing oblique proof of supernatural activities during the retreat. This account, from a lieutenant-colonel at the front, read:

> On August 26th, 1914, was fought the battle of Le Cateau. We came into action at dawn, and fought till dusk. We were heavily shelled by the German artillery during the day, and in common with the rest of our division had a bad time of it.
>
> Our division however retired in good order. We were on the march all night of the 26th and on the 27th with only about two hours' rest.

The brigade to which I belong was rearguarded to the division, and during the 27th we took up a great many different positions to cover the retirement of the rest of the division, so that we had very hard work and by the night of the 27th we were all absolutely worn out with fatigue—both bodily and mental fatigue.

No doubt we also suffered to a certain extent from shock; but the retirement still continued in excellent order, and I feel sure that our mental faculties were still . . . in good working condition.

On the night of the 27th I was riding along in the column with two other officers. We had been talking and doing our best to keep from falling asleep on our horses.

As we rode along I became conscious of the fact that, in the fields on both sides of the road along which we were marching, I could see a very large body of horsemen.

These horsemen had the appearance of squadrons of cavalry, and they seemed to be riding across the fields and going in the same direction as we were going, and keeping level with us. . . .

I did not say a word about it at first, but I watched them for about twenty minutes. The other two officers had stopped talking.

At last one of them asked me if I saw anything in the fields.I then told him what I had seen. The third officer then confessed that he too had been watching these horsemen for the past twenty minutes.

So convinced were we that they were real cavalry that, at the next halt, one of the officers took a party of men out to reconnoitre, and found no one there. The night then grew darker, and we saw no more.

The same phenomenon was seen by many men in our column. Of course we were all dog-tired and overtaxed, but it is an extraordinary thing that the same phenomenon should be witnessed by so many different people.

I myself am absolutely convinced that I saw these horsemen; and I feel sure that they did not exist only in my imagination. . . ."

Yet, you only have to compare that account with the one that follows to see that such phantom horsemen were part of the hallucinatory experiences arising from extreme stress and grinding fatigue. It was provided by Lance-Corporal A. Johnstone, Royal Engineers, and appeared in the *Evening News* on August 11, 1915.

We had almost reached the end of the retreat, and, after marching a whole day and night with but one half-hour's rest in between, we found ourselves on the outskirts of Langy, near Paris, just at dawn, and as the day broke we saw in front of us large bodies of cavalry, all formed up into squadrons—fine, big men, on massive chargers.

I remember turning to my chums in the ranks and saying: "Thank God! We are not far off Paris now. Look at the French cavalry."

They too saw them quite plainly, but on getting closer, to our surprise the horsemen vanished and gave place to banks of white mist, with clumps of trees and bushes dimly showing through them. . . .

When I tell you that hardened soldiers who had been through many a campaign were marching quite mechanically along the road and babbling all sorts of nonsense in sheer delirium, you can well believe we were in a fit state to take a row of beanstalks for all the saints in the Calendar.

5. It's impossible to ignore the maverick account of the *Angel* of Mons related by author Arch Whitehouse. Whitehouse fought in the First World War and authored a number of books based on his experiences. In *Epics and Legends of the First World War* he tells of a single angel that appeared to the Coldstream Guards during the retreat. At Mormal Forest the Guards were the last to be withdrawn and in the half-light of a false dawn they became lost and wandered about trying to join up with their main body. Finding they were completely out of touch they dug in ready to make a stand at daylight. Then, the men saw a bright light approaching them. As it grew closer the Coldstreamers saw the dim outline of a female figure. Then it became more distinct and they realised they were looking at an angel. The sort of angel seen in regimental chapels: tall, slim and wearing a white flowing gown. Around her hair was a gold band, there were eastern sandals on her feet and against her slim back were folded a pair of white wings.

The angel beckoned to them and, after puzzled indecision, the guardsmen began to crawl out of their shallow trenches. They followed the glowing figure across an open field and eventually she led them to the end of a sunken road. She then floated up the bank and pointed towards a covering copse a few dozen yards away. Then, with a smile, she vanished, leaving the guardsmen overjoyed to find the escape route. And, yet having made their escape, no one was ever to find the sunken road again. The Coldstreamers poured over every available map, but not one of them showed the slightest trace of any track that could be identified as the angelic path!

6. There was a childish eagerness during the war to locate omens pointing to victory. Misshapen clouds were sometimes interpreted as patriotic emblems or even supernatural figures. For example, here is a story sent "by a Russian General who is with the army operating in East Prussia." (To Ralph Shirley in October 1914.)

> While our troops were in the region of Suwali, the captain of one of my regiments witnessed a marvellous revelation.
>
> It was eleven o'clock at night, and the troops were in bivouac. Suddenly a soldier from one of our outposts, wearing a startled look, rushed in and called the captain. The latter went with the soldier to the outskirts of the camp and witnessed an amazing apparition in the sky. It was that of the Virgin Mary, with the Infant Christ on one hand, the other hand pointing to the west.
>
> Our soldiers knelt on the ground and gazed fervently at the vision. After a time the apparition faded, and in its place came a great image of the Cross, shining against the dark night sky.
>
> Slowly it faded away.
>
> On the following day our armies advanced westward to the victorious battle of Augustovo.

The French and English troops were a little more cautious though, as the following newspaper story shows:

The Star of Victory—Angiers, September 30, 1914.

Tonight, as the soldiers of England and France lay sleeping in the trenches, sentries noticed what seemed to be a new star in the heavens. Its color appeared strange and novel. They looked again, and to their wonder discovered that it twinkled and shone with the national colours of the Allies— red, white, and blue.

Field-glasses were taken out and groups of officers and men looked up at the wonderful heavenly light. It was an optical illusion, of course, but amongst those who saw it there were men who believed it to be an omen of victory and success (Central News).

7. The public was, in a sense, visually primed in favor of angels by a set of illustrations in the immensely popular *King Albert's Book* published at Christmas 1914. Chandler Christy's wash drawing shows an angel holding a laurel wreath over the head of an exhausted soldier; Briton Riviere shows St. George and the dragon; Frank Dicksee's picture shows a mailed figure carrying a crucifix and a French standard striding across the battlefield, while J. J. Shannon's pastel shows the mailed and winged figure of St. Michael of Belgium supporting a Belgium soldier clutching his country's flag. This last illustration served as the basis for a crudely drawn postcard published by the Church Army. The card showed Christ on the Cross in the background; a sky full of angels and a mailed, winged figure encouraging an infantryman and a sailor, both of them gripping rifles with fixed bayonets. The slogan on the card read: "Enlisted under the Cross! Am I?"

Chapter 12

1. Many myths have their origins in strange, but explicable real-life experiences. And the chances are strong that the lift-crash saga derived from an incident reported in *The Boston Budget* on August 31, 1890.

A strange incident occurred one night last week at one of the Boston Back Bay hotels. It was just before the gas was lighted, and was already growing dusky in the corridors, when a resident guest stepped out of her room to go to the elevator. She touched the electric bell and then went down to the end of another corridor to look out of the window for a moment, while the elevator was coming up. Returning to it, she was about advancing precipitately to the side of it that the door was on, when the sight of a man standing exactly in front of the elevator door caused her to stop short, that she might not be so rude or awkward as to run into him, so to speak, as she was in danger of doing in her rather heedless haste. The hall was dim, but a window opposite the elevator showed the form of the man plainly enough, and the lady waited at a decorous distance. But what was her amazement when the elevator came up, brightly lighted inside, to see, first, that the upper door was wide open, and that thus the entire well of the elevator was exposed. The lady had been a guest for many years in the house, and had never known such a thing as an elevator door left open to happen before. But the second fact was far more startling, *there was no man there!* Now, the appearance of this man, or her impression of his appearance there, undoubtedly saved her from plunging head first down the elevator well. . . .

Now, here is a fact for Dr. Richard Hodgson and his Psychical Society. It may be added that the lady in question immediately went to the hotel desk to report the terrible carelessness of the boy who had left this door open, but not ambitious to acquire the reputation of a lunatic, or even a seer of visions or a dreamer of dreams, she took very good care not to relate the other half of the occurrence, although it was just as palpable a fact that the door was open. Was this the apparition of a spiritual presence, which had materialised to save her from a terrible fate? Who shall say?

Dr. Richard Hodgson of the American SPR knew the lady well and wrote to her. She answered:

My Dear Mr. Hodgson,— No, I did not recognise the form at all. I simply didn't notice—didn't think anything about it, as it is rather the rule than the exception to meet people at the elevator in a hotel. Then, too, I am very near-sighted, and I did not have my eye-glasses on, so I shouldn't have recognised even my most intimate friend in the dusky light and at the little distance.
It occurred on Tuesday night, August 26th.

> Faithfully yours,
> (Signed) A.B.

There is plenty of evidence that the unconscious self can often spot problems and difficulties way ahead of the conscious. And there is ample evidence that subconscious anxieties and expectations can generate hallucinations.

F. W. H. Myers (British SPR) admirably analyzed this case by saying: "Assuming this . . incident to be correctly reported, the least marvellous way of explaining it will perhaps be to suppose that Miss A.B.'s subliminal self perceived the open doorway at a distance somewhat beyond the eyesight of her supraliminal self, and then generated the hallucinatory figure in order to avert the fall."

2. Indiana University Folklore Institute at Bloomington, U.S.A., has a small folder entitled *Urban Belief Tales—Room For One More*. This contains five stories along the lines of the lift crash disaster. All of them except one feature a coach and horses. They're all located in different parts of the United States and one of them is said to have happened to the cousin of a visitor to a Mrs. Carrols of East Lansing, Mich. It is, of course, fiction.

Chapter 15

1. Soal presents his invented dickie bird forecast on page 566 of his Blanche Cooper paper. It reads:

> In the record of my sittings I have found one and only one more slight reference to Gordon Davis. It was during Sitting No. 23, held on Monday, January 30, 1922, 3:40. p.m. This reference occurred during a pause in the middle of the sitting. James Miles had been communicating and was apparently resting. I asked Nada if Gordon Davis could come again.
>
> NADA. Is not coming any more.
> S.   Can't he come and talk to you. He need not use the voice directly.
> NADA. He can't because he's too far away now.
> S.   Try to get him.
> NADA. Only see his house, but it's not clear—can't get anything. There's something about black dickie bird—think it's on piano—not sure about it.
> S.   Would this be in Gordon Davis' house?
> NADA. Think it would be his house—it's very uncertain because he isn't here.
>
> (Frank then speaks and tries to give a book test, which is unsuccessful. Afterwards James Miles is mentioned again and sitting concludes.)

2. I have accepted the difficulty of fully understanding Soal's motives, but other cases drawn from completely different fields can sometimes offer clues. For example the strange case of Georges Fouré, a language teacher of Berlin. In the 1880s, he was one of the top-ranking German philatelists and editor of the *Berliner Illustrierte Briefmarkenzeitung*. He waged, through his paper, an unrelenting war against forgers. At the same time, he used his skill and understanding of the collector's mentality to create completely bogus "early" stamps. As Gustav Shchenk observes in *Romance of the Postage Stamp:* "This dangerous game became a vice and he played out his curious forger's existence like a virtuoso. He took no one into his confidence, so there were no witnesses to his truly magnificent art; he kept his counsel and possessed so little vanity that he was able to live as a lone craftsman without praise or admiration. . . . He must have had a strange streak in his character to derive pleasure in making a mockery of his collegues and fellow experts. . . . His silent laughter over the serious gentlemen of the profession whom he had fooled with his creations was confined to his own room. . . . He was an artist, a tightrope dancer on the adventurous wire of the unreal and the irrational."

3. The real conditions under which the Blanche Cooper sittings were held, were only fully revealed by Soal many years after publishing his results. In 1938, in a letter to the editor of *Psychic Science,* Soal stated that, "There is

no doubt that it required immense patience to listen continuously to these whispering and often inarticulate voices. Over and over again I used to ask for phrases to be repeated until the words were clear and the strain on one's nerves sometimes became almost intolerable." He then went on to add, "If, in fact, it were not for certain episodes in the case of 'Gordon Davis,' I should not be afraid to face the possibility of the hypothesis of a mixture of involuntary whispering on my own part and the occasional reading into vague sounds words that were not really articulated by the medium. The hypothesis of auditory illusion cannot be summarily dismissed. Darkness and an atmosphere of expectation and immense mental strain may favour the mishearing of individual words or even of phrases."

At this point we get the feeling that Soal is opening up and supplying the real source of the voices, while at the same time he recognizes that the "Gordon Davis" case has become a chain that he can't afford to break.

His revelations about the sitting conditions tie in with the independent reports of SPR investigators and journalists. Dr. Eric Dingwall, in his sitting with her on February 23, 1922, reported that: "Whispered voices then began and continued intermittently for one hour and a half interspersed by hymns on the part of the sitters. Scarcely a word could be heard as the music (from the music box) drowned what little noise the voices made . . . The sitting was wholly unevidential . . ." At another sitting a journalist recorded: "A voice that gave no name that I could identify announced that it would give a description of the house in which I lived as a boy. The description was not accurate, and when I asked what the garden was like I got no reply . . . Another 'spirit' appeared in the form of a faint and somewhat hoarse voice that announced itself as 'Grandmother'. When I asked 'What is your name?' she constantly repeated 'Grandmother! Grandmother!'" This gives a good idea of the quality of the material and shows that "house messages" were part of the repertoire.

4. In his "Oscar Wilde Scripts" Soal provided a number of passages that have impressed people greatly. One of these reads: "through the eyes out of the dusky face of a Tamil girl I have looked on the tea fields of Ceylon and through the eyes of a wandering Kurd, *I have seen Ararat and the Yezedes who worship both God and Satan and who love only snakes and peacocks.*"

This particular message was seized on by Hannen Swaffer and quoted by Ida Clyde Clarke in her *The Return Of Oscar Wilde,* while in 1974 *Psychic News* reported that an ecologist who'd made a specialized study of obscure peoples was amazed by these words. The really amazing thing, though, is that they have obviously missed the fact that Soal himself discovered the source of this passage as early as July 1926.

He then wrote to the *Journal* of the SPR saying:

. . . Only quite recently I have discovered what would appear to be its source.

In Vol. I, p. 227, of "People of All Nations," edited by J. A. Hammerton, is a picture of a woman devil-worshipper with the following note.

WOMAN DEVIL-WORSHIPPER OF MOUNT ARARAT.

She belongs to the far scattered sect of the Yezedes who worship both God and Satan and are devoted to peacocks, snakes, water and the sun. They are forbidden to learn reading and writing.

This book was undoubtedly in my possession at the time of the sitting.

Yet another passage was traced to a letter written by Soal to a lady friend and dated October 25, 1915. At that time, Soal was serving in the army. The Wilde Script reads: "Every year Spring throws her green veil over the world and anon the red autumn glory comes to mock the yellow moon." While the war-time letter reads: "But among these wild hills the trees seem dwarfed into insignificance, overshadowed by contrast with the immense contours of the everlasting hills. Here is no ruddy autumn glory to mock the yellow moon, but great empty spaces and windy skies filled at sunset with slate and smouldering crimson."

The rest of this particular letter shows a side of Soal that is absent from his other writings. Indeed his brother said of this letter: "He never wrote to myself or to anyone at home in this descriptive vein, but that is probably because he is naturally reserved with relations." These cryptomnesic borrowings throw extra light on Soal's complexities and they also offer lessons for the study of reincarnationist scripts.

Chapters 16, 17, and 18

1. In the pro-reincarnation camp there are a number of leading figures who are looked up to as authorities. One of these is a Professor Hans Holzer who is described as having ". . . taught parapsychology at New York Institute of Technology for eight years." In 1982, in issues of the magazine *Reincarnation Report,* he twice plugged one of his case histories, for which he made this claim: "Upon reading it, I think you will agree that reincarnation is the only plausible explanation."

And what does this marvelous case consist of? It involves a recurring dream about a Scottish girl. This dream visited 19-year-old Pamela Wollenberg, from Harvey, Illinois, U.S. She wrote to Holzer about this dream in 1967. The dream figure appeared to be trying to tell her something. As Holzer puts it:

Pamela also remembers some alien words which she did not understand. The words were "Purth, Ruthven, Cowrey, Sixteen" and "Towers." The words meant little to me, but short time later, Pamela supplied additional dream details. It was the Scotland of 1600, and additional words included "hansel" and "Gowrie Meadow" as well as "Glamis" and "Angus."

Despite diligent research in available history sources, I could not explain this material until by chance (if there be such a thing!) I found myself at Muchalls Castle near Edinburgh.

Holzer then outlines the key to the puzzle. In Scotland he found out about the Gowrie Conspiracy. This was the high point of a series of intrigues involving the Ruthven family—who provided the Lords of Gowrie. The Ruthven brothers were executed in 1600, in Perth, on the King's orders. Following this, their hereditary titles were wiped out, and even Gowrie Castle was renamed as Huntingtower Castle. All the other fragments mentioned by Miss Wollenberg were associated with that period.

Holzer goes on to ask, "How could a 19-year-old girl from upstate Illinois know this information? Pamela had no Scottish ancestry; she had never left her native state nor even attended college."

In an earlier issue of the same magazine (No. 2) Holzer touched on the same case saying: ". . . Pamela Wollenberg, who received an urgent message from her 'former' self, concerning the names Ruthven, Gowrie and Scotland in 1600, could not and did not know of the obscure plot known as the Gowrie conspiracy which destroyed the Ruthven family of Scotland in the year 1600. My files are full of such cases."

First of all, it's supremely foolish of Holzer to assert that the lady did not and could not know of this conspiracy. He no more knows what Miss Wollenberg has read during her lifetime than he knows what I have read. I don't even know myself—even though I preserve book lists! As for his boast of in-depth investigation, let's see how this case stands up.

I turn to his longest treatment of this particular case. It's found in his *Born Again—The Truth About Reincarnation*. There he takes up 33 pages to tell the slender tale which, at its best, involves only a few pathetic scraps of knowledge. Everything mentioned by Pamela Wollenberg could have been picked up casually from a paragraph or two of a magazine filler.

I gather from his publisher's note that Hans Holzer has written 81 books. I now see how he does it. His volumes are garish candy-floss with little substance. He plays a marvelous game of bluff. He yammers on about research, but it's all so-much hot air. He hasn't even intelligently used his own city's libraries. Had he done so, he would have found that the allegedly obscure Gowrie conspiracy is extremely well documented. No need to go to Scotland. No need to even bother anyone in Britain. If he starts with Hugh Ross Williamson's *Historical Whodunits* (1955), he'll not only find a chapter on the Gowrie Conspiracy, but in its first paragraph he'll read; "Many books have been written since, endeavouring to elucidate the matter."

If he looks further, at something as basic as *The A. A. Illustrated Road Book To Scotland* (1953), he will find there a photograph of Huntingtower Castle, and note of its link with the Ruthven family, the Gowrie title, and the raid of Ruthven. The text also draws attention to the castle's two towers and the space between the towers known as "the maiden's leap."

Then if he opens his eyes a little more, he'll find that this period of Scottish history, culminating in the Gowrie conspiracy, has delighted historical novelists for well over a century. I now present him with a partial list of some such novels: *The Queen's Chair,* by Maurice Hewlett; *Bothwell; or The Days of Queen Mary,* by James Grant; *Gowrie; or the King's Plot,* by G. P. R. James; *Court Cards: Chiefly the Knave of Hearts,* by Austin Clare; *The Witches,* by Jay Williams; and *The Border Lords,* by Jan Westcott.

So much for his case history, which satisfies "all criteria for scientific reincarnation research." And while Hans Holzer is delving into historical fiction, he should take a look at the works of Jean Plaidy. They will prove instructive.

His *Born Again* features a case called "A Tale Of Two Catherines." This involves an English lady, Mrs. Warren-Browne and her royal dreams, set in the time of Henry VIII. After chronicling her dreams and her hypnotic regression, Holzer concludes: "Is Mrs. Catherine Warren-Browne the reincarnated Queen of England Katherine Parr. . . . She does not claim to be, but I think that the evidence points in that direction." Let him now point his nose in the direction of Jean Plaidy's novel *The Sixth Wife.*

Mrs. Warren-Browne's case really begins in 1957. Plaidy's novel of 1953 provides all the seemingly obscure material found in the regression and her dream number two. A brief example will show how.

In dream number two (Holzer, page 225) she relates how Henry walked with Katherine Parr through Hampton Court: "We walked down the long gallery, and in my dream I knew it was where Katherine Howard had run screaming to try to reach the King. Henry seemed to sense this and told me, 'Forget what has gone before.'"

By contrast Plaidy's novel (page 12) has Katherine Parr talking to Nan about the late Queen Catherine Howard. Nan says: "I remember how she ran screaming down the gallery at Hampton Court when the King was at chapel, I can't forget the sound of her voice. . . . It is best forgotten Nan."

In that one novel, he'll find the people Warren-Browne talks about, such as: Thomas Seymour, Lord Burgh (Borough), Lord Latimer, Wriothesly, and Gardiner. Katherine Parr's death and burial at the Castle of Sudley is there as well. So much for Holzer's claim that, in this case, some of the "historical data is not readily accessible to the average person."

2. The reincarnationists are all too ready to make claims about the rarity of the details brought up in their choice regressions. But they positively hate it when it's shown that their claims are bogus—that the "rarity" is purely imaginary. As a good example of this, there is a case in *Reincarnation Report* (No. 6) reported by Lawrence Cortesi. It's all about a Miss Julie Hauptman. This lady had continual neck pains. Surprise, surprise, through psychic investigation it was found that she'd once been beheaded! Incredibly she was once *another* of King Henry VIII's wives—this time Anne Boleyn, who died in 1536. In all solemnity the article tells that, ". . . one point could not be

explained. . . . Julie kept referring to herself under hypnosis as Nan Bullen, a name completely alien to the Royal history of England, and a name that was unknown in historical research of the Henry VIII period."

Having made this inane claim, the article then goes through the usual process of bluff and double-bluff, with talk about inquiries in England and archive records, etc. After these amateur dramatics, we're then ponderously told: "Only someone who had checked those dusty birth records in Norfolk, England, might have learned that Anne Boleyn had began her life as Nan Bullen. Even the English scholars at the university had not known Anne Boleyn's original name. How could Julie have known?"

But this was too much, even for some reincarnationists. And in issue No. 9 of the magazine, Kathleen Kelly wrote in to say, "As I read the article and encountered the name 'Nan Bullen' I remembered at once. . . . I read that years ago in a historical novel. I was appalled . . . to discover Anne Fisher (who did the research) is claiming the name 'Nan Bullen' could have been found only in obscure British records, and Ms. Hauptman's knowledge of it is her main 'evidence'!"

Carla Reamy also wrote in protest, saying: "Miss Fisher claims that only someone who had checked birth records in Norfolk, England, would know that this was Anne Boleyn's original name, and that even English scholars were unaware of it. . . . I am not a scholar. . . . And yet I have known for a long time that Anne Boleyn was christened Nan Bullen at birth. This 'little known fact' is stated in almost every book I've ever read on the subject. One example is the book I've just finished reading, entitled *Elizabeth and the Prince of Spain* by Margaret Irwin."

After that, one would have expected some sort of withdrawal or apology from both Anne Fisher and Lawrence Cortesi. But no. With lofty arrogance Cortesi wrote back to say, "Whether the name Nan Bullen is commonly known or uncommonly known is irrelevant. Anne Fisher and Julie Hauptman were not aware of the name, and only when the psychic convinced her subject that she was the reincarnation of Anne Boleyn did the pieces fall into place for Julie Hauptman." How dishonest can you get?"

3. When examining regressionist claims, it should be borne in mind that the material used to create the fantasy is often juggled around with and modified. As an example, we have another of Dr. Kampman's cases.

This involved a girl who had many "past-lives." At fifteen, she yielded up six different ones. Seven years later, the same girl produced a totally different batch of previous lives. The most striking of this new group involved her "past-life" as a seven-year-old boy who lived at the base of a huge mountain. His father was the captain of a river-boat which sailed on the lake called Issykjokul. The father's name was given as "Aitmatov."

This boy led a lonely life seeing little of his father, though yearning to be with him. And his bleak life reached a grim end when he grew to envy the fish who swam so freely in the river. He longed to become a fish, to swim to the lake and meet up with his father. In a wild fantasy he felt that he really was a fish; he leapt into the lake and drowned.

Out of hypnosis the girl had no memory of the boy, the lake or the father—so a further session was arranged. This time she was asked to remember where she'd first heard the tale of the sad little boy. At once the girl brought out the name of a novel called *Valkoinen Laiva (The White Ship)*. An examination of the book showed that it was set around Lake Issykjokul, and it involved the life and death by drowning of a forlorn little boy. There was no character in the book called Aimatov, but that was, in fact, the name of the author!

Chapters 19

1. The Johnny Coulon item, unlike the other investigations in this book, does not rest on my own research. I include it as, first, a delightful story, and second, as a tribute to the late Joseph Rinn—who has unfolded this story in his *Sixty Years of Psychical Research*. His book has many faults and inaccuracies, but for all that, it offers many hints to investigators and points researchers in many fruitful directions. For example, how many people would remember Mrs. Piper's strange quest for Dean Bridgman Connor if it wasn't for the mention of the case by Rinn?

There is a third reason for the appearance of Coulon and the magnetic-electric girls. Believe it or not, some of the elementary stage tricks involving leverage are now being utilized by psychics to prove that they can harness etheric powers.

Two such phonies are a couple known as Michael and Aurora El-Legion. Recently, this couple did a lecture-tour in Britain and appeared on television and radio programs. One program was the BBC(TV) "Open To Question." In front of the audience of youngsters, this couple claimed that they were, in fact, aliens from outer space, in human form. They also claimed to have originated from the Orion Nebula, and together with many others, including President Reagan and Prime Minister Margaret Thatcher, to supposedly be here to help the Earth come to its senses and solve its problems. On screen they demonstrated their "powers." The lady was easily able to press other people's uplifted arms down. But, when a special crystal was held by these people, she was completely unable to move their arms at all. A psychic crystal, of course!

Having demonstrated their unearthly powers, they went on to talk about the secret space program, which ships kidnapped scientists to a colony on Mars. When asked for the names of the scientists, the audience was referred to the complete account of the kidnapping venture in the book *Alternative Three*. Now "Alternative Three" was the title of a British Television program made by Anglia. It was transmitted on June 20, 1977. Superficially, it looked like an authentic documentary and it led viewers throughout Britain into a state of bewilderment and semi-panic. Many of them jammed television and newspaper switchboards with their worried calls. They asked: "Is the story about missing British scientists true? Are they really living on Mars?"

They soon found out that the program had originally been planned as an April Fool's Day stunt, but had to be transmitted at a later date.

Following the furor over the program, Leslie Watkins wrote a paperback book called *Alternative Three*. It was published by Sphere in 1978 and issued *as fiction*. But, in the text, it kept up the tongue-in-cheek pretense of being fact—an age-old tradition with science-fiction and mystery writers. Unfortunately, many people have been taken in by it and its cover claim that "Life on earth is doomed. The super-power governments have a plan to preserve a tiny nucleus of human survivors. The most astounding and frightening conspiracy ever."

I understand that several other cults are using this book as a support for their bizarre claims. How right Maskelyne was!